The Man Who Predicts Earthquakes

The Man Who Predicts Earthquakes

Jim Berkland, Maverick Geologist

How His Quake Warnings
Can Save Lives

Cal Orey

SENTIENT PUBLICATIONS

First Sentient Publications edition, 2006
Copyright © 2006 by Cal Orey

Cover design by Kim Johansen, Black Dog Design
Book design by Nicholas Cummings
Cover photo of Jim Berkland by Shmuel Thaler, Santa Cruz Sentinel

Library of Congress Cataloging-in-Publication Data
Orey, Cal, 1952-
  The man who predicts earthquakes : Jim Berkland, maverick geologist : how his quake warnings can save lives / Cal Orey.-- 1st Sentient Publications ed.
      p. cm.
  Includes bibliographical references and index.
  ISBN 1-59181-036-1
  1. Earthquake prediction. 2. Berkland, Jim, 1930- 3. Animal behavior. I. Title.

QE538.8.O74 2006
551.22'092--dc22

                                                      2005029384

Printed in the United States of America

10 9 8 7 6 5 4 3 2

SENTIENT PUBLICATIONS

A Limited Liability Company
1113 Spruce St.
Boulder, CO 80302
www.sentientpublications.com

Contents

Acknowledgments

I THANK ALL OF THE OPEN-MINDED SCIENTISTS, INCLUDING JIM BERKLAND, A PATIENT and brilliant man, who encouraged me to write this book. And I recall the people who didn't return my telephone calls or laughed when I mentioned the words *earthquake prediction* or refused to talk about Berkland's quirky quake theories. Now I know what it feels like to be the odd person out when you have a different vision—and people don't get it.

I'll never forget the dedicated earthquake enthusiasts and sensitives on Berkland's website who continue to wow me with their uncanny earthquake predictions and hits. A special thanks to analytical chemist and earthquake sensitive/forecaster/researcher E.D. Glass for his discussions regarding earthquakes and human earthquake sensitivity. I respect all of the hardworking scientists, too, who I discovered are determined to find the missing links between possible precursors and earthquakes, and to fine-tune progressive disaster preparedness and hazard plans globally.

Plus, I praise Jim Cypher, my dedicated literary agent, who kept the faith. He sent out my book proposal for *The Man Who Predicts Earthquakes* to numerous publishers and posted the project on *www.PublishersMarketplace.com*, where we did find an interested publisher, Connie Shaw of Sentient Publications. Not only did Cypher persevere in the beginning of this project, but he also went beyond the call of duty from start to finish of this book. In *The Writer Magazine*, I once tagged him as being my "fairy godfather." To me, he has been just that.

Finally, I'm grateful to my two furry children: my canine companion Simon—a two-year-old Brittany—and Kerouac, a five-year-old black cat, who are both budding seismically sensitive animals. My animal friends kept me grounded during the ups and downs of this challenging project. And my biggest rewards were to fine-tune my own earthquake sensitivity to forthcoming temblors and to develop a sense of inner peace by being prepared, while I continue to live, work, and play on shaky ground.

Foreword

IN 1990, WHILE LIVING IN LOS ANGELES, I HAD MY FIRST EXPERIENCE WITH UNUSUAL animal behavior prior to an earthquake. I was in graduate school at the time, researching the neural basis of learning and memory. I was working in the lab on the fifth floor of the University of Southern California's Hedco Neuroscience Building with three other graduate students and three calm rabbits. Suddenly the rabbits became noticeably agitated. They started hopping around in their cages wildly for around five minutes. Then a 5.2 magnitude earthquake sent the whole building rolling and swaying. This experience made a deep impression on me, and I soon learned that since the beginning of recorded history, virtually every culture in the world has reported observations of unusual animal behavior prior to earthquakes—but conventional science has never been able to adequately explain the phenomenon. Nonetheless, many people believe that these observations may serve to help warn people of impending earthquakes.

Six years after my own experience with anxious rabbits, in 1996, I began researching unexplained powers of animals as part of a collaboration with British biologist Rupert Sheldrake. The initial research that I did became the backbone for the section on unusual animal behavior and earthquakes in Dr. Sheldrake's best-selling book *Dogs That Know When Their Owners Are Coming Home* (Crown, 1999). Since I compiled more material than could fit into the section in the book on this subject, I posted much of this material on my website: *www.animal-*

sandearthquakes.com. As a result of this site I have received hundreds of reports from people all over the world about observations of strange animal behavior prior to earthquakes. Almost every time there is a major earthquake somewhere on the planet, I receive a number of reports—sometimes a dozen or more. The many anecdotes that I have received have been carefully saved in an ever-growing database.

What Is Unusual Animal Behavior?

Unusual animal behavior is difficult to define, and determining if there is a characteristic behavior is not a simple, clear-cut process, although some distinct patterns have emerged. For example, an intense fear that appears to make some animals cry and bark for hours and others flee in panic has been reported often. Equally characteristic is the apparently opposite effect of wild animals appearing confused, disoriented, and losing their usual fear of people. Some other common observations are that animals appear agitated, excited, nervous, or overly aggressive, or seem to be trying to burrow or hide.

Although the majority of accounts pertain to dogs and cats, there are also many stories about other types of animals—in the wild, on farms, and in zoos, including horses, cows, deer, goats, possums, rats, chickens, and other birds. The behavior has been reported in many other animal species as well, including fish, jellyfish, reptiles, and even insects. Deep-sea fish, for example, have been caught close to the surface of the ocean on numerous occasions around Japan prior to earthquakes.

What Are the Animals Reacting To?

A number of theories have been proposed to explain why animals sometimes act in peculiar ways prior to earthquakes, and what the precursory signals that the animals are picking up might be. The scientific theories that have been proposed to explain this phenomenon generally fall into six major categories: ultrasound vibrations, magnetic field fluctuations, electric field variation, piezoelectric airborne ions, brain changes, and precognition—which I discuss in detail on my website. (Refer to Chapter 3, "Berkland Turns to Cats and Dogs.")

The theories that have the strongest support are those that have to do with electromagnetic field fluctuations, piezoelectric airborne ions, and brain changes. The surface of the earth has a constant electromagnetic field, and because telluric current variations (natural electric currents flowing near the earth's surface) have also been noted before some earthquakes, it has been suggested that this may be what the animals are reacting to.

To test this hypothesis, Dr. Motoji Ikeya (author of *Earthquakes and Animals: From Folk Legends to Science* [World Scientific, 2004]) and colleagues at Osaka University in Japan have done studies in which they exposed a variety of animals—including minnows, catfish, eels, and earthworms—to a weak electrical field. Ikeya's laboratory experiments were conducted to see if this type of exposure could elicit the pre-earthquake animal behaviors. Ikeya's experiments produced interesting results. Fish showed panic reactions, and earthworms moved out of the soil and swarmed when the current was applied. (Note: I am presenting this information here purely for scientific reasons, and not because I agree with the nature of these experiments. The respectful and ethical treatment of animals has long been an inherent part of my own research.)

Dr. Helmut Tributsch's (author of *When the Snakes Awake* [MIT Press, 1982]) has suggested that the piezoelectric effect may be responsible for triggering the pre-earthquake behavior in animals. This theory makes sense because of the following facts: When certain crystals— such as quartz—are arranged in a way that pressure is applied along particular portions of the crystals' axes, the distribution of positive and negative ions can shift slightly. In this way, pressure changes produce electrical changes in the crystals' surfaces. On the average, the earth's crust consists of 15 percent quartz, and in certain areas it can be as high as 55 percent.

According to Tributsch, the piezoelectric effect on the quartz is capable of generating enough electrical energy to account for the creation of airborne ions before and during an earthquake. This electrostatic charging of aerosol particles may be what the animals are reacting to, as electrically charged ionic particles have been shown to alter neurotransmitter (chemical messenger) ratios in animal brains. Since some animals have also been observed acting frightened prior to thunderstorms, and are known to flee areas or show signs of distress before a storm arrives, it may be that they have evolved a sensitivity to electrical changes in their environment.

Can Animal Behavior Predict Earthquakes?

The Chinese have employed observations of unusual animal behavior for hundreds of years as an important part of a nationally orchestrated earthquake warning system, with some success. Perhaps most significantly, on February 4, 1975, the Chinese successfully evacuated the city of Haicheng several hours before a 7.3 magnitude earthquake—based primarily on observations of unusual animal behavior. Ninety percent of the city's structures were destroyed in the quake, but the entire city had been evacuated before it struck. Nearly 90,000 lives were saved. Since then, China has been hit by a number of major quakes that it was not as prepared for, and it has also had some false alarms, so its system is certainly not foolproof. Nevertheless, it has made a remarkable achievement by demonstrating that earthquakes do not always strike without warning.

Inspired by China's success, in 1975 Stanford Research Institute researchers William Kautz and Leon Otis ran a study for the U.S. Geological Survey (USGS) called Project Earthquake Watch, which showed promising results. They recruited hundreds of volunteers who lived along the fault lines of California to observe their animals for any unusual behavior, and call a toll-free hotline number to record their observations. Kautz and Otis got significant results—that is, before some earthquakes, more people reported unusual animal behavior—but the USGS stopped funding the study for reasons that no one that I've spoken to so far seems to know. Even harder to understand is why today the official word from the USGS is that no form of earthquake prediction performs better than chance. In fact, the notion that odd animal behavior can help people predict earthquakes is perceived by most traditional geologists in the West as folklore, or an old wives' tale, and is often put into the same category as sightings of poltergeists, Elvis, and the Loch Ness Monster. (Refer to Part 1, "The Predictor," and Part 5, "Politics and Quakes.")

Counting Lost Pet Ads

But not all Western geologists are closed-minded with regard to the phenomenon. When I interviewed James Berkland, I was intrigued by his controversial earthquake prediction methods, which included calculating the number of missing pet ads in the newspapers of earthquake-prone areas. From my animal behavior research, I knew that sometimes dogs and cats flee from their homes prior to earthquakes, so this made sense to me.

Berkland claimed to be able to predict earthquakes with a greater than 75 percent accuracy rate by counting the lost pet ads in the daily newspaper classifieds, correlating this relationship to lunar-tide cycles. Berkland had been meticulously saving and counting lost pet ads for many years, and he said that the number of missing dogs and cats goes up significantly for as long as three weeks prior to an earthquake.

So I set out to replicate Berkland's findings. I sat in the Santa Cruz Public Library for several weeks, rolling through microfilm collections of the *San Jose Mercury News*, counting lost pet ads. I confirmed that Berkland's calculations for one quake were indeed correct: There was a significant rise in the number of missing dog and cat ads in the week prior to the 1989 Loma Prieta earthquake when compared to the previous 12 months. The trouble was that when I checked the number of missing pet ads for the year before, during the same time period, there was also a rise—yet an earthquake didn't follow the rise that year. So more counting needs to be done to determine whether seasonal effects might influence this phenomenon or not, but it does appear that Berkland is on to something significant with his method.

Unfortunately, Berkland's work has not generated much interest among geologists, although there was one study. A geologist at the University of California at Davis, Rand Schaal, evaluated Berkland's method for predicting earthquakes, and published a paper in 1988 entitled "An Evaluation of the Animal-Behavior Theory for Earthquake Prediction." This study was based upon a tabulation of 41,717 daily newspaper reports of missing pets and 224 earthquakes of magnitude 2.5 or larger. Schaal concluded that "a significant positive correlation does not exist between the behavior of pets in the San Jose area and the occurrence of earthquakes within the same area over the three-year period from January 1983 through December 1985."

When I asked Berkland about Schaal's paper, he made some interesting observations. Schaal wrote that he had tabulated "41,717 daily reports of missing pets in the *San Jose Mercury News*." Berkland pointed out that this literally means more than 114 years of daily data, which couldn't be true. Berkland said that the "41,717 daily reports" must refer to the first eight years of data from Berkland's own study, which he gave to Schaal, including daily records for several newspapers. (Berkland received no credit for providing the data in the study, and physicist Antonio Nafaratte—who developed the lost pet ad hypothesis—was not mentioned either.) Berkland also points out that Schaal used only the dog ads and discounted the missing cat data because he said the numbers were too small to be statistically useful.

According to Berkland, that decision wasn't valid and changed the results. "The daily numbers typically ranged from two to nine, and often reached double figures prior to local quakes," Berkland said. Also, adjustments need to be made to the data to compensate for the fact that the numbers of missing pet ads normally escalate right after an earthquake. So there are some questions about the accuracy of Schaal's study. Another more recent study, by an anonymous researcher, analyzed Berkland's missing pet ad data from 1989—taking important factors into account that Schaal missed—and supports Berkland's hypothesis. For more information on this study, see "Do Missing Pets Predict Earthquakes? A Test of the Hypothesis" in the 2005 issue of the *Journal of Unconfirmed Nonsense and Knowledge*, which can be accessed online: *www.sharemation.com/Pedestrian1857/MissingPets-v2.1.html*.

Looking Ahead

Whatever the explanation is for the strange animal behavior that sometimes precedes earthquakes, if you live in an earthquake-prone region of the world, then paying attention to the animals around you may not be a bad idea. People living along major fault zones don't need to be reminded of the devastation that an earthquake can bring, and currently Western science doesn't have any reliable means of forecasting earthquakes. Tens of thousands of lives are lost globally, and billions of dollars in property damage occur on average every year as a result of earthquakes. Any clues that may be used to help us predict when and where the next earthquake is coming should be approached with an open mind.

When viewed in this light, James Berkland's work certainly deserves further attention and study. Berkland's method is so simple and inexpensive that anyone can start tabulating the daily number of lost pet ads and watching the lunar cycles. The results may save your life.

In the pages that follow, Cal Orey provides a valuable contribution to our understanding of this mysterious phenomenon, which fascinates students of the unknown and haunts seismologists. By exploring the colorful life of maverick geologist James Berkland, we not only can learn more about strange animal behavior and forecasting earthquakes, we can also share in a truly exciting adventure on the frontiers of scientific discovery.

—David Jay Brown

David Jay Brown is the coauthor of three volumes of interviews with some of the world's most brilliant and innovative scientists, including *Mavericks of the Mind: Conversations for the New Millennium* and *Conversations on the Edge of the Apocalypse: Contemplating the Future with Noam Chomsky, George Carlin, Deepak Chopra, Rupert Sheldrake, and Others.* Brown holds a master's degree in psychobiology from New York University, and was responsible for the California-based research in two of British biologist Rupert Sheldrake's books on unexplained phenomena in science. To find out more about Brown, visit his website, *www.mavericksofthemind.com.*

Preface

ONE SUMMER DAY, I SAT OUTDOORS IN THE SUNSHINE ON THE DECK OF MY CABIN IN the California Sierra, suffering from writer's boredom. I had just sold my previously published article, "What Kitty Knows," to *PetFolio* magazine. I covered the four-legged potential earthquake predictors. Then, it hit me. I thought of retired geologist Jim Berkland. His quake prediction theories, such as counting lost cat and dog ads in newspapers, always intrigued me.

I wondered, *Did anyone write a book on Berkland?* In the past, I had written articles such as "Will Your Dog Predict the Next Big One?" for *Dog World* magazine, and *Woman's World* magazine purchased my article, "Want a Quake Warning? Ask Your Cat!" Both pieces linked to James Berkland and his entertaining earthquake prediction theories. In fact, I offered to write Mr. Berkland's biography after the 7.1 monster earthquake rumbled through the San Francisco Bay Area on October 17, 1989. But once I received my master's degree from San Francisco State University in 1990, I did a quick flip-flop. I didn't want to write about earthquake predictors—two-legged or four-legged.

But in the summer of 2004, I decided to give earthquake predictor Berkland a call. To my surprise, no book had been written. As we chatted once again, I was captivated by this brilliant and colorful geologist. And I must admit, as a native California girl, I've always been an earthquake enthusiast. Berkland told me that he was still interested in my writing his story, a biography. But he reminded me that the scientific community would make it a bumpy ride. This prediction didn't scare me. I have written books about holistic health and natural remedies—controversial topics, for sure. But I also have written articles about psychics, including pet psychics, and witches, too. I'm an open-minded journalist. And my idea to create a book about a man who predicts earthquakes came with a ready-made guarantee to shake up my favorite season and beyond.

The goals for this book were twofold: I wanted to learn all about earthquake prediction and disaster preparedness and to let readers in on the behind-the-scenes of quakes and the politics of science. Rather than stay uninformed or frightened about when the next earthquake might strike, I could seek Berkland and his peers' knowledge to heighten my awareness at home and around the world. Berkland's unconventional earthquake prediction theories—as well as other quake experts and predictors—would give me priceless information to help me be more aware of Mother Nature.

My passion grew from Berkland's wealth of earthquake expertise and his dedication to helping inform people and dispel their fears about uncontrollable tremors, quakes, and potential deadly superquakes. Some conservative scientists laughed at me; others ignored our interview dates. And some took the time to point out why quake predictors like Berkland are quirky "charlatans." On my telecommuting adventure around the world in the twenty-first century, I learned that geologists, geophysicists, seismologists, and other everyday people were also busy at earthquake prediction and forecasting.

I quickly realized that discussing earthquake prediction was a heated topic. Not only did some scientists clam up, perhaps for fear of losing their jobs, but others became emotional and discussed past, present, and future destruction and loss of lives. After months of legwork, I discovered that you don't have to be scared or powerless even if you live in a quake-prone region (and other quake predictors were quick to point out that I was still living on shaky ground in Lake Tahoe). And so I learned about do-it-yourself quake prediction, whether it be tuning into my own body or paying attention to animal anomalies and earth changes. And I realized that knowledge is power even when it comes to powerful earthquakes.

Jim Berkland has given me an invaluable gift. And I have learned that we all have the power to open our mind and spirit, and be willing to listen—even if we don't have all the answers. Berkland admits he has parts to the earthquake puzzle and is paving the path to understanding the big picture and putting it all together. The treasures that I found on my adventures into the unknown world of earthquake prediction are ones that I will always cherish. And I want to share it all with you.

So, make yourself a cup of tea (remember, I'm a health writer), sit down with the dog or cat (I've also been tagged a pets writer), and grab a pencil (you'll want to take notes!). Meet Jim Berkland. I'll show you, page by page, how his (and other experts') quake warnings can save your life.

Introduction
The Power of Earthquakes

Of all the natural disasters, earthquakes are the most powerful, frightening, and unexpected. Since 1974, I have devoted my life to reducing the fear by increasing earthquake predictability.

—Jim Berkland

I REMEMBER THE GREAT ALASKA EARTHQUAKE OF MARCH 27, 1964, ON GOOD Friday when I was 12 years old. I heard my parents talk about a monster quake and killer waves, like the ones Crescent City, California, residents experienced when a tsunami swept in from the Pacific Ocean early on March 28, the day after the unforgettable quake struck Alaska. It was a surreal and unbelievable nightmare. It was miles away from my safe world in middle-class suburbia. I couldn't imagine such a life-threatening catastrophe.

There I was, months later in the summer on the porch steps of our house in San Jose, California, with my Dalmatian, Casey. It finally hit home. I was awestruck at the *National Geographic* magazine pages of snow-covered ground with gigantic cracks. Anchorage and other Alaskan cities were devastated. And then, I put the pieces together. I, too, was living on shaky ground—near the San Andreas fault, which runs almost the entire length of the Golden State. My life no longer seemed like the perfect *Father Knows Best* safe haven of the 1950s. And things changed.

That was 40 years ago, and today I can still find myself pondering deadly fault lines and many of the earthquakes that I personally survived. Like me and other people, you're likely to be both fascinated and freaked out by the power of earthquakes around the world, past and present.

Earthquakes 101

What are earthquakes? Simply put, a temblor is a shaking of the earth caused by the breaking and shifting of rock or a slip in a fault beneath the earth's surface.

So what causes them, anyhow? Earthquakes are linked to the forces of plate tectonics, which have shaped the earth. These gigantic plates that form the surface can and do create movement over, under, and away from each other, and cause the earth to shake, rattle, and roll. In other words, you can feel the earth move under your feet, as vocalist Carole King belted out years ago.

As one of Jim Berkland's apt pupils, I learned that underthrusting in the Pacific Northwest results in shallow quakes near the Cascadia trench and progressively deeper earthquakes as the epicenters are tracked across western parts of Washington, Oregon, and most of Northern California.

The movement of the Juan de Fuca plate beneath the North America plate is similar to the movements of plates around the circum-Pacific Ring of Fire, where the world's largest earthquakes strike. These areas of underthrusting near seacoasts have been known as subduction zones since 1969, which is considered to mark the birth of the plate tectonic revolution. And it's for these same quake-prone regions that Berkland makes his earthquake predictions.

And note, non-tectonic earthquakes can also be the result of human-caused explosions (i.e., quarry explosions and mine blasting), meteor impacts, sonic booms, and volcanic eruptions. In other words, if the ground shakes, it is, by definition, an earthquake.

When Earthquakes Hit Home

I had my first earthquake experience back in 1963. It was in September. And it was like something out of a creepy sci-fi film. In the late morning, I was taking a shower when I heard the bathroom door rattle. I assumed it was my pesky five-year-old brother. But after I called out his name a few times and didn't get a response, I realized it wasn't child's play. It was a quake. And back in the '60s, my Mom followed the drill, which was to tell us to "Get under a doorway." It wasn't a great earthquake—but it was a rude wake-up call that I was living in earthquake country.

Six years later, a rumor about California falling into the sea began to haunt me. At 17, I lived an hour's drive from the Pacific Ocean. Scientists also claimed that a quake was overdue on the Hayward fault, 30 miles from our house. On October 1, 1969, a pair of quakes of 5.6 magnitude hit Santa Rosa, a place my Dad frequented on business trips. Since I was a teenager with an overactive imagination, my fear of tremors manifested into an earthquake phobia. I shared this fear factor with my wood shop teacher in high school. He listened. He laughed. He tagged me "Earthquake Annie." But his joking attitude didn't stop my serious anxieties and interest in the worldwide geological phenomenon.

I can personally attest that powerful ground shaking from quakes can do much more than get you to cut your shower time. Major quakes collapse buildings and bridges, as I witnessed firsthand in the Loma Prieta 7.1 earthquake in 1989. They can disrupt gas, electricity, and telephone service—and survivors of the Northridge quake of 1994 told me how this affected people and pets. And sometimes, earthquakes trigger landslides, avalanches, fires, flash floods, and huge killer waves, like I saw 40 years ago, and last year.

The great San Francisco earthquake of 1906, the Alaska earthquake in 1964, and the 9.0 Sumatra-Andaman Islands earthquake off the west coast of Northern Sumatra on December 26, 2004 (also given other names, such as the Indian Ocean quake-tsunami of 2004 or the Sumatra earthquake)—which countless people like you and me witnessed in the media—aren't the first great earthquakes, and they won't be the last ones.

The History of Quakes

The power and fear of earthquakes go back to pre-biblical times in

China in 1177 B.C. Earthquakes occurred in Mexico in the 1300s, and in Peru in the 1400s. Quakes in Europe are noted to have happened in the mid-1500s. By the 1600s, the effects of earthquakes were being documented worldwide.

The most deadly earthquake to hit Europe is said to have been the 8.6 quake that rumbled through Lisbon, Portugal, on November 1, 1755, killing 60,000 people, according to the Pacific Disaster Center. The most widely felt earthquakes in North America were a series of temblors that occurred in 1811–12 near New Madrid, Missouri. While the San Francisco earthquake of 1906 was powerful, the Alaska earthquake of 1964 was of a greater magnitude. The longest-duration earthquake in the world happened in Chile in 1960—it lasted four minutes. (And note, I've discovered, as you will too, that the death toll of earthquakes as well as the magnitude can vary when documented by different people or organizations.)

Today, people of all ages understand the power of earthquakes. It's the unexpected and uncontrollable loss of life and infrastructure that makes earthquakes among the worst natural disasters. While it might seem as if we are powerless, earthquake predictions based on Mother Nature are attracting people to pinpoint when and where earthquakes might strike. And I know of one such extraordinary individual who has been predicting earthquakes for more than 30 years.

Jim Berkland, Maverick Geologist

Enter James Berkland. In 1982 when I was a senior at San Francisco State University, I— still earthquake-obsessed—wrote a screenplay, *Palmdale Projection*, for one of my writing classes. I had asked a geology professor what was the most likely place for a great quake to hit in California. He picked Palmdale in Southern California, where a big ground deformation called the "Palmdale Bulge" was believed to be causing stress on the San Andreas. My project was based on that seismically prone area, and my protagonist was a California geologist, based on Berkland. I had read about some of the Santa Clara County geologist's earthquake predictions in the *San Jose Mercury News*. I called him, and it led to a face-to-face interview at the county building in Santa Clara. Many more interviews followed throughout the years for my assigned national magazine articles on earthquake prediction—and this book.

On Monday, December 13, 2004, I was scurrying around my home in Lake Tahoe. It was a special day. It was during Berkland's eight-day seismic window (a period when quakes are most likely to hit), and I was glad he was paying me a visit rather than my traveling toward the shaky Bay Area. Berkland was expected on my doorstep at 1:00 in the afternoon. At 1:01 p.m. I heard a knock at the front door. Jim Berkland was standing in front of me holding books, albums, and papers for me to research for his biography. And I was excited.

As I welcomed a familiar face, I realized Father Time had been kind to the 74-year-old man. For five hours, we chatted about his past and present earthquake predictions. In between bites of cheese, French bread, cheesecake, and chamomile tea, we discussed what was shaking around the nation. Within the past few months, we had read about the long overdue Parkfield quake, Mount St. Helens becoming active again, and even a shaker in New York.

Of course, Berkland was excited about his latest prediction: a 4.5 magnitude earthquake would hit California. To make it even more interesting, he made a wager about it with UCLA's Professor John Vidale. To me, this was all very fascinating. I felt as if I were in the middle of something big, something important.

For several hours, I sat with Berkland in my dining room. As always, this fascinating character had a captivated audience. As he discussed earthquakes nationwide and worldwide, we chatted about anything and everything earthquake related. I remember he handed me a dark, heavy rock that was an Egyptian hammerstone. Like an enthusiastic boy, he told me, "I found it 30 feet off the trail around the Unfinished Obelisk at Aswan, Egypt. When I showed it to John Anthony West, the Egyptologist, he remarked that it was a better example of a dolerite hammerstone than in a showcase of the Cairo Museum." And as a rock hound since childhood, I smiled and admired the rare stone.

That night after Berkland left, I started to organize the research materials he left behind. On Wednesday, Berkland would be traveling to his family's home on the East Coast. It was my job to begin *The Man Who Predicts Earthquakes*. While he did indeed win the earthquake wager, something that happened soon after changed my direction and outlook for the book.

Early in the morning on December 26, 2004, I couldn't sleep. My dog, Simon, was restless, so I took him outdoors. In the light of the full moon, I saw a lone coyote run down the street. It was a weird feeling. Once indoors, I turned on the TV—and that was the beginning of something bigger than life. Reports of the Indian Ocean quake-tsunami woke me up. And for the next several weeks, countless people, like you and me, were fed an enormous amount of earthquake-related information from around the world. Suddenly, the media, literary agents, fellow authors, scientists, and even the neighbor next door were interested in my book about Jim Berkland. (See Part 4, "The Big Wave.")

Predicting the Unpredictable

Despite assurance by many scientists today in the twenty-first century that earthquakes are still unpredictable, Berkland follows his own agenda and opens his mind, heart, and ears to a wide array of earthquake precursors. In fact, he points out that scientific papers have been published that show possible links between temblors and earthquake precursors such as earthquake lights, tides, water changes, tectonic creep rates, sensitive people, and other warning signals.

"Acceptability of some of these precursory effects has varied throughout the years, but most have been totally rejected by the keepers of high wisdom," says Berkland. So I set out to interview Berkland, his followers, and other free-thinking people around the world who believe that earthquake prediction isn't impossible for those who are willing to face the unknown—as did Christopher Columbus, Leif Erikson, and other progressive thinkers and brave explorers who were ahead of their time.

How This Book Can Work for You

Part 1, "The Predictor," gives you the lowdown on Berkland's experience with the World Series earthquake (which he predicted and for which he coined the name). This section gives you details about his growing-up years, his unconventional earthquake prediction methods—monitoring tidal flows, lunar cycles, lost cats and dogs, and strange animal behavior—and how it all led to his prediction of the 7.1 monster quake that rumbled through the San Francisco Bay Area in 1989.

Part 2, "The New Age Movement," discusses fascinating information about seismically sensitive humans, or earthquake sensitives, who are in tune to their body's ear tones, headaches, dreams, and visions that help them to predict earthquakes—and details about other earthquake predictors.

Part 3, "Shakers and Seismic Windows," will help you to understand how Berkland's seismic windows, primary and secondary, have worked in the past and present to predict earthquakes on the West Coast, Pacific Northwest, Midwest, South, East Coast, and around the world. You'll be able to put together the lunar phases, tides, and other regional quake precursors to see the big picture of earthquake prediction at work.

Part 4, "The Big Wave," explains how Berkland's secondary seismic window, on the day of the full moon, and animals' sixth sense was a link to his earthquake theories and the occurrence of the great Boxing Day quake-tsunami on December 26, 2004. (Boxing Day is a holiday celebrated in Britain, Australia, New Zealand, and Canada. It's on the day after Christmas). You'll also learn about the lack of tsunami warnings and how some dedicated scientists did warn people about this potential catastrophe.

Part 5, "Politics and Quakes," includes gritty interviews with conservative U.S. Geological Survey scientists who don't like the word *prediction*, nor do they like Berkland's quirky quake predictions. You'll learn about how Berkland was the first person behind the scenes of an investigation of the great 1906 San Francisco earthquake-fire death toll and why the real death count wasn't revealed for 100 years. You'll discover how both Berkland and Gladys Hansen, the city historian, realized that the phony death lists and missing lists were far less comprehensive than the true list that only God knows.

Part 6, "Bracing for the Big One," will help you to get a grip on what's true and false when it comes to earthquake facts and myths. You'll discover answers to questions about earthquakes from real-life people. National and international earthquake preparedness experts discuss cutting-edge strategies in the works, and will tell you what you can do to prepare for the next "big one." And last but definitely not least, you'll get projections from the USGS, visionary Clarisa Bernhardt, the prophet Nostradamus, and Jim Berkland about earth changes from now to the year 2020 and beyond.

If you encounter any unfamiliar technical words as you're reading, you can check out the glossary at the end of the book.

Part One

The Predictor

1 ⬮ From Kid to Renegade Geologist

October 17, 1989: 5:03 *p.m.*
County Building
Santa Clara County, California

GEOLOGIST JIM BERKLAND LEFT HIS DESK TO JOIN THE EXODUS OF COUNTY EMPLOY-ees who had dashed for the elevators on the fourth floor, rushing home to enjoy the third game of the San Francisco Bay World Series. On his way out, he quickly grabbed the phone at the counter to call the seismological station at the University of California to get an earthquake update. Before he had completed punching the numbers, the 7.1 World Series earthquake hit.

As Berkland tells it, he waved his free hand in the air and cried out, "I got my quake!" But within a heartbeat, he didn't want it. The building swayed, twisted, and bounced. A heavy microfilm reader slammed against the excited stocky, five-foot-nine, 59-year-old man, and he pushed it back, preventing it from crashing onto the floor. There was noise all around him as file cabinets toppled, bookshelves emptied, and many other loose items slid around and fell. He said out loud to himself, "We've got a major quake here. This is a 7!" Then, he considered the human element and thought, I *hope it's centered closer to here than* to *Candlestick*. But the seasoned geologist knew that because the quake was so frightening in the county building that it might be disastrous if centered 40 miles north of San Jose.

Although the ground motion lasted 15 seconds, tall buildings moved back and forth for minutes. As planned, the elevators were out of service, but two were stuck between floors with passengers in various states of panic. Berkland made his way down the stairs and compared notes on the ground with dozens of other county employees.

Some people thought that the epicenter was near Hollister, but Berkland guessed that it was south of Lexington Reservoir, where foreshocks of 5.0-plus had struck on August 8, 1989, and June 27, 1988. He headed home slowly through jammed streets and found that there was relatively little damage in San Jose east of Highway 101. At his home in the foothills, the most noticeable effect was that the water in his swimming pool was about three feet lower than when he had left it that morning. It was one small sign of many big changes that followed.

At that time, Berkland had been the first Santa Clara County geologist for 16 years. For the next week, he worked day and night examining the aftereffects of the deadly shaker, scientifically named the Loma Prieta quake. He studied landslides, fissured ground and roads, and damaged houses, working with private consultants and other governmental geologists and safety personnel on various aspects of the quake. "The San Andreas fault itself did not rupture the ground, but there were spectacular fissures from violent ground shaking. The crack that I was in could be mapped for about one-half mile, but this was where it was the deepest." (See the photo on the cover of the book.)

At night, he tried to answer dozens of telephone calls that had piled up while he was in the field. Evidently, some concerned citizens had heard rumors that the 7.0 monster was a foreshock to an imminent 9.0 superquake. Berkland insists he did his best to dispel such talk and told inquiring people he didn't expect any aftershocks of more than 5.5 to 6.0.

Meanwhile, many people were aware that he had publicly predicted the "World Series quake" in the October 13, 1989, *Gilroy Dispatch*. His call for a 3.5-to-6.0 quake was for the maximum tidal period of October 14–21, 1989. Not for publication, but often stated, were his expectations of a San Francisco Bay Area quake of 6.5–7.0, although none so strong had hit the area since 1911. While his quake warning didn't save any lives—this time—Berkland reports that one Campbell woman saved $6,000 in china and crystal, which she had taken down at his recommendation prior to the quake. Also, he notes, a Lockheed engineer informed him that he had saved thousands of dollars worth of vulnerable disassembled rocket parts by securing the project against shaking, because of his prediction. So Berkland felt satisfied that earthquake prediction was not only possible, it was effective.

Then came his personal aftershock. On October 22, 1989, Berkland was accused of panicking the public with a new prediction for a great earthquake to strike the Bay Area in November. Powerful forces in the scientific and political communities spread the rumor without consulting him, he recalls. Press statements followed.

His wife, Jan, learned of the charges before he did by watching the evening television news. He explains, "She said she was 'shocked in disbelief and was concerned about the possibility of having to survive on her sole income,' as we had done when I returned to college to work on my Ph.D. at UC Davis. She tells me today that she had long recognized her husband as a renegade geologist, but she felt that I would have a reasonable explanation for the county's action. She always supported me 100 percent when it counted."

The result? Berkland was suspended from his job for two and a half months while an investigation took place. While home, he was ordered not to talk about earthquakes with the media. The fact remained, his career was in jeopardy with a capital "J." Son Jay and daughter Krista would find their college futures also at risk. But Berkland believed that his prior actions of forewarning the public of an upcoming earthquake were part of his job description, including that he was expected to conduct special investigations into geological matters to ensure public safety.

Finally, when he returned to work, his life as he once knew it had changed. He was prohibited from discussing the quakes or the "P" word on county time. This punishment was revoked when he convinced management that earthquakes and earthquake safety were both important topics. In order to continue fulfilling his need to "inform rather than conform," about earthquake information, Jim Berkland began his mission to do just that.

While earthquake predictors come and go, Berkland, licensed Engineering Geologist #58 and California Registered Geologist #107, has been predicting quakes for more than 30 years. He's worked in the field with the U.S. Geological Survey, U.S. Bureau of Reclamation, State of California, State of North Carolina, and most notably, as the first county geologist in Northern California.

Berkland's life likely would lack meaning without his passion to provide quake warnings that can save lives. However, while he's the man who predicts earthquakes, Berkland is also so much more than that. To me, he's a multifaceted, unforgettable character. And you'll see exactly how his extraordinary life took an amazing turn on the unbeaten path that few choose to follow.

In His Early Years

Ironically, Jim Omer Berkland was born in the seismic window of July 24–31, 1930, one of only four such windows (the opportune time for an earthquake to strike) for the year. In the following window on the afternoon of August 30, a 5.2 Los Angeles quake rocked his family's cottage in Glendale. His mother fled out of the house with him at her breast and was quickly joined by neighbors who had fled their homes, too.

As Berkland tells it, before his third birthday, they had lived for a time in Long Beach, California, but with a perfect sense of timing, his folks drove back to Iowa for a family get-together. While they were away from California, the 6.3 Long Beach earthquake hit and caused massive destruction on March 10, 1933, the day of a lunar eclipse. More than 135 people died, and it could have been more deadly if it had happened a few hours before 5:54 p.m. Despite the earthquake, the family returned to Glendale, and a sister, Karen, joined the family two years later in 1935.

Growing up during the Great Depression, Berkland took to nature, a free and wonderful pastime. It was in his blood. His father was a rock hound. "My dad worked for the Civilian Conservation Corps for $75 a month, and we didn't see him that much, but twice we got to angle for catfish in a hatchery and visit the Griffith Park Observatory," he tells me.

Berkland also took to science on his own. "I had a good friend, Bobby, whose father was a fireman, and he didn't get home much either. Catching horned toads was a major activity, and I remember grabbing a big one that threw back its head and squirted a red substance from its eyes. I thought I had broken its neck and ran three blocks to a humane society to save it." The vet took one look and despite Jim's tears, sent the boy on his way, but soon the horned toad was acting normally. Years later, in a college biology textbook, Jim read that horned toads could "reputedly" squirt a stream of substance from glands near their eyes as a protection. He thought, "What's this 'reputedly'? I had seen it with my own eyes." That lesson stayed with Jim Berkland through adulthood: "Believe what you have seen more than what you have read or heard from the so-called experts." And I'm not surprised by his statement at all.

In 1936, Berkland's dad passed a state exam and was appointed as an equipment storekeeper at Sonoma State Hospital in the Valley of the Moon. He went by himself to get settled in Glen Ellen, a town of 250 people. Then, by early spring 1937, Jim, his sister, Karen, and mother, Gertie, joined Mr. Berkland in Glen Ellen. And they soon had a great canine companion, Minnie, a border collie. He began an eight-year career at Dunbar Union Grammar School, fished and swam in Sonoma Creek, caddied at the golf course ($1.00 a round, with tips of zero to 50 cents), sold crawfish (at one cent) and French frogs (at 25 cents), gardened, and cleaned chicken houses (25 cents/hour). "It was as close to paradise as I will get while alive," recalls Berkland. And nature lovers can easily believe him.

Turbulent Times

On December 7, 1941, Berkland, at 11, remembers hearing on the radio that the Japanese had attacked Pearl Harbor. As a baby boomer, I can't relate to the '40s, but he recollects this era all too well. "Almost immediately, everything changed. There was rationing of sugar, coffee, chocolate, shoes, and gasoline. Both of my folks went to work on swing shift at Mare Island Naval Shipyard," he recalls. And Berkland won't forget that these were hard times and his dad began to "lose a battle with the bottle." Growing up in a household with an abusive father took a toll on the Berkland family. Divorce was the end result.

Later, things got worse, Berkland told me. In my Tahoe study, in fact, on December 13, 2004, he gave me the details. Berkland's worst nightmare came true when he was 20 years old. In March 1951, he had completed three years of junior college and had no money to go further, because his dad had used his $1,500 in savings bonds to meet current expenses. Berkland had begun working at Sonoma State Hospital as a psychiatric technician at $200 per month, with the hope of continuing his education soon.

One unforgettable night, about 2:00 a.m., Berkland was awakened by a loud argument between his parents. He recalls, "Dad became ever more threatening and held a hammer in his hand. Mom left and returned shortly with a .32 automatic in her hand. 'Put down the hammer, Joe,' she said. Instead, he charged at her with the hammer raised. A single shot penetrated his heart, and he collapsed on the kitchen floor. My mother picked up the phone and called the sheriff's office: 'I've shot my husband.'" The outcome: The grand jury cleared her because there had been a long trail of physical abuse.

Jim Berkland learned that growing up in a family with abuse and alcohol is violent and chaotic. One can't help but wonder, *Could there be an unconscious link to uncontrollable and devastating earthquakes and Berkland's dedication to predict them by giving people warnings to save lives?*

College Days, Field Work

Despite the disastrous family event, as well as growing up in a single-parent household, the facts show me that Berkland remained strong and steadfast, and persevered. He continued his education as planned. He received his A.A. degree in 1950 at Santa Rosa Junior College. He finished his upper-division classes at UC Berkeley, receiving a degree in geology in 1958. He went directly to work for six years with the USGS, involving laboratory and field work throughout the western United States, including Alaska. At the same time, Berkland worked on his master's degree in geology at San Jose State University, completing his course work in 1964.

After six years, Berkland left the USGS because he learned that only Ph.D.'s had a chance for a professional appointment, he says. His master's degree from SJSU wouldn't qualify him, although he notes he passed the USGS examination. "However, using the results of that exam, the U.S. Bureau of Reclamation made me an offer I couldn't refuse, from a GS-5 to a GS-7, still in the Department of the Interior and working out of Sacramento instead of Menlo Park," explains Berkland. So in 1964, he accepted the position as an engineering geologist. For the next five years, he worked on engineering projects involving the storage and moving of water at a number of dam sites, tunnels, and canals in California and Oregon. (See Chapter 9, "Pacific Northwest to Alaska.")

After more than 10 years with the Department of the Interior, he resigned his position in order to work on his doctorate at the University of California at Davis between 1969 and 1972. He recalls that this was an exciting time to share in the new revolution in earth sciences, as the theory of plate tectonics fleshed out the discredited concepts of continental drift. At the same time, Berkland became a house husband, and father to Krista, his daughter, while his wife, Jan, provided their sole income as she continued her career in teaching.

In 1972–73, Berkland held the position of assistant professor of geology at Appalachian State University in Boone, North Carolina, where he shared in the discovery of evidence for Pleistocene glaciation in the southern Appalachians.

One year later, after his teaching assignment, he and his family were in a station wagon homeward bound to the West Coast. "Beneath a canvas on the luggage rack were some suitcases and a large cardboard box with my precious, though unfinished, Ph.D. dissertation," Berkland tells me. After a side trip to Niagara Falls, when they were driving 70 miles per hour on Interstate 90, fate took a twisted turn, and Berkland's typed manuscript—complete with diagrams, tables, and photographs—blew out the window. It was like a scene straight out of *Wonder Boys* when Michael Douglas lost his only copy of a 700-page unfinished novel on the road. But thanks to good-hearted onlookers, with their help Berkland did manage to salvage his papers—several years of field work. Sadly, this event foreshadowed the future. While Berkland passed his Ph.D. oral exams, he didn't complete his dissertation within the required seven years, which is one of his few regrets.

From County Geologist to Quake Predictor

Once Berkland returned to California, he found a postcard that had been relayed from North Carolina. "It was from Santa Clara County and said they still had not found a suitable candidate to be its first county geologist. I had taken the highly competitive oral exam months earlier, and assumed that the position had been filled," he recalls. But the job was still available. Thus, Jim Berkland became the first county geologist for the most populated county in Northern California. He held that position from 1973 until his retirement in 1994.

It was during this period that Berkland noted that many earthquakes occurred at the same time as maximum tidal forces linked with the twice-monthly alignments of the Sun and Moon. He began to make informal predictions, scoring six out of eight during 1974, including the 5.2 magnitude Thanksgiving Day earthquake on November 27. "This one hit the day after I predicted it at a meeting of USGS geologists, and it shook my daughter and me while we were attending the movie *Earthquake*," he points out.

Despite Berkland's successes in earthquake prediction (using tidal flows and abnormal animal behavior), he found it almost impossible to publish on the subject in scientific journals. His career began to suffer, although his credentials included a fellowship in the Geological Society of America and membership in the Association of Engineering Geologists, Earthquake Engineering Research Institute, American Association for the Advancement of Science, Sigma Xi science honor society, Peninsula Geological Society (PGS), and Seismological Society of America; he's also been recognized in about eight *Who's Who?* publications, including the most prestigious, *Who's Who in America*.

Perhaps the greatest triumph and challenge in his career followed his prediction, in the *Gilroy Dispatch*, on Friday, October 13, that a major World Series earthquake would happen in eight days. It happened. After his suspension for two months, because he was misquoted by a reporter in *The Oakland Tribune* about predicting a larger quake and creating panic, he was allowed to resume his career only after promising not to predict any more quakes on county time. Then, Berkland followed his heart and his predictions continued on in his publication, *Syzygy—An Earthquake Newsletter*.

Since mid-1997, Berkland has developed an Internet website (*www.syzygyjob.com*), which has received more than 130 million hits, says Berkland, as he predicts earthquakes and reports these warnings every month on the site.

As you'll discover, Berkland is not only an energetic man. He also is well-traveled, a humanitarian, a nature lover, and an animal person. Plus, he got Mintu (Minnie two), a border collie mix, once he returned to Glen Ellen in the summer of 1997. Most important, this dedicated geologist, a poet at heart, has taken the less-traveled road to provide quake warnings to help save lives.

Now that you know *who* Jim Berkland is, I want to let you in on the details about exactly how this unconventional scientist fell into his "far-out" prediction theories linked to Mother Nature. Read on—and learn all about how Jim Berkland relies on the height of tides and the positions of the Sun, Earth, and Moon, and counts missing dogs and cats to predict earthquakes.

EARTHSHAKING FACTS
TO DOG-EAR

-◆ Don't always believe what you read in the newspaper or hear on the TV or radio. The media can and do overstate or understate earthquake predictions.

-◆ And note, the media often don't provide the complete or honest story about earthquake predictors.

-◆ Do understand that the government often conceals information about quake warnings to prevent public panic. (See Chapter 14, "Where Are the Quake Warnings?")

-◆ Use your head when you hear quake predictions. Don't panic, but get prepared for your safety's sake. In earthquake country, you and your family should always be ready.

-◆ Remember, earthquakes are uncontrollable events and happen every day. However, a quake warning for a significant earthquake might help to save your possessions, property, or life.

2 ⬥ Mother Nature's Forecasters

I'm often asked, "Why did you start predicting earthquakes?" I usually answer, "No other geologist was doing it, so I fell into it by default."

—Jim Berkland

IT ALL BEGAN MORE THAN 30 YEARS AGO. ON JANUARY 8, 1974, JIM BERKLAND read about a press release from the National Oceanic and Atmospheric Administration (NOAA) that warned of the potential for damaging coastal flooding because of an unusual astronomical alignment. "It referred to the first full moon of the year only 90 minutes from the closest approach of the Moon in two years, and a few days after the closest approach of Earth to the Sun. Thus, the three major tide-raising forces were almost coincident," recalls the geologist, a progressive thinker. He realized that these same tidal forces might deform the earth slightly and trigger earthquakes.

Berkland continues, "A quick review of the six most recent earthquakes in the San Francisco Bay Area revealed that all six had occurred at the times of the maximum astronomical tidal stresses on the earth. I made my first earthquake prediction on January 8, 1974, and called for a 4.0 to 5.0 magnitude quake locally within a week. Two days later, a 4.4 hit south of San Jose, and I thought how simple it was. Using similar criteria, I was correct for six of eight predictions that year, including the 5.2 magnitude Thanksgiving Day quake." But there's more…

The Prince of Tides and Moons

There are countless noteworthy events of tides and Berkland's quake predictions, too. For instance, two weeks before the highest tides of the century hit between December 29, 1986, and January 5, 1987, Berkland warned the Peninsula Geological Society that a 3.5-to-5.5 quake would hit the San Francisco Bay Area. Then, a 4.6 centered near San Jose, my hometown, struck on the first day of that seismic window. "The president of PGS sent me a letter of congratulations saying, 'I'll never doubt you again.' I thought he was endangering his 35-year career with the USGS until I later learned he had retired at the end of the year, two days after the quake," recalls Berkland.

But other scientists continue to doubt Berkland, who turns to the full and new moons every month to help him pinpoint upcoming quakes. As a creative ghostwriter for my cat Kerouac, I can tell you that he too uses lunar phases in his bimonthly horoscope column. However, Berkland's full moon phases and links to earthquakes are more than cat's play. Take a look at the links between these earthquakes and lunar phases:

- Long Beach earthquake, March 10, 1933: day of a lunar eclipse

- Hebgen, Montana, earthquake, August 19, 1959: day of the full moon

- San Fernando earthquake, February 9, 1971: day of a lunar eclipse

- Tabas, Iran, earthquake, August 17, 1978: day of a lunar eclipse

- Parkfield earthquake, September 28, 2004: day of the full moon

Says Berkland, "I don't think it's coincidental that the high tides of the September 28, 2004, full moon were on the day of the long-awaited 6.0 Parkfield earthquake, and that the January 16, 1995, Kobe, Japan quake, when at least 5,530 people were killed, was also on the day of the full moon and the high tide." In his 30 years of studying the tide-quake correlation, he has no doubt that it's real and that it has been recognized worldwide.

But some mainstream scientists and earthquake enthusiasts insist that Berkland can take any number of other great quakes and put them into a non-full-moon tide phase. They boldly point out to me that Berkland tends to emphasize the earthquakes that did hit during a lunar phase and tune out the ones that did not. So, is it just coincidence?

In December 2004, Berkland proved to one skeptical geologic colleague that his method is more than an accident and more valid than looking at the stars for answers. As Berkland tells it, he put his wallet where his mouth was and bet Dr. John Vidale, a seismologist at UCLA, that there would be a 4.5 magnitude quake in California during the perigean spring tide period of December 10 –17, 2004. On December 12, there was an earthquake southeast of Eureka that was reported as a 4.1 and then a 4.3. On December 13, when Berkland paid me a visit in Tahoe, I figured he still had time to hit it on the money. But he already had done just that, sort of.

"On December 14, I contacted the Berkeley Seismological Station and learned that the final determination was 4.3. However, the map of North America showed the epicenter and labeled it as 4.5 magnitude. Dr. Vidale indicated this was rounded up from 4.46 magnitude, which would be less than the required 4.5. Because of the ambiguity, we agreed to consider the wager as a draw. I was happy not to lose $500 in this widely discussed wager, but there was a final satisfying touch in the form of an email that I received on December 20, 2004:

Re: Blue Lakes Quake of Dec. 12, 2004

Hi Jim,

A correction to the previous email from my colleague. The initial Mw report was 4.3, but has since been revised to M4.5.[1] We will be revising the catalog shortly.

Lind S. Gee
Seismological Laboratory, UC Berkeley

---

1. According to Berkland, you can think of Mw (or M) as representing "whole magnitude." This is the symbol for moment magnitude on recent measurements of earthquakes that is intended to replace the Richter Magnitude (ML), which understates the total energy released by large tremors. M4.5 refers to the magnitude of an earthquake. The symbols Mw and M are used interchangeably.

Berkland's prediction of a California quake did indeed hit during the perigean spring tide of December 10–17, 2004. (By the way, perigean spring occurs two to five times per year. Spring tide alone occurs 26 times per year, so perigean spring is much more significant, explains Berkland.) But that's not all…

There's more confirmation from other quake experts on tides and earthquakes, according to Michael J. Kozuch, Ph.D., President/CEO of geoForecaster, Inc. Says Dr. Kozuch about Jim Berkland, "He has been a brave soul going against a very skeptical establishment, using tides for his forecasts. There is some merit to the correlation between tides and earthquakes even though the triggering forces are very small forces. I saw this years ago and have seen it in several papers."

He adds, "The problem with tides is that it raises overall seismicity [e.g., the number of total earthquakes] for large regions, but it does not tell you if a particular event will happen or not. So, as a forecast tool, you might use tides to say there is a heightened state of stress during high tides and you might issue some kind of general alert."

And month after month, year after year, Berkland has done just that. He looks at the tide table and publicizes his quake warnings, often before an earthquake hits.

The Power of Syzygy (Sizz'-a-Jee)

Twice a month, Berkland checks out an alignment of the centers of Earth, Sun, and Moon at the time of syzygy (new or full moon). He says the second most key tidal effect is the closest approach of the Moon to Earth at perigee. "This effect is dramatically enhanced when syzygy and perigee occur on the same day, but this occurs only from two to five times a year. Such a coincidence always creates what I call an eight-day seismic window," explains Berkland.

"The tide-raising forces are directly proportional to the mass and to the cube of the distance between the masses. Thus the Moon has 2.2 times the tidal effect that the Sun has on Earth, despite the much greater mass of the Sun. Based upon the rapid daily rise to peak tides, my seismic window may open up to three days before syzygy," he adds.

And it did just that, according to the Pacific Disaster Center, on November 1, 1755, when an 8.6 quake hit Lisbon, Portugal, just three days prior to the highest tidal forces of the year. According to the U.S. Geological Survey, after a tsunami and fire, 25 percent of Lisbon's population perished. (And note, the death toll, injuries, displaced people, and total structural damage, etc., caused by natural disasters can vary a lot depending on the source of the data.)

"Professor Vidale has stated repeatedly that the alignment of the Sun, Moon, and Earth at syzygy has no demonstrable effect on earthquakes. Yet he has coauthored a study in which he found a significant correlation between some earthquakes and extreme daily oceanic tides, apparently ignoring the fact that these maximum diurnal tides occur at the time of maximum biweekly syzygeal (near syzygy) tides. He can't have it both ways," insists Berkland.

Berkland's Seismic Window Theory

Actually, it was a past earthquake event that led Berkland to his seismic window theory. Back on July 1, 1911, the 6.6 magnitude Coyote earthquake shook a wide area in California, causing a salesman in San Francisco to die of a heart attack, notes Berkland. And, it was this strong Coyote quake that helped Berkland develop his seismic window theory in early 1974.

"It struck just five days after the top perigean tide of the year on June 26, 1911, when the new moon and the closest perigee of the year occurred only nine hours apart, which was a very rare synchroneity. There was also a 9.0-foot range of tides at the Golden Gate at that time, which was within 0.2 of the maximum in history," he explains. Synchroneity refers to the hours between syzygy and perigee. It is less than 25 hours only two to five times per year.

Every January, Berkland distributes the "Top Windows" list for the year, and makes his earthquake predictions of time, place, and magnitude. The magnitude and his confidence level are often adjusted upward as the critical period nears, and current local phenomena make it advisable to inform the public. For example, in 1989, he had given an

80 percent chance for a San Francisco Bay Area quake of 3.5 to 5.5 between October 14 and 21, based upon the highest tidal forces in three years. "During September and early October, there were many clues that the quake would be much stronger," recalls Berkland, "so I upgraded my confidence level to 85 percent and my prediction of magnitude to 6.5 to 7.0." (To learn what these many clues were, see Chapter 4, "The Grr-eat Cat-aclysm".)

Soon after Berkland became the first county geologist for Santa Clara County, he enjoyed sharing information with Edgar Bailey, a USGS geologist and his geologic mentor, whom he worked closely with during his six years' experience with the USGS. Bailey once told Berkland, "I don't know much about your seismic windows, but at least you have introduced an interesting word (syzygy) into the popular lexicon. Jim, it is clear that you will never convince your severest critics about the validity of your theory. Your goal is to outlive them, or have your ideas outlive them." And in the twenty-first century, Berkland's seismic windows are doing just that.

Berkland notes a list of killer quakes posted on the *LiveScience* website (*www.livescience.com*). On the following page, take a look at the death toll of each, and how 85 percent fit Berkland's eight-day seismic window theory related to syzygy. Plus, according to Berkland, 17 of 20 quakes were from syzygy minus 2 to syzygy plus 6 in seismic windows; 16/31 days equals 52 percent for the chance expectation to fit the theory. He adds, "It doesn't take a statistician to note that this is a significant correlation with higher tidal forces."

Berkland Does Windows for the World

While Berkland does mention quakes around the country that occur in or close to his primary seismic windows and secondary seismic windows, he doesn't do specific predictions for states in the Midwest, South, or East Coast. "I don't predict there because I don't have updated local information as I do for the West Coast."

But Berkland does urge residents of states in those regions to make use of his seismic windows for their own earthquake prepared-

Place	Date	Death Toll	New Moon/Full Moon ± Days
Iran	Jun. 20, 1990	50,000	NM - 2; P - 1
Calabria, Italy	Feb. 04, 1783	50,000	NM - 3 days Miss
Quetta, Pakistan	May 30, 1935	30,000-60,000	FM - 1; P + 5
Sicily, Italy	Jan. 11, 1693	60,000	NM + 3
Silicia, Asia Minor	1268	60,000	No data
Peru	May 31, 1970	66,000	F + 11days Miss
Gansu, China	Dec. 25, 1932	70,000	NM - 2;P + 0
Lisbon, Portugal	Nov. 01, 1755	70,000	FM - 2;P - 2
Tabriz, Iran	Nov. 18, 1727	77,000	FM - 1
Shemakha, Caucasia	Nov. 1667	80,000	No data
Chihli, China	Sept. 1290	100,000	No data
Messina, Italy	Dec. 28, 1908	70,000-100,000	NM + 5
Ashgabat, USSR	Oct. 05, 1948	110,000	NM + 3
Tokyo, Japan	Sept. 01, 1923	143,000	NM + 6
Ardabil, Iran	Mar. 23, 893 +	150,000	NM + 1
Gansu, China	Dec. 16, 1920	200,000	NM + 6
Damghan, Iran	Dec. 22, 856 +	200,000	NM - 3 days before syzygy
Xining, China	May 22, 1927	200,000	FM + 6
Aleppo, Syria	Aug. 09, 1138	230,000	NM + 5
Sumatra	Dec. 26, 2004	283,106	FM + 0
Tanshan, China	Jul. 27, 1976	655,000	NM + 0
Shansi, China	Jan. 23, 1556	830,000	NM + 3

ness, and to learn if they have the same time frames. The key is that he doesn't read more into his window than the facts justify. "I am not psychic," he emphasizes. And note, Berkland's seismic windows apply to the United States as well as worldwide, especially the quake-prone region of the Pacific Ring of Fire. (See Chapter 13, "The Great Quake-Tsunami of 2004.")

Counting the Number of Lost Pets

Another variable in Berkland's earthquake-predicting formula (and you can use this whether you live in Phoenix, Chicago, Omaha, or New York City) is nothing more sophisticated than the number of missing-cat ads in newspapers. According to Berkland, cats and dogs go AWOL when they feel an earthquake coming.

For more than 25 years, Berkland has performed daily tallies of the number of missing felines and canines listed in the lost and found sections of the *San Jose Mercury News*, *San Francisco Examiner/Chronicle*, and the *Los Angeles Examiner*. He applies this missing cat and dog approach to a combination method of predicting earthquakes, which is based primarily on the height of the Pacific tides. Also remember, he observes the alignment of the Sun, Earth, and Moon, plus the proximity of the Moon and Sun to Earth. He then considers the seismic windows. And undeniably, this dedicated avant-garde scientist readily admits that the furry four-leggers have been very useful in his earthquake forecasts. The tides tell him when. The animals tell him where with an indication of how big.

Berkland probably never would have thought of this missing cat system if it hadn't been for physicist Antonio Nafarrate of San Jose, who began to count lost cat advertisements in the local newspaper in April 1979. When Nafarrate originally telephoned Berkland to explain his method of earthquake prediction, he told the geologist that his upcoming seismic window was indeed correct—because the cats were disappearing again. Berkland, somewhat dumbfounded by his caller's statement, replied, "Oh, how do you know that?" The physicist answered, "I looked at the lost and found column in the *San Jose Mercury*

News." Yet the once no-nonsense geologist who specializes in dealing with the physical nature and history of the earth told me he almost hung up on the man who initiated the quirky but doable missing cat system.

Instead of hanging up, Berkland took into consideration his own cat, Rocky, who had gone AWOL on Berkland's birthday, July 31, 1979, six days before the strongest quake in the county since 1911. This was the Coyote Lake 5.9 quake of August 6 in California. "I never considered putting an ad in the paper, and most people don't place lost cat ads. So when you see an advertisement it probably represents at least ten—maybe a hundred—cats. And when you see it jump from two to eight cats missing, that's usually significant," Berkland told me. Berkland didn't systematically look at lost cat ads until Rocky reappeared after six months on January 20, 1980. The cat was evidently in excellent health, which indicated to Berkland that Rocky had stayed at another home for the time of his absence and escaped the Livermore, California, earthquakes on January 24 and 26 of 1980, which registered at a 5.5–5.9 magnitude.

This convinced the geologist, as he had personally experienced that his own cat actually anticipated the tremors by a few days. Berkland combined his missing pet occurrences along with maximum tidal forces to verify his seismic window. Continuing studies by Berkland validated Nafarrate's missing cat system and that the lost and found column is a good, objective indicator of how many frightened animals are out there just before an earthquake arrives. A caution is that a significant flight of pets also follows violent thunderstorms and the annual Fourth of July fireworks. For most years, the annual maximum of missing pet ads is noted between July 8 and 12. If the numbers exceed that amount during another time of year, it is a quake warning that should not be ignored.

Since 1974, Berkland's findings have been logged in a system he calls his "CATalog," which documents the numbers of missing felines and canines listed in California's three major newspapers. The "Fe-line" is a graph that makes a pictorial representation of what's in the

CATalog. The missing cat system is part of a three-pronged method of earthquake prediction that Berkland calls his "Three Double G" system. Part 1 relates to the gravity gradient, or the forces exacted on the earth by the gravitational pull of the Sun and the Moon. Part 2 is named "Gone Gatos," as it pertains to the missing cats (gatos is Spanish for cats). Berkland believes that cats and other animals are able to detect changes in the earth's magnetic field, and the magnetic field changes drastically a few hours or days before a quake. Part 3 is "Geyser Gaps," in which Berkland monitors erratic behavior of a Napa Valley, California, geyser called Old Faithful. When the geyser fails to erupt every 45 minutes, Berkland has discovered a quake usually follows.

These far-out theories of Berkland's also include strange animal behavior such as homing pigeons losing their way during races, worms wriggling up out of the soil, snakes deserting their dens, and confused swarms of bees flying into churches as harbingers of earthquakes. (See Chapter 3, "Berkland Turns to Cats and Dogs.")

Short-Term Clues about Earthquakes

While scientists continue to ignore earthquake prediction and tend to focus on long-term earthquake forecasting methods, Berkland, like the film Phenomenon's character George Malley (John Travolta), doesn't tune out phenomena linked to oncoming quakes.

"I have never considered quakes to be random events, despite assurance by many experts of high science that they were unpredictable," says Berkland, who points out that many scientific papers have been published that show possible correlations to short-term signals of earthquakes. These earthquake precursory effects include large new reservoirs, pumping in deep wells, heavy rainfall, time of the year, time of day, patterns of small tremors, seismic velocity changes, atmospheric pressure changes, seismic gaps in time and/or space, tectonic creep rates, strain rates, earthquake lights, earthquake sounds, sensitive people, etc. "Keep in mind," adds Berkland, "most have been totally rejected by the keepers of high wisdom."

And while lunar phases, tidal flows, lost cats and dogs, strange animal behavior, and other earthquake precursors are still ignored by USGS scientists, Berkland believes otherwise, as you'll discover in the next chapter.

EARTHSHAKING FACTS
TO DOG·EAR

- ◀ Each month note on your calendar the dates of the new and full moons and eight-day seismic windows.

- ◀ Take note of the tidal stresses each month. Consider purchasing an annual tide calendar, like Berkland does every year.

- ◀ Only the "when" of earthquakes can be provided by the tides and the lunar phases.

- ◀ The "where" and "how big" require additional clues you can find by detecting them in your local region (i.e., strange animal behavior, earth changes, etc.).

- ◀ Beware of the powerful alignment of the centers of Earth, Sun, and Moon at the times of syzygy (full and new moons).

- ◀ If it is a seismic window, and your pet is acting strangely, tally up the number of lost pets in the classified ads.

- ◀ Also for a quake warning, be aware of uncharacteristic animal behavior both indoors and outdoors.

3 ⫸ Berkland Turns to Cats and Dogs

Nature has much to teach us if we will only listen.

—Jim Berkland

SINCE I'M A CALIFORNIA NATIVE, I'M USED TO THE GROUND SHAKING VIOLENTLY. And as a pet person, I know getting a heads up from kitty isn't an unheard of phenomenon before a tremor. In fact, a cat's sensitivity to an oncoming earthquake can occur much earlier than what you may have observed, according to Jim Berkland. He believes cats can sense an imminent quake and often react with various abnormal behaviors, including leaving a week or so before it hits.

From the first moment I spoke with Berkland back in 1982 (the same year *The Jupiter Effect*, the intriguing but erroneous book, was popular), I could tell he is a Type A person. He's on a lifetime mission of sorts. By that I mean that this brilliant man cares about people, his community, the nation, and the world. It's his passion. It's his purpose in life. And as a dedicated senior scientist, he exudes enthusiasm with a capital E about his work—and that is our bond. Plus, our big working connection is still animals.

Odd Feline Behavior

Early in 1982, Berkland was on his way to purchase a tide table. He unexpectedly walked inside The Cat Clinic and introduced himself to James Stiles, D.V.M. The geologist said boldly, "This may sound weird, but I think cats can tell about quakes before they happen." Dr. Stiles answered, "Oh yeah? Tell me about it."

The 43-year-old vet easily recalled the behavior of three separate patients before the 1980 Livermore, California, earthquakes of January 24 and 26 hit. In fact, the animal doc's records pinpointed cats affected with feline urological syndrome (FUS) on January 2, 19, 23, and 28, and February 2. Simply put, FUS includes common disorders such as cystitis, infections, urethral blockage, and uremia. Some common symptoms a cat with FUS will experience include straining to urinate, frequent trips to the litter box, and urinating in inappropriate spots. Today, we know that stress can trigger FUS, but at that time, the vet's records had nothing to do with earthquake forecasting. Nevertheless, Dr. Stiles always thought that since the syndrome seemed to occur in rashes prior to quakes, it was strange.

How Do They Know?

According to Berkland, dogs are more sensitive to movements of the earth's crust because of their heightened sense of orientation. He suggests that dogs are able to detect minute changes in the earth's magnetic field, due to magnetite in their bodies; magnetite is magnetic iron oxide grains that are common in many rocks. Recent research on magnetite suggests it is the cause of homing pigeons' navigational ability, along with that of dolphins, salmon, sharks, whales, butterflies, and other migrating animals.

The magnetic field fluctuates a few days or hours before a quake, Berkland says. Then animals are disoriented or frightened, and some run away. Many dogs find their way home by pulling a "homeward bound" journey and trek hundreds and sometimes thousands of miles. "They're not using psychic ability or smelling their way home," Berkland says. "They actually have a sense of orientation, thanks to the magnetite and the earth's magnetic field." Berkland says the magnetic field gets distorted locally because of upcoming earthquakes. The stress in the earth's crust causes magnetite to change its magnetic properties. And dogs and other animals seem to pick up these rather abrupt changes in the magnetic field. For small quakes, they get warnings of seven to ten days, but up to three weeks prior to large quakes, such as the California tremors in Loma Prieta in October 1989 and the Northridge quake in Los Angeles in January 1994.

Having raised homing pigeons in the 1940s, Berkland was one of the first people to recognize that they use the earth's magnetic field for homing, and that they become confused prior to earthquakes. "In the 1970s, I became aware of studies that proved magnetite was produced behind pigeons' eyeballs and that when they fly in circles prior to homing, they were becoming mini-generators by breaking lines of magnetic flux with their own magnetic material. They become disoriented when the magnetic field becomes anomalous and produce 'smash races,' where many of the homing pigeons become lost," he explains.

Berkland adds that he met a longtime pigeon racer, Nick Corini of Morgan Hill, California, and for several years coordinated pigeon races with him. "I warned him of upcoming quakes so that he held back his most valuable birds," he notes. "His top bird, Roving Girl, flew the coop the night before the World Series quake and didn't return for a week."

However, Corini didn't know of any link to quakes until he gave Berkland several dates of mysterious smash races, which seemed to correlate with earthquake epicenters in time and space. Nick recalled that the most disastrous pigeon race in Bay Area history had happened years ago when only 10 percent of the birds returned. It took him several days to go back through more than 30 years of the pigeon fancier's record books. As Berkland described it, "When Nick gave me the date of their worst known smash race, I got a chill down my spine. It was March 24, 1964. That was the Good Friday earthquake in southern Alaska. There was a huge magnetic anomaly prior to that quake." As a result, the theory, points out Berkland, is that electromagnetic emanations from the earth prior to tremors explain most of the strange animal reports, whether it is pigeons or lost cats and dogs. (See Chapter 9, "Pacific Northwest to Alaska.")

Back in 1989, Bruce Presgrave, a former geophysicist for the National Earthquake Information Center (NEIC) in Golden, Colorado, told me that immediately before humans detect an earthquake, animals can often perceive it. "In those cases we are talking about tens of seconds," Presgrave said. "Basically, animals are more sensitive to the P-wave (the first arriving wave), which humans are insensitive to. So at that point they're not predicting the earthquake; they're just feeling the earthquake sooner than we can. As for whether animals can sense an earthquake coming before they've actually felt those seismic waves (which indicate that the earthquake has actually happened) requires more research."

I know from my own experiences that dogs can and do bark, whine, or run to cover before earthquakes strike. One dog was reported to have run about the house for 10 seconds before a tremor shock was felt, and then it jumped out of an open window down one story to the ground. Some bitches have brought their puppies to what apparently seemed to them safer quarters. The most common report, however, regarding the behavior of dogs before a tremor is their howling during the night preceding the earthquake.

Birds (and Other Animals) Do It, Too

Odd animal behavior before quakes is nothing new. Reports exist from survivors of earthquakes like the one in Haicheng, China, on February 4, 1975. Chinese seismologists claim that during the few days before the quake, frogs and fish killed themselves trying to break through the ice in rivers and ponds; horses, cows, and pigs ran off. A few days after the strange animal behavior began, a 7.3 quake flattened the city, destroying 90 percent of the buildings. But because city officials took heed of the animal warnings, the city was evacuated hours before the quake. As a result, fatalities were far fewer than they could have been. But the Chinese weren't able to forecast the earthquake in July 1976, which killed more than 600,000 people.

So, with unforgettable hit-and-miss reports such as these and on into the present day, experts at the USGS don't give much credence to animal behavior as a source of scientific evidence of an oncoming earthquake. Scientists at the U.S. Geological Survey in Menlo Park, California, admit that they have not yet reached the point where they can predict earthquakes reliably. Meanwhile, Berkland is still busy at work. He counts lost cats and dogs and looks at the sky to predict quakes. And many different newspapers, such as the *Chicago Tribune*, *San Jose Mercury News*, *The Arizona Republic*, and *The Washington Post*, have published Berkland's quake predictions before and after they became history.

Keep in mind, Berkland is hardly the first scientist to recognize that some animals can become aware of some earthquakes before they occur. "I am the first to record daily for 25 years the lost and found pet ads in several newspapers," he notes.

Is It ESP?

Cats have an amazing ability to sense earthquakes. Whether it's ESP (extrasensory perception), superior senses, feline intuition, or a change in routine, your cat may sense danger, and you should know about it.

On August 12, 1998, Central California experienced an earthquake measuring 5.4 on the Richter scale, which struck the San Andreas fault near San Juan Bautista and was felt in San Francisco, 90 miles away. Cat lovers reported odd behavior in their cats hours—even days—before the earthquake occurred. "My feisty, semi-feral calico cat, Bonnie, was crying incessantly that night. She got more and more adamant as the night progressed," says a resident of San Ramon, a town 67 miles from the quake's epicenter. "The next morning, she was quiet and calm," she says, adding, "my other cats acted normally."

Berkland predicted that the quake would occur between August 7 and 14, calling the seismic window "a hint of things to come. I had rated the probability of such a quake at 80 percent because of the tides associated with the lunar eclipse on August 7," Berkland says, "augmented by the near-record 24 missing cat ads on July 30, in the *San Jose Mercury News*."

A British TV crew was interviewing Berkland at his Glen Ellen, California, home on August 12, 1998, and asked him for specific quake predictions on camera. He recalls, "Encouraged by high numbers of missing pets and the recent syzygy eclipse, I told them, 'Today I am predicting an earthquake of at least 4.5 within three days.'" That night in their San Francisco hotel, the British media crew were shaken by the 5.4 quake in the South Bay (before they could fly from San Francisco to Japan the next day), reports Berkland. "They called to congratulate me," he adds.

My geologist pal also told me, "Cats are better than any black box or electronic equipment." He believes some cats hold mysterious psychic powers as well, citing his past pet bobcat, Cee Cee, as an example. "When Cee Cee remained at my Glen Ellen home with my mother during my irregular commute trips, he would behave abnormally just before I would return. About 20 minutes before my arrival, Cee Cee would stop whatever he was doing and stand expectantly at the front door, awaiting my entrance," he told me. Even many housecats (and dogs) are ready and waiting for their owners to walk in the door. So, was Cee Cee psychic? Or was he merely used to a routine?

For Berkland, that was no "routine," since the time and day of his returns varied from week to week. "Watch dense flights of birds or schools of tropical fish and note instant twists and turns without chaotic behavior and appreciate the fact that the motions are like individual cells in a human body, reacting as if by some electrical connection," explains Berkland.

Playing the Odds on Tabby

Interestingly enough, the quake radius maximum in connection to the missing cat system is not just workable in the vicinity where the lost and found ads are placed. Berkland explains that if he suddenly sees a lot of missing animals in the San Jose region and not in San Francisco, then he believes there may be a quake due east or south of San Jose, rather than north toward San Francisco. On the other hand, if he sees a lot of missing cats or dogs in the Los Angeles Times and in the San Jose Mercury News, then he estimates a quake could be somewhere in between, and has made a number of successful predictions using such data.

Awareness of odd feline and animal activity used as a method of earthquake prediction is still a controversial subject today. The USGS does not give much credit to uppity cats or wayward whales as a source of scientific evidence of an oncoming earthquake. Jerry Eaton, a former seismologist for the USGS in Menlo Park, told me that not very many people are in the game of trying to predict earthquakes with the sort of material he is using. "All these strange things animals do," said Eaton, "they do every day." (But, I ponder, how would he know?) And according to most seismologists, there is no firm scientific evidence that cats or other animals can sense the advent of an earthquake.

Still, others do believe it's a good idea to tabulate lost cats and dogs. "I'm all in favor of using the behavior of pets to predict earthquakes, and the Chinese have done a great job in applying this," notes British author Rupert Sheldrake. And Japanese researcher Kiyoshi Shimamura, a public health doctor, has done just that and claims dogs can sense oncoming quakes.

"Shimamura noted that the unusual behavior, such as incessant barking and biting, had begun about one month before the disastrous 6.8 Kobe earthquake of January 16, 1995. The behavioral anomalies were 60 percent higher compared with the previous year," Berkland notes, and points out seismically sensitive animals are a valuable tool in earthquake prediction—and one he puts to work.

A Man's Best Friend: Quakes and Four-leggers

While the USGS believes there is no correlation between pets and earthquakes, Berkland insists that dogs and cats can and have sensed quakes before they actually hit. Take a look at this prediction list (compiled by Berkland), which covers hits of 23 primary quakes of 5.0 to 7.1 in the San Francisco Bay Area in the 30 years from 1973 through 2004. As Berkland puts it, "I successfully predicted all within one day, except the last one, which was predicted by my seismic window theory, but not directly by me."

100% hit

Thanksgiving Day quake (5.2), Nov. 28, 1974

Prediction:	Top seismic window, Nov. 29–Dec. 6. Predicted 3.5–5.5M to Pick & Hammer Club on Nov. 27.
Pets:	Missing dog ads increase from 35 to 54 in 5 days by Nov. 23.

100% hit

Stone Canyon quake (5.0), Oct. 18, 1977

Prediction:	Top seismic window list, Oct. 12–19.
Pets:	No missing animal data.

100% hit

Coyote Lake quake (5.9), Aug. 6, 1979

Prediction:	Top seismic window, list for Aug. 07–14 (FM – 1). Predicted to USGS. Maximum magnitude since 1911 in Bay Area. Maximum tides in 6 months. Fourteen hours early, but several aftershocks met prediction entirely.
Pets:	Missing dog ads increase from 37 to 52 in 4 days by July 27. Missing cat ads increase from 3 to 8 in 4 days by July 31.

90% hit

Livermore quake (5.9), Jan. 24, 1980

Prediction:	Top seismic window for Jan. 16–23. Maximum quake located in Contra Costa County. Maximum tides in 6 months.
Pets:	Missing dog ads increase from 35 to 46 in 4 days by Jan. 26. Day late.

100% hit
Eureka quake (7.4) , Nov. 8, 1980

Prediction: Predicted 6.5+M to USGS Hotline tape for Earthquake Watch at noon on Nov. 7. Historic maximum geyser interval, 3 hours 12 minutes on Nov. 7.

Pets: Missing dog ads increase from 27 to 46 in 4 days by Nov. 5. Missing cat ads increase from 4 to 14 in 4 days by Nov. 8 (maximum total for 1980).

100% hit
Coalinga quake (6.7), May 2, 1983

Prediction: Top seismic window, Apr. 26–May 3. Evacuated Santa Clara County Building. Record precipitation and flooding in San Joaquin Valley.

Pets: Missing dog ads increase from 20 to 53 in 5 days by Apr. 23; also 31 to 50 overnight by Apr. 27.

100% hit
Point Sur quake (5.4), Jan. 22, 1984

Prediction: Top seismic window for Jan. 16–22. (FM + 4; P + 3). Predicted to *Sonoma Index-Tribune* on Jan. 21.

Pets: Missing dog ads increase from 31 to 50 in 2 days by Jan. 18.

100% hit
Morgan Hill quake (6.2), Apr. 24, 1984

Prediction: (FM – 9). Predicted Bay Area 6.0+ for 1984 to SEEQ Technology, SIRs (a San Jose electronics firm, Sons in Retirement Society), Milpitas City Council, Campbell Chamber of Commerce. Predicted for March, April, or

October following all-time record annual precipitation in 1983. Previous record precipitation was in 1889 followed by 6.5 on Apr. 24, 1890.

Pets: Missing dog ads increase from 14 to 42 in 2 days by Apr. 18.

100% hit
Bear Valley quake (5.0), Jan. 13, 1986

Prediction: Top seismic window for Jan, 8–15. (NM + 3; P + 6).

Pets: Missing dog ads increase from 26 to 52 in 2 days.

100% hit
Super Bowl quake (5.5), Jan. 26, 1986

Prediction: Predicted to *Hollister Free Lance* on Jan. 24. In special prediction window Jan. 24–31.

Pets: Missing dog ads increase from 19 to 43 in 3 days by Jan. 22. Missing cat ads increase from 5 to 11 in 5 days by Jan. 25.

100% hit
Mount Sizer quake (5.7), Mar. 31, 1986

Prediction: Top seismic window 24–31. (FM + 6; P + 4). Predicted to *San Jose Mercury News* on Mar. 29. Time Research Co-prediction. Repeated prediction for larger quake following 4.0 in East Bay on Mar. 29.

Pets: Missing dog ads increase from 23 to 56 in 6 days by Mar. 15.

100% hit

Bishop quake (6.6), July 21, 1986

Prediction: Top seismic window of July 20–27. (FM+; P + 2). Predicted in *San Jose Mercury News* on July 20.

Pets: Missing dog ads increase from 29 to 51 in 5 days by July 19. Missing cat ads increase from 3 to 8 in 2 days by July 16.

100% hit

Cabernet quake (Hollister) (5.5), Feb. 20, 1988

Prediction: Top seismic window Feb. 16–23. (NM + 3; P + 3). Predicted to *Gilroy Dispatch*.

Pets: Missing dog ads increase from 15 to 74 in 4 days by Feb. 20. Missing cat ads increase from 7 to 15 in 3 days by Feb. 20.

100% hit

Alum Rock Park quake (5.4), June 12, 1988

Prediction: Top seismic window June 12–19. (NM – 2; P + 8). Predicted to *Milpitas Post* and to Lions Club. It hit during the meeting.

Pets: Missing dog ads increase from 15 to 39 in 5 days by June 11. Missing cat ads increase from 3 to 8 in 4 days by June. 21.

100% hit

Redwood Estates quake (5.5), June 27, 1988

Prediction: Top seismic window June 27–Jul. 04 (FM – 1; P – 3).

Pets: Missing dog ads increase from 23 to 47 in 4 days by June 25.

100% hit
San Jose quake (5.0), Apr. 3, 1989

Prediction: Top seismic window Apr. 3–10 (NM – 2; P – 2).

Pets: Missing dog ads increase from 20 to 41 in 4 days by March 24. Missing cat ads increase from 9 to 15 in 4 days by Mar. 31.

100% hit
Lake Elsman quake (5.5), Aug. 8, 1989

Prediction: Top seismic window Aug. 1–8, (NM + 7).

Pets: Missing dog ads increase from 26 to 36 in 4 days by Aug. 4. Missing cat ads increase from 9 to 15 in 4 days by July 28. Dog ads increased from 26 to 36 in four days by Aug. 4.

Multiple critters' hit
Loma Prieta quake (7.1), Oct. 17, 1989

Prediction: Top seismic window Oct. 14–21, (FM + 3; P + 3). Predicted 6.5–7.0M to *Gilroy Dispatch* on Oct. 13. First 7M Loma Prieta quake on Oct. 8, 1865 (FM + 4; P + 4) was under identical astronomical conditions. I had predicted to KCBS radio and the *San Francisco Examiner*.

Pets: Missing dog ads increase from 33 to 58! in 4 days by Oct. 13; also 21 to 57! in 4 days by Sept. 22. Missing cat ads increase from 11 to 18 in 3 days by Oct. 13; also 13 to record 27 in 3 days by Sept. 22. Pigeons lost; whales beached locally; hot springs became cooler.

100% hit
East Gilroy quake (5.6), Jan. 15, 1993

Prediction: Top seismic window (FM + 7). Predicted in *Syzygy*; to TV crew for SciFi Channel, on camera at my home. Four hours later, they were startled in a San Jose motel. (My prediction was verified in credits at end of TV show.)

Pets: Missing dog ads increase from 25 to 56 in 4 days by Jan. 15; also 17 to 47 in 4 days by Jan. 8. Missing cat ads increase from 11 to 23 in 5 days by Jan. 10.

100% hit
Gilroy quake (5.6), Aug. 12, 1998

Prediction: Top seismic window Aug. 07–14 (FM + 5; P + 1). On Aug. 11 at 5 p.m. I predicted a 4.5+ within 3 days to BBC TV crew. Fourteen hours later, they were shocked in San Francisco hotel before they flew to Japan to complete their show.

Pets: Missing dog ads increase from 12 to 25 in 3 days by July 30. Missing cat ads increase from 13 to 21 in 3 days by July 30.

100% hit
Bolinas quake (5.0), Aug. 17, 1999

Prediction: In top seismic window Aug. 10–17. (NMe + 6; P + 10). Strongest San Andreas fault quake north of San Francisco since 1906. Six days after total solar eclipse.

Pets: Missing dog ads increase from 8 to 15 in 4 days by Aug. 13. Missing cat ads increase from 7 to 14 in 4 days by Aug. 6.

100% hit
Napa quake (5.2), Sept. 3, 2000

Prediction: Top seismic window Aug. 27–Sept. 03 (FM + 6; P + 8).

Pets: Missing dog ads increase from 12 to 26 in two days by August 25. Missing cat ads increase from 9 to 13 in 4 days by Sept. 2.

100% hit
West Gilroy quake (5.2), June 12, 2002

Prediction: Secondary window, June 11–18, (FM + 0)

Pets: Missing dog ads increase from 4 to 11 in 4 days by May 10. Missing cat ads increase from 3 to 6 in 3 days by May 11.

Meanwhile, some scientists who study geological fault lines or monitor seismometers in an attempt to predict earthquakes think Jim Berkland is a "charlatan" and a "clown." However, the USGS admits that it still has not yet reached the point where it can predict earthquakes reliably, whereas Berkland claims a 75 percent accuracy rate of forecasting quakes. Keep in mind, 20 years ago, I wrote this same sentence for magazine articles, and the words haven't changed at all.

So, at sunrise Berkland reads the newspaper headlines and then turns directly to the lost and found ads. But most important, Berkland told me in a soft tone of voice, "I hope it won't take the 'big one' to wake people up." Possibly, Berkland knows that counting missing cats is way out on the fringes of science, but then again, this creative geologist's CAT-alogs and Fe-line graphs may mark the beginning of a recognized phenomenon. Perhaps Berkland may be on the edge of a major breakthrough regarding accuracy of earthquake prediction, which our cats and dogs could very well be part of forecasting.

But note, not all animals can and do predict earthquakes or sense when their humans are coming home, like Cee Cee, the sensitive bobcat. And speaking of odd animal behavior, before the World Series quake, were the cats and dogs in the San Francisco Bay area responding to earthquake precursors, or were they behaving strangely due to other causes? Read on—and discover exactly what pets were doing before the big quake hit home.

EARTHSHAKING FACTS
TO DOG-EAR

—⦙⦙► If your cat is making frequent trips to the litter box, straining or meowing when he tries to go, it's time to go to the vet. If Felix is diagnosed with FUS, it may be time to check Berkland's seismic window for the month.

—⦙⦙► In some ways, cats and dogs know more than you do.

—⦙⦙► So if your cat or dog starts acting really strange, it may be time to stock up on disaster survival supplies. On the other hand, your cat may just be out of sorts because of a new cat on the block.

—⦙⦙► Next time your pooch howls at night, give Rover a doggie treat to reinforce psychic behavior. Plus, consider it a Lassie-type warning and get your survival kit items all in a row.

4 ⫷⫸ The Grr-eat Cat-aclysm of '89

Animals knew this quake was coming weeks ago.

—Jim Berkland

I REMEMBER MY FOOD-LOVING, SENSITIVE, ORANGE-AND-WHITE CAT ALEX DID NOT eat on the morning of October 17, 1989. At 5:04 p.m., a 7.1 earthquake rumbled through the San Francisco Bay Area. It was a frightening experience for me, my three cats, my dog, and other pets and their people. It was a hot, Indian sum mer day that I will never forget. I still have memories of the eerie sound of the quake, like a freight train roaring through my San Carlos bungalow, as the windows rattled. I grabbed my yellow Lab Carmella and headed for the front doorway. It's basic instinct for any California native when the earth shakes, rattles, and rolls. But this monster was intense. It was big. It was unforgettable.

After the quake hit, I sat jittery and glued to the TV (now put on the floor) for days, watching the incredible damage to Santa Cruz, San Francisco—places I've lived, places I love. At night, I slept in the living room with my dog and two cats, Gandalf and Ashley. (Like many people who chose to sleep outside, Alex, my super sensitive feline was too spooked to come inside the house.) For weeks I kept the light on, a dog leash and tennis shoes beneath me. I, like countless other Bay Area residents, was trying to cope with the trauma of the 7.1 monster quake and its multiple aftershocks.

During the weeks that followed, as a devout pets writer and long-time fan and friend of Jim Berkland, I landed five national magazine article assignments. It was my job to document the aftermath of the

San Francisco Bay Area earthquake and how it affected Californians. I sat on edge in my study, writing copy in between nerve-wracking aftershocks. Often clad in a white T-shirt with the orange words "I Survived the World Series Quake," I could not help getting an adrenaline rush each and every time I interviewed Berkland.

On Friday, October 13, 1989—just four days before the quake—Jim Berkland had called a local newspaper to report this was a "perfect" time for a tremor to hit. Years later, I read the short article, which made me wonder and smile about Jim Berkland, the so-called charlatan geologist.

Gilroy Dispatch
October 13, 1989

Is "World Series" Quake Coming?

While the Bay Area is rumbling with excitement over the first-ever Bay Bridge World Series, the Earth may be putting on a show. A county geologist is predicting an earthquake to hit the Bay Area anytime from tomorrow to the 21st of October. It will be the "World Series Quake," according to Santa Clara County geologist Jim Berkland. The temblor, he predicts, could be anywhere from 3.5-to-6.0 on the Richter scale. Berkland is basing his prediction on the unusual gravitational pull of the Moon and Earth.

What led this California geologist to stick his neck out this way? Cats and dogs. While Berkland relies on moons and tides before pets, this time was different. (See Chapter 2, "Mother Nature's Forecasters"). Too many "Felixes" and "Rovers" in the Bay Area had disappeared, and that always makes Berkland uneasy. Three weeks before he phoned the *Gilroy Dispatch*, there were 27 missing cats, a record high compared to an average of four or five. There were also 57 dogs missing in late September, again a record high number except for the usual Fourth of

July fireworks scares.

Four days after he notified the newspaper, at 5:04 p.m., just as the third game of the 1989 World Series was about to begin, the ground shook violently for 15 seconds along the San Andreas fault. It was the deadliest earthquake to jolt Northern California since the San Francisco quake of 1906, which measured a hefty 8.3 on the Richter scale.

Berkland wasn't surprised. While most experts could pin down the next California quake within a 30-year span, Berkland was right to the week!

Cat Cues to Quaking

Animal people often get purr-fect cues from their cats (and dogs) before an earthquake. My former neighbor Nate Murray of San Carlos, California, had five cats. On August 7, 1989, he noticed "two of my cats were fighting. The others didn't want to eat and were quieter than normal all day. Around one in the morning on August 8, the house shook and the windows rattled. When I looked for my cats, there wasn't one around."

My Siamese-Manx insisted on going outside immediately after the tremor, I recall after experiencing the 5.6 quake on August 8, 1989. Ashley didn't want to come back inside. Later that day, we had two strong aftershocks. In fact, my once indoor cat changed her main residence to outdoors in the violet morning glory bushes—up until the day after the World Series quake hit.

A day before the quake, Maggie, a feisty Siamese, confused her owner, Charles Abbott, another San Carlos resident. Charles recalls that the morning before the quake, his cat was reacting out of the ordinary. "Maggie was clingy. She was extremely affectionate, and more vocal than usual. She didn't want to let me out of her sight."

Gary Manuel of Oakland claims his cat, Spider, began to act bizarrely on the Saturday before the quake. "She'd run through the house, pause in my bedroom, then run out of the room quickly. One minute I'd let her outside, then in a matter of a few minutes she'd meow, demanding to be let in."

Alice Johnson, of Daly City, thought her cat had been acting fairly strangely on Tuesday, the day of the devastating quake. Usually gregarious and playful, the three-year-old mixed breed had refused to eat all day. Johnson didn't think much about it until after she finished cleaning up a few dishes that had broken during the earthquake. "It really struck me. It was like she knew something wasn't right."

Larry Tritten, my writer friend of San Francisco, recalls his cat's behavior. "Three weeks before the quake, our cat Calliope wouldn't come inside. We thought it was because of a skin infection she had that was making her angry because we would medicate her when she came inside. We figured she was staying outside to sulk."

Jack Thorne, a resident of the Santa Cruz Mountains about ten miles from the epicenter, recalls Sunday, two days before the monster quake. He called Jim Berkland and said, "My cat Botie absolutely detests the other two cats I brought into the family six months ago. He yowls and attacks them if they get close, but the last two nights he's been sleeping with them."

Dog Hints to Shaking

Pre-quake strange behavior wasn't just a cat thing. Many dog owners in the San Francisco Bay Area can also recall their dogs acting pretty strangely before the terrifying earthquake of 1989. For instance, in San Carlos—for one week before the October 17 quake—my own dog was behaving rather strangely. My easygoing yellow Lab? Well, Carmella, who usually had a tennis ball in her mouth, changed her usual demeanor. For seven days, she would periodically pace in the living room, then run up to the front door and bark. When I'd go to the door, no one was there. And then other times, before the period of countless aftershocks we experienced, she would stretch her head up in the air and cock her ears. This display of odd behavior may mean that dogs were sensing the unforgettable quake of 1989 before it happened. Bay Area dog owners' stories are varied:

Karen Meisenheimer, former director of education at the Peninsula

Humane Society, brings her five-year-old female Australian shepherd/spaniel mix to work every day. On Tuesday at lunchtime, she noticed her dog Alice was more hyper than usual. "She was jumping at noises. I had her walk in an area that she's used to, but she was acting like she was in a place where she was brand new to it." The dog always liked to sleep right next to the wall. But two days before the October 17 earthquake, the dog would not go near the wall. She had a strange look and began shaking her head at different intervals.

Berkland recalls a trained standard poodle belonging to a family residing in Redwood Shores, south of San Francisco. The dog wouldn't eat his favorite food. He also snapped at his human early on the day of the quake and then went upstairs to hide under the bed. Just before 5:00 p.m. the sensitive canine joined his family and stood nervously in the middle of the living room and spread his legs, as if to brace them. When the 7.1 quake struck a few minutes later, the poodle did a flip in the air and ran about.

The following week, the family took the dog with them when they traveled to pick up a Halloween pumpkin at Half Moon Bay. While they were going over the causeway across Crystal Springs Reservoir, the poodle went crazy in the car. He started snapping at the glass and scratching underneath the seats. When the family got up into the hills, the dog settled down, only to repeat his performance hours later at the same place during the trip home. Apparently, the dog was reacting to something underneath the causeway where the San Andreas fault lies.

So is it possible that something was radiating from the fault line that our dogs sensed before the quake of 1989 occurred? It wouldn't be difficult to convince Berkland or this sensitive poodle's owners that our dogs may get cues to quakes that we humans don't.

The Proof Is in the Pets—Or Is It?

The number of lost dog ads peaked a day or so before the October 17 quake. Yet in the middle of September, before the quake of 1989, keep in mind, there was an astoundingly high number of 57 missing dogs in a Bay Area newspaper's lost and found column.

"To me it was unbelievable," Berkland told me. "I couldn't believe my eyes. The numbers kept going up and up. Around the office I was pretty confident we were going to have a quake. Then we didn't. The numbers continued to stay high, and I discovered a new phenomenon." The numbers of missing dogs in September began decreasing. But after October 10, the missing dog list got longer. On October 13, there were 58 missing dogs listed in the *San Jose Mercury News*. That led Berkland to predict that the October 17 quake was going to be a big one. The larger the quake is going to be, the more the number of lost animals will rise.

Ten days after the big quake of 1989, the dog list hit 81 missing. "They just plain got driven away by the fright of the earthquake," Berkland explained. It's interesting that the number of missing dogs had been higher twice before in the past. The number hit 88 on July 8, 1980, and 85 on July 9, 1982, because of the Fourth of July effect, according to Berkland. So the earthquake did not frighten the dogs as much as Independence Day. In fact, many animal experts believe the chaos of New Year's Eve and the flash and noise from the mid-summertime holiday can drive some dogs bonkers for a while.

Most folks did not pay attention to the earthquake prediction article published in the *Gilroy Dispatch* on Friday, October 13. But some did. Perhaps next time Felix starts acting strangely, more people will consider heading for safer ground, or at least make earthquake preparedness plans.

Berkland's Theories Come Together

While the animals played a big part in short-term prediction of the Loma Prieta earthquake, Berkland's other theories were at work, too. He had predicted a 6.5 to 7.0 magnitude with 85 percent confidence for the seismic window of October 14–21. His determination was based on the highest tidal force in three years on October 14 (full moon just four hours from a very close perigee). But there's more…

- Very rare beaked whales washed up alive at San Francisco just before a rare pygmy sperm whale washed up at Santa Cruz, within five miles of the epicenter. Seagulls flew miles inland and acted strangely; homing pigeons got lost and one of the top homers flew the coop the night before the quake. Andy, a gelding, panicked in his corral in the Santa Cruz mountains, 20 minutes before the quake fissures ruptured the ground near him.

- The Gilroy Hot Springs cooled and slowed down in volume, just as it had before the 1906 San Francisco earthquake, the 1952 Kern County quake, and the 1979 Coyote Lake quake.

- Earthquake-sensitive people called in large numbers to the Time Research Institute and Marsha Adams.

- There had been a foreshock of 5.6 at Lake Elsman two months prior to the quake.

- The first Loma Prieta quake of October 8, 1865, had identical astronomical conditions: Both were in the top window for the year, both triggered a 7.0 quake, both caused landslides blocking the road between San Jose and Santa Cruz, both severely damaged filled ground at the marina in San Francisco, and both were on the San Andreas fault near Loma Prieta.

A Real-Time TV Earthquake

Author Stephen Spignesi didn't hesitate to add the Loma Prieta earthquake to his book *Catastrophe!: The 100 Greatest Disasters of All Time*. "The reason it was included was because it was one of the few disasters in history ever to be broadcast on TV as it was happening." Plus, the cost of the damage—with half of that in San Francisco alone—was far greater than the 1906 quake's toll.

"Also," he adds, "I tried to factor in the long-term effect of a disaster when compiling the ranking. Severe damage to the infrastructure of a modern, technologically advanced city like San Francisco has a ripple effect—primarily financial—that lasted for months following the actual events. All of these elements contributed to include it."

While earthquake clues were happening prior to the temblor, the aftermath won't be forgotten by pets and their people.

Yep, I remember that one. I lived in San Fran at the time. I was at school at SFSU, and I was getting ready to go to a weight-training class. When the quake hit, the freestanding lockers started to sway, and the overhead lights were swinging. Nothing came crashing down, but I did stand in the nearest doorway. I was living at the time out of San Francisco, and so I stayed at a friend's apartment. No lights, no electricity, no phones, but I think we had water. We heard all these crazy stories that the Bay Bridge had collapsed. That Interstate 280 had huge cracks and cars were falling in. Basically it was the end of the World Series. That night, I could see the sky was sort of orange-y and that was because of all the fires in the Marina district.

—Rebecca Chiller

I was working at Lonely Planet at the time, in their Oakland warehouse. On that day I had the opportunity to work some overtime. I had planned on staying until seven o' clock, but around 4 p.m. I started getting antsy and wanting to leave. I had a forty-five minute argument with myself, going back and forth, should I go/shouldn't I go. I left at 4:45 and walked up to the bus stop. It was located right next to the Cypress structure.

All of a sudden the tree that was next to the bench started dancing. A woman stopped her car in the middle of the intersection and got out screaming, thinking that her car was going to blow up. The ground underneath me began to undulate, and in order not to fall off the bench I needed to grab onto it with both hands and tuck my feet as far under the bench as possible and just ride out the wave. It was very much like surfing. . . It wasn't until I got home to Berkeley three hours later that I found out about the amazing extent of the damage.

The next day I went to the Lonely Planet offices and the section of the warehouse where I was working the day before. It was covered in a massive amount of red bricks that had collapsed from a firewall and through the roof, 20 feet above. I had always trusted my intuition, but October 17th, 1989 was the day that I finally realized to trust my intuition above all else.

—Kimberly Kradel

When the Loma Prieta earthquake hit, it wreaked havoc at the East Bay Vivarium—a business that sells reptiles. The store was then located only 50 feet west of the collapsed Interstate 880 freeway. Owen Maercks, former owner, describes the scene:

The freeway falling was a disaster, because it created its own secondary earthquake, which is what knocked over everything in the store. Literally, all of the contents of the store were on the floor. We had no power for 12 hours. It was a nightmare. All of our glass tanks went over. I was collecting snakes, lizards, and frogs and throwing them as fast as I could into whatever containers I could find that weren't broken. Several king snakes that had gotten out of their cages were in the process of trying to eat other snakes and lizards as I was trying to catch them.

—Owen Maercks

How the World Series Quake Jolted Jim Berkland

Jim Berkland speaks out about predicting the 7.1 monster quake that shook the San Francisco Bay Area, rattled nerves for weeks, and affected lives forever, and the personal consequences for him, which jolted his own life as he once knew it.

Many people were aware that I publicly predicted the World Series quake in an October 13, 1989, newspaper. When I was accused of "panicking the public," with my predictions, I received hundreds of phone calls and dozens of letters in my support. And these supporters did not even know that my job description included the expectation that I conduct special investigations into geological matters connected with public safety.

After I returned to work, I found a great many changes had occurred, including a ban on my discussing the subject of earthquakes on county time. This was rescinded when I convinced management that earthquakes and earthquake safety (although not necessarily earthquake predictions) were vital everyday topics for California geologists.

In July of 1994, I retired after more than 37 years of government service, almost 21 of which were with Santa Clara County.

The personal "aftershocks" of the October 17, 1989, earthquake cost me thousands of dollars and resulted in shortening my government career by at least several years. However, I would do it all again. I did it my way, and I have yet to see any of my detractors develop a more effective method of earthquake prediction.

The Intensity Scale that Can Rock Your World

I remember flipping through the pages of those dry earthquake textbooks in college. I recall scrutinizing the different levels of the modified Mercalli scale, a measurement of an earthquake's intensity. I tried to envision what it would feel like to experience a 10 superquake. It took the Loma Prieta quake for me to get a clear idea of how intensity can really shake people and objects. Take a look at this updated version of the different levels combined with the Richter scale ranges. But note, there can be overlap, depending upon local geological conditions, types of faulting, the effects of earthquakes, and types of structures, says Berkland.

Intensity	Magnitude	Felt Duration (shake)	Distance Felt (miles)
I. Not felt except by a very few under especially favorable conditions.	-3.0 to 1.5	1 second	Possibly felt over ground
II. Felt only by a few people at rest, especially on upper floors of buildings.	1.5 to 3.0	1-2 seconds	5-10
III. Felt quite noticeably by people indoors, especially on upper floors of buildings. Many people don't recognize it as a quake. Standing motor cars may rock slightly. Vibrations similar to the passing of a truck.	3.0 to 3.5	2-3 seconds	10-20
IV. Felt indoors by many, outdoors by few during the day. At night, some awakened. Dishes, windows, doors disturbed; walls make cracking sound. Sensation like heavy truck striking building. Standing motor cars rocked noticeably.	3.5 to 4.0	3-4 seconds	20-30
V. Felt by nearly everyone; many awakened. Some dishes, windows broken. Unstable objects overturned. Pendulum clocks may stop.	4.0 to 4.5	4-5 seconds	30-60
VI. Felt by all, many frightened. Some furniture moved; a few instances of fallen plaster. Damage slight.	5.0 to 5.5	5-10 seconds	60-120

Intensity	Magnitude	Felt Duration (shake)	Distance Felt (miles)
VII. Damage negligible in buildings of good design and construction; slight to moderate in well-built ordinary structures; considerable damage in poorly built or badly designed structures; some chimneys broken.	5.6 to 6.5	10-20 seconds	120-250
VIII. Damage slight in specially designed structures; considerable damage in ordinary substantial buildings with partial collapse. Damage great in poorly built structures. Fall of chimneys, factory stacks, columns, monuments, walls. Heavy furniture over-turned.	6.5 to 7.0	30-40 seconds	250-300
IX. Damage considerable in specially designed structures; well-designed frame structures thrown out of plumb. Damage great in substantial buildings, with partial collapse. Buildings shifted off foundations.	7.0 to 7.5	30-40 seconds	300-400
X. Some well-built wooden structures destroyed; most masonry and frame structures destroyed with foundations. Rails bent.	7.5 to 8.0	40 -60 seconds	400-500
XI. Few, if any (masonry) structures remain standing. Bridges destroyed. Rails bent greatly.	8.0 to 9.0	1-3 minutes	
XII. Damage total. Lines of sight and level are distorted. Objects thrown into air.	9.0 to 9.9	3-10 minutes	700-1,000

Sources: USGS and Jim Berkland

10 Facts FYI

Here's everything you wanted to know but were afraid to ask, about the World Series quake, predicted by Jim Berkland. These facts were gleaned from a variety of sources: Jim Berkland, the USGS, and other organizations.

1 — The 15-second quake, centered 60 miles south of San Francisco on a 30-mile segment of the San Andreas fault, was felt as far away as San Diego and western Nevada.

2 — Cypress Street section of I-880 in Oakland collapsed, causing most of the deaths. Sections of San Francisco-Oakland Bay Bridge collapsed.

3 — Areas including Santa Cruz, Watsonville, Hollister, and Los Gatos suffered heavy damage.

4 — Over 12,000 people were left homeless. Over 18,000 homes were damaged, and 147 were destroyed.

5 — The depth was 11 miles, unusual for California earthquakes, which are usually four to six miles deep. A 5.2 aftershock occurred 25 minutes after the mainshock; in the week following, a total of 300 more of 2.5 or greater and 20 greater than 4.0 occurred.

6 — It was the first major rupture along the San Andreas fault since 1906. This rupture was unusual for the San Andreas fault, because past earthquakes have been the result of horizontal slip of the ground on the two sides of the fault, with the southwest side moving northwest relative to the northeast side.

7 — The Loma Prieta earthquake included not only horizontal movement, but also a significant thrusting of the southwest side up and over the northeast side. Peak ground shaking as strong as 0.65g occurred in the epicentral area. This means that shaking exceeded the force of gravity, which is why objects were knocked down.

8 — Runway at Oakland airport, bridge along the Pajaro and Salinas Rivers, and the San Jose State Marine Station in Moss Landing were all damaged by liquefaction.

9 — Caused thousands of landslides as far north as just south of San

Francisco. Large fissures opened throughout the Bay Area.

10 ⎯⫴⫴⫴ A major fire occurred in the Marina district, along with 34 other fires in the area; also mains supplying water to the district burst.

In 1989, when I wrote my post–Loma Prieta earthquake articles for national magazines, I ended each piece: "But since USGS scientists admit they aren't yet able to reliably predict earthquakes, is it really so silly to monitor missing cats and dogs?" That was more than 15 years ago. And today, the USGS still stands by its words. "Changes in animal behavior cannot be used to predict earthquakes. Even though there have been documented cases of unusual animal behavior prior to earthquakes, a reproducible connection between specific behavior and the occurrence of an earthquake has not been made. Animals change their behavior for many reasons and given that an earthquake can shake millions of people, it is likely that a few of their pets will, by chance, be acting strangely before an earthquake." (See Chapter 13, "The Great Quake-Tsunami of 2004.")

Meanwhile, while countless anecdotes of pets sensing the Loma Prieta earthquake are remembered by their humans, there are human earthquake sensitives who also sense oncoming quakes. In Part 2, "The New Age Movement," you'll meet some amazing people who "hear" and "feel" the earth move before a quake hits.

SHOCKING EFFECTS

Quake: 1989, Loma Prieta, California (October 17, 5:04 p.m.)

Richter magnitude: 7.1

Mercalli intensity: IX

Number of people affected: 63 dead; 3,800 injured

Property damage: $10 billion

EARTHSHAKING FACTS
TO DOG-EAR

⤙ While the 7.1 Loma Prieta quake was a major earthquake, it wasn't the big one.

⤙ Caution: You can be suspended from work (or worse) if you predict an earthquake, especially if the media misinterprets your prediction.

⤙ Check out the lost dog and cat ads in your local newspaper to get a heads up of an oncoming quake.

⤙ Tune into other strange animal behavior and natural oddities (i.e., whales, geyser activity, etc.) and earth changes to get a clue if an earthquake might hit.

⤙ Earthquake prediction can help you to prepare and protect your valuable possessions, and your life.

⤙ Consider the pros and cons of getting earthquake insurance. (See Chapter 19, "Don't Be Scared—Be Prepared!")

⤙ Since mainstream scientists admit they aren't yet able to reliably predict earthquakes, monitor lost pets, strange animal behavior, and earth changes, for your safety's sake.

Part Two

The New Age
Movement

5 ～⫿⫿⫿～ Tuning in to Earthquake Sensitives

When there is no magic bullet, use the whole arsenal.

—Jim Berkland

ON JANUARY 24, 1980, Mark Waterman, a young man from Walnut Creek, California, heard ringing noises in his ear before an earthquake jolted Livermore. And his parents affirmed he had warned them about the imminent quake the day before it hit. This 5.5 earthquake injured 44 people, and most of the $11.5 million in damage happened to the Lawrence Livermore Laboratory, according to the California Governor's Office of Emergency Services. It's not that Waterman predicted the earthquake, but he certainly sensed it and others for more than two years, with a success rate of more than 80 percent for local quakes exceeding 3.0, reports Jim Berkland.

Sound silly? Not to Berkland, who's fascinated by it all. Or to me, who won't forget the intense 1980 rolling quake in San Jose. But, to be certain that this is a feasible earthquake prediction method, he tuned into his own sensitivity. "One afternoon I was at the public counter of the county building when I heard a ringing in my own ear. I asked my coworker if he had heard anything, and he denied it. Then I admitted to him that it might mean a local quake within a couple of days, and he was rightfully incredulous. Before we left work that evening the office building rocked slightly from a 3.5 magnitude quake centered about 10 miles away," remembers Berkland.

After a few more similar incidents, Berkland began to file his earthquake-sensitive symptoms with Marsha Adams, founder of the former

Time Research Institute in Woodside, a community in the San Francisco area. (Currently, she tells me that she's busy studying earthquake lights, another intriguing earthquake precursor.) He says that she told him after about 12 such reports that he was scoring about 80 percent with his ringing quake precursors. But it didn't stop there.

On October 31, 2004, at 10:45 p.m., Berkland heard a strong ear tone. Instead of ignoring it, he posted on his own website the following information:

> Folks,
> I just had the first ear tone in at least a month. It sounded strongly in my right ear for ten seconds at a lower pitch than usual. My ear tones usually occur within three days of a 3.0-to-5.0 quake within 100 miles.

His report was followed on November 1, 2004 by:

> Folks,
> Boulder Creek had a 3.6 quake just after 2 p.m. today on November 1. This was less than 14 hours after I had suggested that such a 3.0-to-5.0 would occur within 100 miles. The epicenter of the 3.6 was about 90 miles south of my Glen Ellen home...

Berkland added that the earthquake was also predictable for other reasons. Not only did it occur in the secondary window of October 26 to November 2, 2004, that accompanied the total lunar eclipse of the prior week, but there were also reports of unusual animal behavior before the quake happened. So, was it coincidence or an acute sensitivity?

Sensitive to Earth Changes

Are humans *really* seismically sensitive? "A person with a very sensitive body may also have some subtle reaction to whatever animals react to," says Reneau Z. Peurifoy, M.A., a broad-minded therapist and author of *Anxiety, Phobias & Panic*.

How? How is this possible? It's threefold, explains Peurifoy, "The first would be electrical signals from what is known as the piezoelectric effect. This occurs when crystals acquire a charge when compressed, twisted, or distorted. Since the earth's crust runs from 15 percent to 55 percent quartz, the building of pressure prior to an earthquake often produces electrical charges. Sometimes this causes what are known as 'earthquake lights.' Low-frequency electromagnetic signals prior to earthquakes have also been reported. The stresses prior to an earthquake also produce low-frequency vibrations. Finally, experiments have been done [monitoring] radon emissions prior to earthquakes as the means of earthquake prediction. It is possible that animals and humans may be responding to any one of these three things."

But not all humans are sensitive to an oncoming earthquake. "If people are picking up on the same cues that are affecting animals, it would simply be that they are especially reactive to those cues. It is similar to individuals who might be more sensitive to noise, light, or medications," explains Peurifoy.

So, What Are Your Symptoms?

Earthquake sensitives, like Waterman, Berkland, myself, and countless others, can and do feel physical and mental reactions to environmental threats that can take many forms—including ear tones and ringing, dizziness, headaches, aches, pains, anxiety, dreams, visions, and much more. So, are these symptoms imagined—or are they real?

"Some people are more in touch with this side of themselves than others. It could very well be that the physical factors described above are affecting the normal physiology of their bodies more than the average person. It could also be that the unconscious awareness is producing increased anxiety that could easily account for the various symptoms reported," explains Peurifoy.

Earthquake sensitives will tell you that headaches are a common symptom. I know from firsthand experience that a killer migraine can link to a killer quake. For instance, on October 17, 1989, I had a terrible sinus-type headache. In the late afternoon, I tried to escape my throbbing headache by taking a nap in my San Carlos, California, bungalow. Thus, I was awakened by the 7.1 World Series quake.

Later, I discovered that headaches are a common symptom prior to an earthquake. Berkland will tell you 13 women and one man have reported to him about headaches that develop in their foreheads several days before local quakes. "In each case," he tells me, "the pain and pressure end less than an hour prior to the quakes." He says that these reports began before a 1984 revelation at an American Geophysical Union meeting in San Francisco: The mineral magnetite had been found in the human forehead over the pineal gland (where psychics tell you the third eye is believed to be). Magnetite is the most highly magnetic natural material on earth.

Ear tones or ringing in the ears is another sign of an imminent quake, claim earthquake sensitives. Peurifoy explains it this way: "This would be similar to a person with panic disorder, whose fear of panic attacks makes them so aware of their body that they become frightened whenever the fight-or-flight response is triggered. This would include the host of normal everyday occurrences that we respond to such as a door slamming or the realization that we are late for an appointment."

During the writing of this book, I experienced ringing in my ears three times: The first time was when I was interviewing Jody, a sensitive with an amazing track record; the second time it was an intense one-minute ringing in my left ear; and the third one followed that night when I told Berkland about it during a phone conversation. The next morning, an earthquake hit in Japan. I thought, *Left ear, west toward Japan?* I dismissed it as another coincidence. But other people worldwide use their ear tone-based warnings to publicly predict earthquakes.

Lee Cheng-chi, a resident in T'aichung, Taiwan, for instance, got a personal ear tone warning in November 2004. He made an earthquake prediction that included magnitude, time, and epicenter. He had sent a cell phone message to the local media giving them a heads up that a

5.0 quake would hit Taiwan on November 12 or 13. A 4.1 earthquake struck eastern Taiwan on November 12. How did he do it? Cheng-chi gave credit to an ear condition that causes him to hear a ringing in his ears. It was reported that he said the symptoms become noticeable before a quake is going to happen.

Plus, Cheng-chi has publicized other earthquake predictions. On October 15, 2004, he warned of an oncoming quake based on ringing in his ears (reported as tinnitus symptoms). That day, a 7.0 quake hit Taiwan. Then he predicted three more quakes for October and November; two out of three hit. (Actually, he got two for one on October 28.) But when his prediction for an earthquake of 5 or 6 magnitude failed, the Central Weather Bureau was warned that he was violating the law. He agreed to stop making public predictions; if he continued to do so, he could be fined.

Meanwhile, sensitives in America continue to make predictions and are congratulated by fellow sensitives for their efforts. Visionary Clarisa Bernhardt, a pioneering California earthquake sensitive, now living in Manitoba, Canada, was long ago given by U.S. Geological Survey personnel the sobriquet, "The Earthquake Lady." Bernhardt says, "People must be strongly aware that everyone on the planet is affected by atmospheric shock waves from earthquake energy, not just the epicenter of the area hit by the quake. This can cause an increase in binge eating and drinking or excess of anything, including reckless driving." She tells me, "Earthquakes can be fattening! They can cause insomnia! They can cause heart attacks! They can cause tempers to explode! And they can cause some people to be disoriented!" And due to my personal experience, as well as the observation of sensitives, her words ring true.

But one sensitive is reprimanded and others are ignored or considered kooks and hypochondriacs. Why? Why don't conventional science and medicine accept earthquake sensitivity as a reality? "Many scientists simply feel that reported earthquake sensitives are similar to palm readers and astrologers. Once a group has been labeled as such, they don't bother to look at the evidence," answers Peurifoy. But I'm com-

pelled to peek. I'm awed by past and present predictions from seismically sensitive humans.

Super Sensitives

Charlotte King is a classic earthquake sensitive who resides in
Salem, Oregon. Like Berkland, she predicted the first Mount St. Helens
eruption of March 27, 1980. But her prediction wasn't based on lunar
cycles or animals. King tuned into her body and felt the pain before she
sent out a quake warning. "I was very ill," she recalls. The day before
the great volcanic blast of May 18, 1980, she called the local TV station. "I said, 'Okay you guys want to know when the volcano is going to
blow? It's going to blow in 12 hours. Log my call for 8:20 p.m.' It blew
in 12 hours and 12 minutes." She was 12 minutes off the timing of the
eruption. Thirty-one people were killed, according to the USGS. Plus,
approximately fifty 4.5-plus quakes occurred near Mount St. Helens
before the eruption.

While scientists tell me again and again that people can't predict a
quake or volcanic eruption, King is proof that it's simply not true. She
pioneered biological earthquake prediction, heading a volunteer
research project tagged "Project Migraine." As is noted at King's website (www.viser.net/~charking/info.html), the focus of this project was to
prove, beyond coincidence, that quakes and volcanic eruptions could
be predicted—by targeting time, magnitude, location, and probability.

As time passed, it was apparent that King was hardly alone. There
may be hundreds, and even thousands, of other people worldwide who
might be able to "feel" and "hear" quakes and volcanic eruptions
before they hit. What's more, King is behind the "popcorn theory,"
which is that people might crave popcorn before a quake hits. As a
health writer, I have written that carbs such as popcorn have a naturally
calming effect, which may be due to brain chemistry. According to
research at the Massachusetts Institute of Technology (MIT), eating
carbohydrates revs up levels of serotonin, a natural tranquilizer found
in the brain that can help people calm down.

In a past interview, King noted to a reporter that before the Loma

Prieta quake of 1989, all the stores in her neighborhood were sold out of microwave popcorn. Of course, it must be pointed out that munchies and beverages are in high demand for TV viewing of the World Series.

Jody and Rhonda are two other amazing earthquake sensitives who post earthquake predictions at Berkland's website. Before you say I sound like Sandra Bullock talking about "Cyber Bob" in the film *The Net*, listen up. These two sensitives put their senses to work, time after time—and deliver results. Here's the proof.

Jody, based in Concord, California, gives thanks to Berkland's site, *Syzygy*, where she learned she was an earthquake sensitive several years ago. "Everyone there owes Jim Berkland and Will Fletcher a great debt of gratitude for the environment they created for growth in the very new field for saving lives." She points out to me, "Mr. Berkland wasn't the only one who predicted Hokkaido in September 2003— there was Vladimir Keilis-Borok and me, too! I posted on September 10 through September 30, 2003, for a 6-to-7-plus quake in Japan and Russia. Both hit within two to three days of each other: an 8.3 in Hokkaido followed by a 7.3, then a 7.4, in Russia, and all the aftershock hits from both."

She adds, "Nobody on earth called both locations in one prediction like I did. Keilis-Borok called for Japan only, and Mr. Berkland predicts by syzygys affecting the Ring of Fire. I predict by ear tones only, so I could hear Japan and I could hear Russia in the same tone. Thus, I combined both into that prediction. This is how I can locate quakes." According to Jody, it's taken her years of practice and trial and error to be able to pinpoint where a sound is coming from. She says she can also detect the range of magnitude and then determine the timing for that range of quake.

If you're wondering how you can hear your ear tones and connect them to earthquakes, like these two earthquake sensitives, just ask Rhonda, aka "Quakeroo," in Ohio. (She uses an alias because she doesn't want to be ridiculed by nonbelievers.) She'll tell you, "Everyone seems to have his or her own particular tones corresponding to specific locations. Once you learn to recognize your tones, you will know if your left ear is for north, south, east, or west. Same for your right ear tones."

Quakeroo has been listening to her ear tones for more than 20 years, she says. As a regular poster on Jim Berkland's "Super Sensitives" message board, she claims, "I'm still trying to get it right. If I could get it right, then I could help people save lives and property. But it's so frustrating—the not knowing!"

Born in Ohio, Rhonda moved to California, where she realized that she was an earthquake sensitive. "In 1986 Jim Berkland referred me to Marsha Adams, who was involved in a privately funded study of earthquake sensitives. I remained in that study for about six years, dropping out after the Loma Prieta quake, which I accurately predicted three weeks before it happened." Then, after the 1989 Loma Prieta quake, she moved to Arizona to "evade the earthquake stuff." Once that didn't work, she finally moved back to Ohio, trying to find a place where she felt safe and could disassociate herself from the ear tones and other symptoms earthquake sensitives can experience.

Her uncanny earthquake predictions have wowed me again and again. For instance, on Monday, February 14, 2005, she sent me an email:

RE: Biggie tone for AK/PNW/N. Cal[2]

Hi Cal—
Just had a very intense tone that sounded the same as the last Alaskan quake only BIGGER. Since I haven't really honed this tone down to an exact location...all I can say is: AK/PNW/N. Cal—but probably Alaska? 5.0 to 6-plus and should hit before Friday, but probably by Wednesday night.

On February 16, I received another email from Quakeroo: "RE: Alaska just hit." Thus, a map of a southern Alaska 5.4 popped up with

---

2. Alaska / Pacific Northwest / Northern California

her email. This is just one of dozens of hits, from China and Japan to Argentina and Ohio, that Quakeroo sent to me over a few months. Is it another coincidence?

She suggests following these tips: Locations have signature tones due to the makeup of the rock at the site of fracture/pressure. Granite sounds are different from quartz. Keep a journal. Log your tones; wait approximately three days. Check the quake lists and note what earthquakes have come in. Sooner or later, you'll begin to see the pattern for your specific tones.

Are Sensitives for Real?

In my book *Doctors' Orders: What 101 Doctors Do to Stay Healthy*, I discuss the reality of fibromyalgia and toxic amalgam fillings, two controversial health topics that many mainstream doctors ignore. So, will conventional doctors ever give credibility to super sensitives as holistic medical practitioners have to aches and pains and a link between teeth and body woes?

"If this is a real phenomenon, it will eventually be shown to be so. Many people believe if a scientist can't measure it, it doesn't exist. This is another reason why scientists don't take the idea of earthquake sensitives seriously," says Peurifoy. He adds that this might change if someone devises a way to measure in a consistent and reliable way the thing that's producing these effects, such as ear tones.

One earthquake enthusiast who chooses to stay anonymous suggests that the only way to get a good pool of ear tones with disparate, definite locations is by expanding the group of ear tone reporters. He says that while including exact location in longitude/latitude is necessary, posting that information could be a security problem for many people. He recommends expansion of a group of ear tone reporters to a larger number of reliable people spread out geographically. Plus, he's quick to point out that this task will be both a technical challenge and a people skills challenge.

Another anonymous person attempted to glean data from super sensitives after the Christmas week Indonesia quake-tsunami on

December 26, 2004, and after the Sumatra quake on March 28, 2005. This poster, named "Monitor," posted his or her all-too-familiar post on the Syzygy Super Sensitives message board: "REQUEST to ALL Sensitives."

So what type of feedback did Mr./Ms. Monitor receive? After the December 26, 2004, Indian Ocean catastrophe, some sensitives were skeptical but many did respond. Three months later, sensitives weren't as cooperative. It didn't help matters that Monitor was cryptic, nor did he/she explain where or how the personal data would be used.

The fact remains, most sensitives are shy about expressing their symptoms (unless it's among themselves), because often they're tagged hypochondriacs or are believed to be obsessed with earthquakes. Plus, some feel that people such as Monitor may want to scrutinize them, like getting hold of E.T. *the Extra-Terrestial*, and they'll be poked and needled like an alien creature. So it's understandable that sensitives avoid attention from curious or skeptical onlookers. Currently, whether earthquake symptoms are a real phenomenon remains a very controversial topic in mainstream science and hasn't yet been scientifically proven.

In the next chapter, I'll show you how predictive dreaming and visions come into play for predicting earthquakes—and why your own dreams can hold important warning signals in your life.

EARTHSHAKING FACTS
TO DOG-EAR

- Got a headache or craving for popcorn? It may be that you like popcorn, or it could be a warning that an earthquake is coming.

- If you hear ringing noises in your ears, don't dismiss them.

- Check the Internet to see if a quake hits in your region within three days. One good site is Latest Quakes, Recent Earthquake Activity in the USA, found through *www.earthquake.usgs.gov.*

- While some sensitives claim ear tones can work locally, other experienced sensitives use their ear tones to pinpoint quakes globally.

- Learn to recognize your tones, and log them. Once you see a pattern develop, your ear tones might be more useful to you and others.

- Share your symptoms with other seismically sensitive and earthquake savvy people at *www.syzygyjob.com.*

6 ⚡ Dreams and Visions

If you ignore your dreams, you may never live them.

—Jim Berkland

JIM BERKLAND GOT a unique warning before the Sharpsburg earthquake rocked Maysville, Kentucky, on July 27, 1980. On July 14, he had a long dream of being trapped in a dark mansion with false doors, long halls, and countless rooms. Then he heard a voice in the doorway. It belonged to a stocky man, about the size of his long-dead father. "I heard the voice saying, 'Did you hear about the big earthquake back East?' I said, 'No. How big was it?" '5.5 to 6.0,' came the response. I replied, 'Wow, that was a big one for back there. Where was it, in the Boston area?'" Berkland heard only a garbled voice and he awakened from the intriguing dream.

Two weeks later, on the afternoon of July 27, the day of a lunar eclipse, Berkland was at home on the weekend, preparing for a barbecue. His friend Stanton T. Friedman, a nuclear physicist, joined him that day, bringing potato salad to the event. Friedman's first words were, "Did you hear about the big earthquake back East?" Berkland had a déjà vu experience when he asked, "How big was it?" and heard the response, "5.8." Berkland told Friedman about his dream 14 days earlier, and both men marveled at the coincidence. According to the revised reports, the 5.1 quake lasted 15 to 45 seconds, rocked 14 states, and caused no deaths or injuries, but hundreds of buildings, mostly in Maysville, sustained damage from shattered windows and toppled chimneys to cracked foundations.

A coincidence? Perhaps not, says dream researcher/analyst Craig Webb, executive director of the DREAMS Foundation in Montréal,

Québec, Canada, who's fascinated by it all. "It is true that people have verifiable precognitive dreams of actual events that later take place that they had no normal way of knowing about beforehand. There is no question in the minds of those who experience such dreams or visions that they are indeed real. Although much headway is being made, the topic of precognition is still looked at rather skeptically in various places." So, while scientific studies are needed, it doesn't mean that you should tune out your dreams. They can hold signs to what's happening, or might occur in your life.

She Sees Earthquakes

This inspirational woman gets visions of oncoming earthquakes. Back in early November 1974, Clarisa Bernhardt received a very vivid vision. Bernhardt was shown a calendar; the date was circled, which happened to be Thanksgiving Day, and as she puts it, "The word 'earthquake' was stamped across it. Then I heard it would be about 3 p.m. and that no one would be hurt." So the visionary spread the word.

Seeking opinions and documentation to back up her prediction, she contacted the San Jose Mercury News, the local Los Gatos Weekly Times, and the police department, and she made her prediction public.

Two days before Thanksgiving, as she puts it, on her radio show, her guest proved so interesting that she almost forgot to make her earthquake prediction. But she got it in. She suggested that if listeners wanted to avoid their turkey dinners sliding across the tables, wait until after 3 p.m. on that coming Thursday afternoon to dig into turkey and all the trimmings, because a moderate earthquake would strike the San Jose, California, region. At exactly 3:01 a 5.2 quake did happen as predicted.

As a result, says Bernhardt, "The United States Geological Survey set up a program to investigate the potential of psychic earthquake prediction. They invited me to participate in the study, which I did." Not only did she receive more kudos for her accuracy of earthquake prediction, she says she had numerous visions of other quakes, too (*www.clarisabernhardt.com/quakes/predict.html*).

For instance, she visited Northern California just before a quake rumbled through the state. She recalls that she found it disorienting during her visit, and she shared her feelings with numerous friends as well as the Monterey Salinas Airbus company driver, Bryan Mick, who drove her to the San Jose Airport. "It seemed good that I was leaving, because I definitely felt the increased quake energy. The driver of the airbus confirmed this to me, as he had become disoriented after he picked me up. We got lost and he drove around unable to find the address even though it was in an area that he said he knew well. And then I explained to him that disorientation is a symptom of a pending quake." By Tuesday of the next week, on September 28 (the day of the full moon), the 6.0 Parkfield earthquake did jolt Central California, and lasted about 10 seconds, according to the USGS. (Berkland notes, "This was the long-awaited quake that the USGS had forecast would occur during the window of 1984 to 1992. Twelve years late is better than no quake at all.")

I decided to call Mick and check out his side of the story. Yes, he did admit to getting off track on familiar ground. I asked him how he felt after the earthquake happened. He says, "I was astounded. It felt creepy." These days, Mick and other skeptics are more open to the fact that indeed both pigeons and people can lose their sense of direction before the ground shakes. (For "The Earthquake Lady's" earthquake projections, see Chapter 20, "Future Shocks, Wow!")

Calico the Psychic

Carol Shumaker (her clients call her "Calico") has been predicting earthquakes for many years. As a resident of Ventura, California, 60-year-old Calico claims she's been sensitive and psychic all of her life. "I used to get ringing in my ears. Either one would start ringing loud. It was like a piercing radio signal in my ear."

Then, one afternoon she heard a voice. "It happened during a calm walk in the park. Unlike other times, when I had been distracted by my surroundings, I stopped and closed my eyes to become more aware. To my amazement, I heard the words: 'China. 7.2.' There was a shrill ringing in my left ear." She knew she was onto something big. She noted the time, date, and prediction that a major earthquake of 7.2 magnitude would occur in China. Two days later, she heard on the news that a 7.2 quake struck China.

That event led Calico to feel and document her "vibes." She started reporting them to local TV and radio stations. "Eventually, I found that reporting them to the USGS was in everybody's best interest. Even though I managed to obtain documented proof in the form of congratulations from Caltech in Southern California, I was disappointed to find out that no warning could be given due to the understandable fact that panic would ensue."

Meanwhile, Calico calls her vibes ELFs, or extremely low frequency electromagnetic vibrations. And she continues to make earthquake predictions as well as post them on her website, (*www.calicothepsychic.com*).

Berkland isn't surprised by Calico's sensitivity to ELFs. He explains, "Perhaps related to solar activity are the outbursts of ELF and ULF (ultralow frequency) electromagnetic radiation that have been shown to occur prior to significant earthquakes." He also points out that huge anomalies like these were detected a few hours before the great Alaskan earthquake of 1964, as well as the Loma Prieta quake of 1989. "This last anomaly was clearly recorded by Tony Fraser-Smith of Stanford University for the Navy during investigations unrelated to earthquakes," he adds.

The Millennium-Ending Earth Changes

While Bernhardt's visions of earth changes have both hit on the money and failed, another visionary, Edgar Cayce (1877–1945), known as the Sleeping Prophet, can't be trusted 100 percent either, according to Berkland.

He notes some of the following Cayce forecasts that you will notice didn't happen before the end of 1999: New land will appear in the Atlantic and Pacific Oceans; most of Japan will slide into the sea; the southern Atlantic coast of Georgia, South Carolina, and North Carolina will also fall into the ocean; the Great Lakes will empty into the Gulf of

Mexico; and the West Coast of North America will be engulfed by the sea for hundreds of miles inland, perhaps making Phoenix, Arizona, a seaport. (See Chapter 17, "Good-bye, California?")

Berkland concludes, "I can't speak authoritatively on Edgar Cayce's ability to diagnose illnesses while separated by time and space, but I can advise you that I have never had a speck of respect for his version of millennium-ending earth changes." So if you can't rely on famous visionaries, can you trust your own dreams of future earth changes?

Other Sensitives' Dreams and Visions

While Berkland, Bernhardt, and Cayce have had their share of dreams and visions, other people have had earthquake dreams, too. Some have come true, others have not. I can personally attest that I've had dreams about impending doom that happened—and sometimes it didn't. Dreams that appear to be precognitive may occur because something else is on your mind. For example, if you dream of a tsunami hitting your home, it could simply mean you're overwhelmed with work or emotions. The bottom line: I've learned to pay attention to both my "good" and "bad" dreams and consider them to be a special message.

Here are some dream predictions that came true that were posted on Berkland's site:

Pre-2004 Sumatra quake/tsunami, posted before December 16, 2004:

I was a tourist to this place. I know that they had exotic animals like lions and tigers. I believed it to be near western Australia and the Indian Ocean. The part that stood out was the tsunami. I was in some kind of medium-sized boat that was still at the beach. Looking out to sea, the sea was strangely way out, and then suddenly started coming in with a huge-looking wave. I was a passenger in a jeep with some other people in it, and there were other jeeps and vehicles racing out of there

away from the beach and to higher ground. I saw what
appeared to be a rhinoceros (maybe a hippo?) submerged in
water, and there was water coming in everywhere. I was afraid,
but thinking hopefully we would get out of there, and to higher
ground.

—Priscilla Barry, Olympia, Washington

Anonymous pre-2004 Sumatra quake/tsunami vision:

At the time of the first vision, on December 16, I had gone out
to dinner with a friend whom I had not seen for several
months. After dinner, we sat in the truck and talked, because
the restaurant had closed. Outside the restaurant is a large,
roughly rectangular rock. Right in the middle of an explanation
of something, the rock seemed to develop the features of a
dead young man, and the idea of drowning came to me, along
with the idea of many people. I sometimes get these small
scenes before great disasters, but this one seemed so unlikely
to be true that I did not inform my friend of what I was 'seeing';
instead, I pushed that thought away, and went on with the conversation. However, the scenes stayed with me for several
days. Then the December Sumatra quake occurred a little over
a week later.

Pre-2004 Sumatra quake/tsunami dream:

I had three dreams before the Sumatra quake. I live in Redondo
Beach, California, about two miles from the beach. The dreams
are more like videos I'm made to witness. They are so clear and
with so much detail of area that I'm seeing that they are real.
This happened right after Thanksgiving, for three consecutive
days. The first was stepping out my back door in brackish water
that covered my feet. The next day I was awakening in bed as if
floating in water although not completely submerged; my nose

was still above the water level, about three feet aboveground, and I was approximately about 100 feet or more above sea level. The next day I was seeing the single-story house across the street submerged in water. The strange thing was there was no debris nor any damage to the structures or terrain. It was obviously salt water. As if a very gentle tide had completely submerged the area, or that the land had gently sunk. [See Part 4, "The Big Wave."]

—Justice Doherty

Natural Disaster Dreams

Meanwhile, I, Berkland, and other earthquake sensitives who pay attention to their dreams and visions are hardly alone. According to Craig Webb, many famous people have had precognitive dreams. He notes the pharaoh's dream from the Bible that Joseph correctly interpreted. The result: "It saved the entire region and possibly the whole Egyptian civilization from famine and ruin. There's other famous examples of precognitive dreams," he adds, "such as Abraham Lincoln, who verifiably dreamt his own death; Harriet Tubman, who freed and saved many slaves with such skills; and Bishop Joseph Lanyi, who had a vision about the event that triggered the first world war."

While famous people have dreams or visions about quakes, one average man listened to his dreams—and decided to move, like animals flee before a big earthquake hits. Central California native Mike Nelson, 44, made the decision to pack his bags and flee the Golden State about four years ago when bad dreams began to haunt him. He recalls, "The dreams began taking an ugly turn—massive geological changes (i.e., earthquakes, landslides, etc.) and burning cities. This started affecting my waking thoughts. And soon, my unease was like a not so quiet voice whispering you have to get out before it's too late. I discussed this with my family and closest friend, who had a feeling he had to get out as well, and we both decided to move our families and businesses to upstate New York last April." Now residing in Marion,

New York, Nelson has discovered Berkland's website, and reports of future earthquakes and past accurate predictions in California seem to validate his actions, he says.

"Since living in New York the last year, my dreams have returned to normal. I still dream of California occasionally (always in disaster), maybe because so many people I love still live there. But I truly believe I have saved both my and my friend's families, and my own, lives. When I see the birds flying seasonally here, it strikes a chord in my mind about parts of the dreams I've had. I can't shake the feeling that a darkness has spread its wings over the West Coast. It's just a matter of time before an earthshaking event will take over the headlines. I pray for all those folks that can't get the message."

I got the message loud and clear for not one but several earthquakes. In an email I sent to myself after watching 10.5, an earthquake disaster film about the west coast being hit by deadly earthquakes, I wrote:

Message: 10.5
Date: 7/25/2005 12:46:39 PM Pacific Standard Time
From: COrey39184
To: COrey39184

Watched it last night for amusement. Then, had a dream. Northern CA/NV and even Wyoming got significant quakes. Dogs alerted me and then there were newspaper headlines about the earthquakes. In the dream, very real shaking of the ground. So perhaps this means more to come.

On July 26, 2005 a 5.6 moderate earthquake hit Western Montana. "The strongest Montana quake in more than 30 years occurred on the night before the last day of my July Seismic Window. This was widely felt in Seattle, Washington and in Calgary, Alberta," points out Berkland. Plus, the quake was felt in Yellowstone National Park, Wyoming–just like in my dream.

Also, on July 26, a minor 3.0 tremor occurred offshore Northern California. On July 27, a 3.0 earthquake happened at 12:51 a.m. in Wyoming; and a microearthquake hit Nevada at 1:05 p.m. What's more, a missoulian.com news article, "Earthquake Left Dillon Residents Shaking," published on July 25, 2005, reported that Western Montana residents recounted that the dogs gave the first warning that something was up.

While some people think that precognitive dreams are a silly notion, or that the small quakes in my past dream that came true weren't earthshaking enough to note, I'm not laughing. I'm tuning into my dreams to help improve and perhaps one day save my life.

How to Keep a Dream Journal

Whether you live on the West Coast, Midwest, East Coast, or in another country, keeping a dream journal may help you to recall precognitive dreams, and get prepared. "Making a consistent effort to remember and record your dreams will help your waking mind to ally itself more closely with your dream experience. It's also an excellent way to increase imagination, creative and intuitive capabilities, which are all intimately connected with dreams," explains Webb. Here are his five dream recall techniques, to help you remember more dreams:

- You've got to want it. You must feel that it will be useful to you, if not extremely valuable. Without this, motivation will soon disappear. More important, the desire acts as a magnet that draws your dreams into memory.

- It's a matter of focus and attention. Dream recall is like a mental muscle—the more you use it, the stronger it becomes.

- Follow a bedtime practice. Before sleep, reread your dreams from the previous night(s). This allows you to begin to connect with your dream memory, and is also an opportunity to interpret your dreams and spot connections to the day's events. Then, as you go to bed, ask yourself to remember your dreams. Any time you awaken, keep your eyes closed and remain motionless. Gather as many images, feelings, or impressions as you can, then rise and immediately record them in a journal.

- Be playful, patient, and persistent. Try to maintain a relaxed and playful attitude of looking forward to your dreams while being willing to let them come all in good time. Once you start on a cycle of focusing on recall, stick with it for at least a few days, because consecutive nights can have an addictive effect.

- Join a dream study group. People who have a shared interest in dreams are unmatchable for sustained motivation and inspiration.

Courtesy of The DREAMS Foundation, *www.dreams.ca*.

EARTHSHAKING FACTS
TO DOG-EAR

~ If you recall your dream or have a repeated dream, it may be a warning about what is going on in your life presently…

~ …Or a dream might be a key hint to what can happen in the future.

~ Explore your own personal dreams, which can be tools to learn about your fears, goals, and power to change your fate.

~ Decode your dreams. It may be a quake warning or it could be something else.

~ Keep a dream journal to help you recall or pinpoint your precognitive dreams.

7 ⎯⎻⎺⎺⎻⎯ Other Quake Predictors

Earthquake prediction is easy. Anyone can do it. The hard part is being right.

—Jim Berkland

JIM BERKLAND IS KNOWN AS THE CALIFORNIA GEOLOGIST WHO PREDICTS EARTH-quakes—not by expensive seismic monitoring, but by checking daily tides and tallying up the number of lost cats and dogs in the classified ads. He is hardly alone. There are other people worldwide, both conventional and unconventional, who do predict and forecast earthquakes, too.

Jack Coles, for one, an earthquake predictor with his own link on the *www.syzygyjob.com* site, uses radio and TV waves to predict quakes. He hears static on the TV and radio and interprets it the way others interpret ear tones. He can also *see* the interference on TV. Berkland told me, "Some of Jack's predictions have been uncanny, such as the first one I knew of. A geologist friend pointed out a small advertisement in the *San Jose Mercury News* from someone claiming to have predicted the Loma Prieta quake and offering his predictive services. I decided to check him out and phoned his number that evening in early 1990. 'Oh, Mr. Berkland,' he said when I identified myself. 'I have been following you for years. It's funny that just as the phone rang I got a warning for a local 4.0 quake from the static on my TV.'" Sure enough, the next morning a 4.2 quake shook Livermore, says Berkland, who can verify at least three more predictions from Coles that were on the money. "Hewlett Packard admired what he was doing and lent him a $50,000

Frequency Analyzer which was most helpful. Of course," he adds, "there were also some notorious failures, but nobody said that earthquake prediction would be easy."

But Coles doesn't make it look hard. In early April 2005, I noted his forecast was posted on *www.syzygyjob.com* for a quake to strike the area from San Francisco to Los Angeles, California, effective through April 20, 2005. The percentage of probability was 57 percent that a shaker would occur between 4.4 and 5.5. The likely dates were April 6, 7, 8, 19, and 20. As a San Francisco Bay Area native, I had a special interest in this prediction. On April 16, I read on the Internet that a moderate 5.1 earthquake occurred 12 miles from Mettler, California.

Then, on July 28, 2005, Coles phoned Berkland and reported his heightened concern about the area of Japan. Evidently, he didn't know that there had been at least seven quakes there of 5.0-plus near Honshu since the 6.1 on July 23 that he had correctly predicted two weeks in advance. "I continue to be amazed at how much Jack can do with so little," says Berkland. Once again, I realized that earthquake prediction can and does work despite what conventional scientists and skeptics believe.

Saying the "P" Word

To get a well-rounded perspective for this book, I set out to track down a middle-of-the-road earthquake expert (or two) to discuss earthquake precursors and prediction theories. This wasn't an easy task to do, especially since the two words *earthquake prediction* are often frowned upon in the scientific world, especially in the United States.

I first went to Professor Roger Bilham at the University of Colorado at Boulder. His response to my request was, "If you have been reading the reports from the U.S., in China, in Japan, and elsewhere, on attempts at earthquake prediction, you will know that earthquake prediction is not currently possible. Earth scientists have much to gain by successfully predicting the earthquakes (fame, saving people's lives, saving insurance losses). All have failed. A number of people appear to be predicting earthquakes, but when you look at the details you discover that they identify vague areas, or vague times, or vague magnitudes."

I was disturbed by Bilham's word choices, "all," "failed," "vague," and "fake claims." So I decided to continue my quest to get a quick overview on earthquake prediction methods. So I contacted Colorado-based Roger Hunter, a retired USGS programmer (and frequent prediction evaluator poster on Berkland's website), and seismologist Roger Musson of the British Geological Survey in Edinburgh to provide some working definitions for earthquake precursors.

10 Popular Earthquake Precursors

- Clouds. There have been reports of strange clouds seen before earthquakes. As one folk philosopher put it, "Before the earthquakes, there was always some sort of weather going on."

- Electrical activity in the ground. "A number of individuals have suggested that ground currents will fluctuate before a quake. The best-known project involving this is the VAN project in Greece. VAN refers to Drs. Varotos, Alexopoulos, and Nomicos of the University of Athens, which has tried to use electric field measurements between electrodes buried in the earth to predict earthquakes in Greece. It is the focus of great criticism and dispute," asserts Hunter.

- Changes in rock behavior. One promising line of approach depends on the fact that rocks under stress change the way in which seismic waves travel through them. Therefore, if you can keep observing how seismic waves from explosions or distant earthquakes travel through the part of the earth's crust that you are interested in, you can detect changes that may be the precursor of an impending quake. In theory, this method is attractive; in practice, it is hugely difficult and expensive to even test.

- Groundwater changes. Changes in the level of water in wells have sometimes been reported before earthquakes.

- Radon emissions. Radon is a slightly radioactive gas found in rocks, and changes in stress before an earthquake may affect the rate at which it is released.

Dr. Musson explains that earthquake theories that aren't based on physical precursors lend themselves more to forecasts than precise predictors such as these:

- Dilatancy-diffusion. "In 1973, Christopher Scholz, Lynn Sykes, and Yah Aggarwal of Lamont-Doherty Earth Observatory proposed the dilatancy-diffusion theory. This was based on observed effects in rock under pressure and says that microcracks form that fill with water and weaken rock." Says Berkland, "Dilatancy is the tendency of coarse soils that transit fluids to behave like quicksand if shaken, explains Berkland The dilatancy theory was in vogue for about five years, and then it failed time after time." This led to the Parkfield prediction, adds Hunter, who points out that failed as well.

- Seismic gaps. When one spots places in a belt of high seismic activity where there have been no major earthquakes for many decades, but there have been recent major earthquakes on either side, then it seems likely that the gap is going to be filled by a larger earthquake sometime.

- Stress transfer. It seems fairly straightforward that one result of a large earthquake that releases stress on one part of the fault, is that the burden of stress is passed on to another part of the same fault, or to a neighboring fault. Recently, methods have been developed that actually calculate how the stress has shifted after a big quake. Knowing which faults are now more highly stressed doesn't tell you when they will break, however.

- Time-predictable. "This involves looking for the recurrence interval, the time it takes for a quake to happen again in the same place. Parkfield is an example. It repeated every 22 years until the site was instrumented before the next one was due. Then the cycle failed. The last one was much later than expected," explains Hunter.

- Triggering theory. If a fault is highly stressed and about to break, then some minor force such as tides or the alignment of the Sun and Moon may be enough to set it off. This is fairly useless as a prediction method, as if the fault is not about to break, then no amount of planetary alignment will set it off.

Meanwhile, while Berkland continues to put his own earthquake methods to work, he's not an earthquake faddist prone to jumping on seismic bandwagons. He says, "I have seen the surge and demise of earthquake theories about P-wave velocity (dilatancy), long-term earthquake cycles (like the supposed 22-year pattern at Parkfield), and computer picks of foreshock patterns (such as the 2004 failure of Keilis-Borok in Southern California). I believe that interest in earthquake clouds will meet a similar fate."

Hunter adds, "After the past failures, scientists got gun shy about making predictions. It's gradually wearing off as some of the predictions finally panned out. The amateurs, not needing funding, are free to predict all they want, and some of them come true."

Speaking of earthquake predictors, take a look at a few past and present ones and their methods.

The Predictors

Marsha Adams is an electrobiologist who worked with the Stanford Research Institute for several years. She studied subjects such as earthquake sensitives, strange animal behavior prior to quakes, and unusual fogs, and often independently corroborated Berkland's predictions.

Vladimir Keilis-Borok is a UCLA seismologist and geophysicist who has said, "Earthquake prediction is called the holy grail of earthquake science, and has been considered impossible by many scientists. It is not impossible." In June 2003, Keilis-Borok and his team of scientists from Russia, the United States, western Europe, Japan, and Canada predicted an earthquake of magnitude 6.4 or higher would occur within a 9-month time frame in a 310-mile region of Central California, including the San Simeon region where, indeed, a 6.5 quake hit on December 22, 2003.

In July 2003, the team predicted a quake in Japan of magnitude 7 or higher by December 28, 2003, in an area that included Hokkaido. An

8.1 quake hit Hokkaido on September 25, 2003. Both predictions were based on observations of small earthquakes that happen daily. However, Keilis-Borok's team's prediction wasn't fulfilled by an earthquake of at least a 6.4 by September 5, 2004, in a region that includes the southeastern portion of the Mojave Desert.

Berkland notes that the Keilis-Borok predictions (for which Berkland says he "never saw the evidence") were headlined in January, March, and July 2004 in newspapers, magazines, and the Internet, each time as if it were new. "It was another huge setback for earthquake prediction from high science (and indirectly a setback for the rest of us depending upon public credibility)."

Iben Browning is a late biologist who was behind the scenes of widely publicized earthquake predictions for the New Madrid zone back in 1990. Browning predicted a greater than 50-50 chance that a major 7-plus magnitude earthquake would strike the area within two days of December 3, 1990. He based his prediction upon the highest tidal forces in 27 years. While Berkland agreed that the December full moon would bring a high potential for quakes in many seismically active areas, he didn't agree that a major quake could be reliably predicted for a specific place and time months in advance.

On the Eddie Schwarz show (WGN Chicago) on September 24, 1990, Berkland expressed his anti–Iben Browning prediction and gave his own prediction for a 50-50 chance of a 3.0 to 5.0 magnitude tremor in the New Madrid area between December 2 and 10. Less than two days after his interview, such a 4.6 magnitude quake actually rumbled within 40 miles of New Madrid. (See Chapter 10, "Midwest Movements, Southern Shakes.") Berkland points out that he had observed that there was an unusual number of missing pet ads in *The Commercial Appeal* of Memphis, which he had been monitoring thanks to a radio station arranging to mail a subscription to him for the months of September to December 1990 so he could keep an eye on the Browning prediction for the area.

GeoForecaster is a dedicated team of two men, Drs. Lowell Whiteside and Michael J. Kozuch (*www.geoforecaster.com*). This duo once forecast earthquakes in California, but because neither of them has a geologist's license, like Berkland does, the California Board for Geologists and Geophysicists made this an issue. So the earthquake forecasters continue to offer their forecasts globally—but exclude California.

"We don't specifically say how we do our forecasts, as that is our intellectual property. However, we do say that our forecasts are data driven and not based on a model of how faults interact or some other physical model." Plus, rather than look at a specific region or fault, these forecasters "look at the earth as a whole and approach the problem holistically. Using our own pattern recognition algorithms and earthquake statistics, the physics is inherent in our results," explains Dr. Kozuch.

In addition, geoForecaster claims to use data from over 40 agencies throughout the world; they claim an average score accuracy rate of 83 percent for magnitudes greater than 3.0 and over 90 percent for magnitudes greater than 6.0.

Zhonghao Shou ("Cloud Man") based in Hangzhou, China, has turned to clouds for his short-term earthquake prediction method. He notes, "I have been predicting earthquakes since June 20, 1990, when I observed a long line-shaped cloud with a tail pointing in the northwest direction. Eighteen hours later, a magnitude 7.7 earthquake struck Iran and killed or injured 370,000 people." (Berkland also notes that June 21, 1990, was the day of a rare perigean spring tide.) Adds Shou, "Because the earthquake was the only one bigger than 7 to the northwest of my hometown, Hangzhou, China, for 333 days from May 31, 1990, to April 28, 1991, I believed that there must be a strong relationship between the cloud and the earthquake."

Beware of Shaky Predictors

Berkland recalls pre-Iben Browning days when he publicly "pooh-poohed" the major scares for Californians from (1) the Jupiter Effect theory in which the planets were to trigger devastating earthquakes; (2) the multiple misinterpretations of psychic archaeologist Jeffrey

Goodman in *We Are the Earthquake Generation*; (3) the unique and unjustified prediction by stock market analyst Joe Granville; and (4) the ad, which ran for a full month in the *San Jose Mercury News*, prior to March 22, 1990, in which a major quake was predicted for the Hayward fault on that exact date.

"The events predicted for those times and places failed to occur; in fact, there were not even 3.0 to 5.0 magnitude quakes, which might have made the predictions mildly interesting. The lesson is obvious. Don't allow yourself to get shaken up prior to a nonevent by a predictor without a track record," cautions Berkland.

Also, Berkland says he went to the county media center to denounce the Orson Welles TV narration of "The Man Who Could See Tomorrow," about the supposed Nostradamus prediction of a great Southern California quake in May 1988. "I received calls from frightened people who were preparing to close businesses and leave the state. I decided it was time for my own anti-prediction. As it developed, an alarming interpretation of Nostradamus quatrains again was wrong and I was right." (See Chapter 20, "Future Shocks, Wow!")

Whom Can You Trust?

So Berkland and other quake predictors continue to make earthquake predictions and forecasts, publicly or underground (on Internet websites). "The Chinese, Japanese, and even the USGS have made projections for many events, which haven't occurred. The California State Office of Emergency Services made headlines with the forecast of a 6.0-plus magnitude aftershock within a couple of months following the major Loma Prieta quake of October 17. Such a quake has yet to occur," says Berkland.

Meanwhile, "It is very easy for a charlatan to fake a good prediction record," points out Musson, "and misleading track records may also be assembled in good faith by those whose belief in their ability exceeds their gift for statistics. The easiest way to fake a record is to produce one's predictions only after the earthquake and still take credit for them."

Adds Hunter, "If you boast about the hits and cover up the misses, you can look pretty good. Or if you make sunrise predictions (as in 'I predict that the Sun will rise tomorrow morning') you'll get a lot of hits to impress the gullible."

So, when it comes to earthquake predictors and forecasters, whom can you really trust? "Whenever you hear predictions from anyone," says Berkland, who has publicly predicted hundreds of earthquakes and has scored time after time with his method, "you must use your personal filter of skepticism, created by your own experiences and knowledge."

Most important, preparedness is key. "Earthquakes are going to continue to occur whether or not they're predicted. There are plenty of excuses for missing predictions, but there are no valid reasons for being totally unprepared, especially when you live in known earthquake country," concludes Berkland. (See Chapter 19, "Don't Be Scared— Be Prepared!")

Meanwhile, take a look at Part 3, "Shakers and Seismic Windows," to see how Berkland's windows and other earthquake precursors link to rattling tremors around the world.

EARTHSHAKING FACTS TO DOG-EAR

⚓ Be aware of short-term earthquake precursors (i.e., clouds, changes in rock behavior, groundwater changes, etc.) and you might get a heads up of an imminent earthquake.

⚓ Be wary of unknown earthquake predictors who pop out of nowhere. Consider their credentials and track record before you put faith into their latest earthquake prediction or forecast.

⚓ The USGS continues to make long-term forecasts, while other quake predictors predict earthquakes that might hit in the near future.

⚓ While earthquake predictors are interesting, the key to remember is that no matter what the prediction is, be prepared for self-preservation.

⚓ To read or post a prediction, go to *www.syzygyjob.com*, *earthwaves.org*, or *earthboppin.net*.

Shakers and Seismic Windows

8 West Coast Vibrations

If California weren't famous for quakes, we would have twice the population.

—Jim Berkland

At 4:31 a.m. on Martin Luther King Jr. Day in Reseda, California, a big tortoiseshell tabby started acting strangely. "Our cat woke me up about five minutes before the quake. Squeaky was running and yowling. I remember that it was so bad I put him in the living room and shut the door, and then went back to bed. A couple of minutes later the quake struck," recalls Dawn.

That day, on January 17, 1994, it was recorded that this early-morning jolt was a 6.8 Northridge (Los Angeles), California, earthquake. Sixty people died, more than 7,000 were injured, and 20,000 were left homeless, according to the Pacific Disaster Center. This earthquake was centered in Reseda, but the damage was more deadly in Northridge, 11 miles away. "First I felt a roll like being on a wave; then we got thrown across the room. It felt like the floor dropped out about 10 feet from under us. I ended up at the foot of the bed. My husband was thrown into the hall," says Dawn with awe. When it was over, Squeaky fled his home and didn't return for a few days. What made Dawn's cat react in such a way? Some people say it's ESP (extrasensory perception), or a sixth sense. Others claim cats aren't gifted, just blessed with well-developed or heightened senses—scent, sound, and sight—that are far superior to our own.

Many people who live through terrible earthquakes believe their pets knew something before these quakes struck. But whether or not pets really can predict danger is still an open debate.

Meanwhile, Jim Berkland and other pet people continue to turn to sensitive cats and dogs and other animals for predicting earthquakes in California. In fact, he has achieved accurate results for dozens of San Francisco Bay Area earthquakes that exceeded 5.0 since 1973, and for hundreds of others in the Golden State. Read on and decide for yourself if the animals sensed earthquakes were coming.

Northern California

Eureka Earthquake of 1980

On November 7, 1980, Berkland predicted the Eureka earthquake 14 hours before it rumbled through the Northern California town. His prediction was recorded on the Earthquake Watch hotline, which was sponsored by the U.S. Geological Survey and included up to 1,800 observers. About eight months later, Berkland was informed by a secretary that the tape recording containing his prediction of the largest California quake in 28 years had somehow been lost in the mail between Menlo Park and Palo Alto. The tape also contained, said Berkland, the standout evidence of San Jose's Youth Science Institute, which had left a telephone message about agitated animals just four days before the Eureka earthquake.

"Every time I think of my November window, I recall with some resentment my experience with high science after I had predicted the 7.4 Eureka earthquake, based upon the new moon, a record gap between eruptions at the Calistoga geyser, and the 1980 record number of missing cat advertisements in the *San Jose Mercury News*," he says with conviction.

Berkland notes that significant changes in eruption cycles often precede significant earthquakes in the region. Old Faithful holds the longest gap on record (3 hours, 12 minutes), which occurred the day before the Eureka quake of November 8, 1980—the strongest in Northern California since 1906—he points out. Plus, this earthquake was the first major seismic event in California since 1952, and no greater than a 6.5 had struck Northern California since 1966. There were no deaths, eight injuries, and there was $1.75 million property damage, according to the California Governor's Office of Emergency Services.

Morgan Hill Earthquake of 1984

I remember this 6.2 quake, on April 24 at 1:15 p.m., with an epicenter about nine miles east of downtown San Jose, my hometown. As a graduate student at San Francisco State University, and a resident tucked away in the privacy of the Santa Cruz Mountains, I experienced the strong and scary afternoon jolt. Living amid tall redwoods, I realized as I ran outdoors (like people do, and shouldn't for safety's sake) that I was looking up at the towering trees, brick chimneys, windowpanes, and other deadly hazards. Despite the lack of damage to my home, it was a wake-up call. (I hadn't experienced a significant jolt since the frightening 5.5 Livermore quake on January 24, 1980, when I lived in an upstairs apartment in San Jose. That quake caused one death, 44 injuries, and $11.5 million in property damage.) This time, four years later, I was all alone that day in the mountains; it was an isolated area. Nobody, absolutely no one, was outdoors in the afternoon. And when you hear windows rattling and feel the ground shaking without another human around, it can be a chilling sci-fi type of event, perhaps like dying alone. But this quake caused no deaths. Twenty-seven people were injured, and there was $10 million in property damage, according to the California Governor's Office of Emergency Services.

The Morgan Hill quake was no surprise to Berkland, who noted that it was the first 6.0-plus earthquake in the immediate Bay Area in 74 years. Also, I remember that he had told me more than once that April is one of the three most seismically active months in the San Francisco Bay Area.

Berkland recalls the Morgan Hill earthquake, too. "I rode it out on the seventh floor of the Santa Clara County Building, and my pendulum began to sway more than three feet, until I stopped it so that it would not bang against the window," he recalls. "I drove up Mount Hamilton Road to where it was crossed by the Calaveras fault in order to see if there was any surface offset (none there). Two geologists from the USGS were already on the site, and were soon followed by a couple of more investigators who dejectedly informed us that the nearby tilt meter record had been lost because the roll of recording paper hadn't been replaced on schedule."

He adds, "The strongest aftershock, a 4.6, of the Morgan Hill quake hit in my predicted window on September 26, 1984, while a reporter was phoning to kid me about 'Where's that quake you predicted?' Then my office began to shake, and I told him to 'Hold on! I think this one will make it!'" According to The Virtual Museum of the City of San Francisco, the 6.2 Morgan Hill earthquake was centered at Morgan Hill and was felt in San Francisco. Damage was estimated at $10 million.

Southern California

San Fernando Earthquake of 1971

In Southern California, many people may remember what happened at 6:01 for 60 seconds on the morning of February 9, 1971. "That was the moment for the San Fernando earthquake, the most destructive in Southern California between 1933 and 1994. It seems hardly coincidental that both the March 10, 1933, Long Beach earthquake and the San Fernando quake occurred on the day of a lunar eclipse. What are the odds?" asks Berkland. About three weeks before the 6.7 quake hit, there had been the most devastating marine mammal beaching in the history of Southern California. Berkland says, "About 200 dolphins beached themselves on San Clemente Island, within 75 miles of San Fernando." According to the USGS, 65 deaths occurred, more than 2,000 people were injured, and property damage was estimated at more than $500 million in the San Fernando earthquake (also known as the Sylmar earthquake).

"As severe as the damage was," Berkland adds, "the destruction and loss of life could easily have been far greater had not the Van Norman Reservoir been partially drained for annual inspection of the dam. The shaking of this outmoded hydraulic fill dam produced partial collapse with fissures nearly down to the lowered water level. There was great concern that the water could easily erode the dam and the water could flood the homes of 80,000 residents below, especially if there were a strong aftershock." But the dam didn't end up producing another catastrophe. In fact, the event spawned new dam safety regulations in California, and the lower Van Norman Dam was rebuilt.

Brad Nelson recalls the Sylmar quake. At nine years old, he was living in the San Fernando Valley with his family, who were earthquake virgins. "I remember I woke up about five minutes before the quake. I looked out my window into my backyard, and there was an eerie quiet. No birds were chirping, no dogs barking, just a quiet calm. I just lay in bed staring at the ceiling, and then it struck. It was a rolling motion, like waves. I ran into my sister's room. I tried to shake her awake. She was in shock, so she stayed in bed. I was yelling at my older brother and sisters to get up. I remember the sound of the quake; it was like a deep rumble and very loud. I could hear our house shaking, windows rattling, walls bending. I thought it was the end of the world." The young boy ran down the hallway, bouncing in between the walls as he made his way to the kitchen, where stuff was flying out of the cabinets and onto the floor. Then, the earthquake stopped. "Then a second quake hit," he adds, "almost as big as the first one. I could feel the earth moving in waves."

"I remember looking out the kitchen window and looking at the full moon low in the western sky, and directly across in the eastern sky, the Sun was coming up. I thought that was odd at the time," he points out in retrospect about the quake. (See Chapter 5, "Tuning into Earthquake Sensitives.") "We had to be evacuated for about a week till they drained the Van Norman Dam. There was a huge crack in it, and the officials were afraid of the potential tidal wave flooding if it blew. We stayed at our friends' house in Canoga Park, because they were considered high ground and a safe area. Our house made out okay, but it had a lot of cracks. Our water and electricity was out for about a week, so it was good we stayed at our friends' house, which was fine. After this quake, I started my interest in earthquakes and learning everything about them." So, is Nelson alone? Not at all. Often it takes a personal experience like this one to nudge people to want to understand "why?"

While the San Fernando quake did indeed occur on the day of a fully eclipsed moon, as Nelson pointed out, it's not the only California quake that might have been linked to lunar effects, according to Berkland:

CALIFORNIA QUAKES AT FULL MOON

Date	Year	Magnitude	Location
Nov. 20	1915	7.1	Northern Baja California (shook much of Southern California)
Feb. 15	1927	5.0	Santa Cruz
Mar. 10	1933	6.3	Long Beach
May 14	1954	6.2	Santa Rosa Mountains
June 7	1963	4.0	Antioch
Apr. 15	1965	4.5	San Bernardino
Sept. 10	1965	4.8	Pittsburg
Aug. 6	1979	5.9	Coyote Lake (day before full moon)

Northridge Earthquake of 1994

Jim Berkland predicted that an earthquake measuring between 3.5 and 6.0 on the Richter scale would strike the Los Angeles area between January 9 and 16 in 1994. Though Berkland's prediction did not hit the bull's-eye—the Northridge, California, earthquake arrived at 4:31 a.m., on January 17—he was close enough to raise a few eyebrows. Sixty people were killed and more than 7,000 were injured, according to the USGS.

Berkland's methods were in full gear, too. He recalls that on January 18 there was a missing dog peak of 50 (double the total of January 5). The cat ads also doubled (from 5 to 11) between January 10 and 14, and he emphasized it on his catalog of daily ads. "And it became part of my justification to warn my cousin in Northridge about my January 9–16 seismic window when we visited on January 1–2, 1994. That was when I urged her to protect her lifelong collection of Hummel ware." But that's not all.

As usual, Berkland followed the trend of Los Angeles Times dog ads from December 15, 1993. "Even my detractors have no problem with the amazing record of 92 on January 29 and relating it to the 6.8 magnitude quake 12 days earlier. The same thing happened 10 days after the Loma Prieta quake, when the San Jose Mercury News dog numbers leaped to a record total of 82," points out Berkland. He adds, "But what explained the 54 total of December 31 before the quake? That number was the highest in more than 21 months, when there were 68 dog ads in the Los Angeles Times on March 20, 1993. That number can be explained by the fact on March 19, 1993, there were three separate quakes east of Los Angeles (3.5 Barstow, 3.6 Riverside, and 3.9 magnitude Yucca Valley), an extremely rare concentration of quakes on a single day."

While Berkland's numbers were pointing toward an imminent quake, Mark Ehrman recalls just how the Northridge earthquake hit as he was packing socks into his duffel bag to go to Europe. As his story goes, he was boiling some pasta on his stove, and went to pack. "The lights went out, and I have no memory of how I got up from where I was kneeling to hugging the doorway between my bedroom and bathroom." He'd experienced other California quakes, but this one was the only one that really frightened him as he listened to sounds of rumbling and glass breaking through his apartment. When the earthquake ended, Ehrman saw that the pasta was still on the stove, but the flame seemed abnormally high, perhaps because there wasn't electricity and the burner was the only light on. He turned off the stove and sat on his front-porch steps wrapped in a blanket. He listened to car alarms ringing throughout the neighborhood, wondering what to do next.

"When the phone started working again, I called the airline. At first, they wouldn't let me change my ticket and said I would forfeit it if I didn't make the flight. But I screamed about how we just had a major earthquake, and no one knew whether the freeways were safe. They agreed to let me leave the next day," he says. "I always have been a bit nervous about flying, but after 24 hours of aftershocks, I felt nothing but relief when the wheels lifted off the ground and I watched the city slide out from under me." (See Chapter 17, "Good-bye, California?")

EARTHSHAKING FACTS
TO DOG-EAR

-ᐤᕈᐠ- If you get a heads up from your seismically sensitive cat, dog, and other animals, consider it a blessing and prepare yourself for a potential quake.

-ᐤᕈᐠ- Once you create an earthquake prediction, make two copies so you'll have a backup if you get a hit.

-ᐤᕈᐠ- When there's a full moon and you observe other earthquake precursors, consider it a blessing from Mother Nature, and prepare yourself for an oncoming quake. (Refer to Chapter 7, "Other Quake Predictors.")

-ᐤᕈᐠ- If an earthquake hits and you're amid towering redwood trees or pine trees, don't run outdoors. Instead, duck for cover under a sturdy table.

-ᐤᕈᐠ- If you're near the ocean, a lake, or a dam, and a quake hits, head for higher ground.

9 ~ Pacific Northwest to Alaska

Maximum tidal forces help to tell us when but not where or how big.
—Jim Berkland

TIMOTHY SMITH, 51, A HIGH SCHOOL TEACHER IN SOUTHERN CALIFORNIA, RECALLS a haunting quake-tidal wave memory in Ouzinkie, more than 200 miles from the epicenter of the great Alaska earthquake on March 27, 1964. Born in Kodiak, Timothy will always have vivid images of Good Friday, when he was 10 years old and preparing for Easter with his family.

It was around 5:30 in the evening, and the daylight was beginning to fade. It was calm, and the channel between the islands shimmered like a mirror through the trees. Dad looked up and glanced out the window. "Did you hear that?" There was no need to answer, for the next instant there was a roar like a hurricane or a thousand freight trains, followed by the sickening sensation that the world was falling apart. The floor began to heave and roll, and I, well familiar with life on the open sea, was appalled to observe the walls and the ceiling pitching as though in a broadside swell. After only a few seconds, which felt like an eternity, our senses were racing, so both Dad and Mom said, "We'd better go outside." We sloshed through the thick snow that still lay crusted in the backyard, and huddled together on the rock outcropping. It was hard to stand up, even for experienced boat men like ourselves. So we huddled together and hugged each other, for practical purposes as much as comfort, until the quake was over.

While the long and violent earthquake had ended, the next catastrophe had not even started. Once Timothy's dad turned on the radio and heard static, he remarked that the quake must have been huge. "We finally found KFQD, an Anchorage station operating on emergency generators and broadcasting news that sounded like it was the narration of the apocalypse. Compelling as the drama in Anchorage was, it was not local news," recalls Timothy. Once they tuned to the station on the Navy base in Kodiak, it was even more frightening: A voice told listeners to head for high ground—a tidal wave warning had been issued.

Timothy remembers that they had several families from homes next to the water stay the night at their home, since the basement was 45 feet above the tide line. "I did awake several times in the night," he recollects, "startled by the bump of an aftershock, then became aware of a roar like a huge waterfall coming from the direction of the bay, a sound of rapids caused by the tide receding from terrain that had always been far under water before."

Once the sun rose on Saturday morning, the young boy saw something was dreadfully wrong with the tides, which still lapped up around the grass and trees that once had been far from the water's edge. "What we did not know yet," concludes Timothy, "was that the entire north end of Kodiak Island had sunk six feet lower. That meant the tides were now hopelessly wrong, changing the shoreline forever."

Okay, that may seem a bit dramatic, but today, as countless people in the Pacific Northwest know, earthquakes followed by tsunamis can and do happen. And, yes, if you experience a great quake, it will have a dramatic effect on your life as it did for Timothy. Did Jim Berkland's earthquake theory of tidal forces, the moon, and strange animal behavior fit the great Alaska quake of 1964 as well as other earthquakes he predicted, for California, Oregon, Washington, and Alaska? Read on and decide for yourself.

Pacific Northwest: Oregon and Washington

The Nisqually Quake of 2001

This earthquake hit during the secondary seismic window for February 2001, five days after the new moon. Berkland's former webmaster, Will Fletcher, had predicted a 7.0-plus quake for February 22–March 1. "For the Seattle area, he had specified a 3.5 event, and as it happened, the only Washington quake to meet that minimum in February was the 6.8 Nisqually earthquake that hit on the 28th. Unfortunately, with the severity of this quake, he somehow felt some degree of responsibility for it, and has vowed not to predict any more quakes," explains Berkland.

Berkland adds, "On my website, there were also several predictions of a significant quake in Washington for the last half of February. I made copies of them but can't find them now. As I recall, they were mainly from dreams or psychic impressions, but the result of the posts is just a bit spooky."

Speaking of eerie, remember Priscilla Barry, the Olympia, Washington, 55-year-old woman who had a tsunami dream? This self-professed earthquake sensitive recalls a variety of symptoms that hit her in late February 2001. She says she endured intermittent jabs and jolts in the back of her left leg behind the knee. Each time it occurred, she believed that a local Washington earthquake was near.

She notes, "Other sensitives in the area keep reporting in on Syzygy too, as well as reporting abnormal pet behavior like whales close up and personal in Budd Inlet in Olympia. Then finally there was that right-sided face pressure, and some white noise ringing, and then finally a loud tone. This tone came in just before 7:00 p.m. on February 27 in my right ear (which would indicate south of me). Combined with the face pressure, I believed a quake would hit southwest Washington. In fact, I stated so that evening in my post on Syzygy Sensitives, of which I will quote the first part:

Hi all,

First, SW Washington Emergency tone received in right ear just before 7:00 p.m. tonight. This means it should be local, meaning fairly close to me and also south of me.

The alleged time of Priscilla's post was before midnight on February 27. The Nisqually earthquake rocked Olympia and Seattle at 11:54 the next morning. Priscilla was on the 37th floor of the Washington Mutual Tower in downtown Seattle.

"I ducked under a table and counted it out—20, 21, 22—and continued up to about 30 seconds. We saw bricks had fallen from the facade of the old buildings across the street on 2nd Avenue, and they announced on the intercom that we could not use the elevators until they were inspected. I was excited and really not concerned too much about my safety.

"Since I was expecting a quake, I probably 'ducked and covered' just a bit more quickly than I would have if it were a total surprise," she says, which backs up Berkland's awareness of hearing earthquake sensitives and how tuning into your body can save your life.

"I believed a good shaker was coming and that it was probably coming within 72 hours. I knew I could not decide to call in sick and not go to work. I reasoned that being at work was only approximately one-third of the daily hours, so there was only 30 percent chance the quake would happen while I was at work in downtown Seattle. So I probably would not be there when it hit. Turns out that I was at work, but I knew that was a possibility, too, so I was prepared mentally for it happening."

Puget Sound Quakes

In June 2003, during the last day of Berkland's seismic window, the Puget Sound was struck by a 2.5 quake on June 19. While Roger Hunter, a retired USGS "detractor," wasn't impressed, Berkland decided to check out the frequency and timing of past Puget Sound quakes. Take a look at the list of 15 quakes:

PUGET SOUND QUAKES AND SYZYGY

Year	Date	Magnitude	Syzygy+	Type of Seismic Window
2000	Jan. 30	4.1	FMe + 10	Jan. 19-26, miss (4 days late), primary
	Jan. 30	3.6	FMe + 10	Jan.19-26, miss (4 days late), primary
	Apr. 21	3.6	FM + 04	Apr.18-26, hit, secondary
	Oct. 15	3.6	FM + 02	Oct. 13-20, hit, primary
	Dec. 24	3.5	NMe - 01	Dec. 24-31, hit, secondary
2001	Feb. 28	6.8	NM + 06	Feb. 21-28, hit, secondary
	June 10	5.0	FM + 05	June 5-12, hit, secondary
	July 22	4.3	FM + 02	July 19-26, hit, primary
2002	June 16	3.7	NMe + 05	June 10-17, hit, secondary
	June 29	4.5	FMe + 05	June 22-29, hit, primary
	June 29	3.8	FMe + 05	Jun 22-29, hit, primary
2003	Apr. 24	3.9	FM + 08	Apr 15-22 (80 percent, 2 days late), primary
	Apr. 25	4.8	FM + 09	Apr. 15-22 (70 percent, 3 days late), primary
	May 29	3.7	NMe + 0	May 28-Apr. 04, hit, secondary
	June 19	3.5	FM + 05	June 12-19, hit, primary

According to Berkland, of these 15 quakes, there was a significant link between the maximum twice-monthly tides and earthquakes in the Puget Sound area. "Also intriguing is that seven of the 15 quakes closely followed perfect syzygies (FMe or NMe), which were eclipses of the Moon or Sun," points out Berkland. But, while these hits don't prove his seismic window theory, it does make you wonder if a correlation between tides and quakes is more than a coincidence.

And Berkland also sees the correlations between solar flares and earthquakes. "I have no doubt that such a correlation is real, but the mechanisms are obscure," he says. As a Californian, he says he's impressed by examining a list of the 25 greatest solar storms, especially the severest types, such as coronal mass ejections (CMEs), of the past 30 years. He discovered that within two days of those events, the largest quake in the San Francisco Bay Area since 1906 hit—on October 17, 1989, as well as the second strongest Bay Area quake, April 24, 1984. Plus, the 7.4 Eureka earthquake that hit on November 8, 1980, was the strongest quake in Northern California between 1952 and 2004; all of these temblors were predicted publicly by Berkland.

Meanwhile, on March 6, 2005, another believer of the effects of solar activity on quakes is Seattle-based producer Mitch Battros of Earth Changes TV. He, in fact, noted his personal observance of new earthquakes in his Earth Changes TV Newsletter, after receiving a U.S. Geological Survey report of a 5.2 tremor off the coast of Oregon— the area where now over 3,800 quakes have occurred. Not only did he include two news reports pointing out that scientists are interested in the quake swarm off southern Vancouver Island, he also provided his opinion about what may be happening.

Battros believes there may be a connection between the Sun and Earth's magnetic field shift and earthquakes. His research related to the Sun-Earth connection doesn't focus on solar events and earthquakes specifically. "I know there are some in the field of geology and seismology who might make this leap showing some kind of causal effect on tectonic plates, and they may be correct. I simply cannot, at least at this time, affirm such a connection," he says.

His studies have been targeted toward solar activity and its link to weather, not climate. While he notes that there are scientists who have shown research linking solar cycles and climate cycles, he doesn't. What makes his research different is his suggestion of a "more immediate cause-effect. So immediate, I am suggesting a 48- to 72-hour time-linked means."

So, what is Battros's equation?

Sunspots → Solar Flares (CMEs) → Magnetic Field Shift → Shifting Ocean and Jet Stream Currents → Extreme Weather and Human Disruption

That said, Battros admits that he's "uneasy" with the present-day underwater quakes near Washington, Oregon, and Vancouver Island. "The idea of tectonic plates 'pulling apart' as opposed to 'shifting' is one scary scenario,'" he adds.

And speaking of water, Berkland hasn't forgotten how the tides affected the Pacific Northwest years ago.

The Great Alaska Quake of 1964

Berkland will be the first to remind you that the great Alaska earthquake of March 27, 1964, was on the full moon at the time of the extreme low tides. He will also tell you that he got eyewitness accounts of rats and mice running in the streets of Seward as well as seagulls disappearing from the harbor. "An unprecedented 100 gamma magnetic anomaly was measured from the ionosphere by new equipment on Kodiak Island," recalls Berkland, who says this earthquake precursor was an eye-opener after the quake hit.

While Berkland notes the earthquake precursors before the earthquake, he also recalls exactly where he was before the historical quake hit. "I was in Seattle with the USGS, where I gave a paper on Franciscan chert [a term for rocks]. I stayed in a USGS houseboat that reacted to a 4-foot tsunami in the harbor, but no big deal," he remembers. "This quake was called 8.5 Richter and upgraded to 9.2. For three and a half minutes, it was almost impossible to stand up in Anchorage. The only longer quake I know of was the Lisbon disaster of November 1, 1755, which was also preceded by strange animal behavior and magnetic anomalies (magnets temporarily lost their strength, although physicists say that is impossible). The Good Friday quake in Alaska became the most investigated since the 1906 quake in California." And residents who experienced the deadly earthquake will not forget its wrath either.

SHOCKING EFFECTS

Quake: Prince William Sound, Alaska, 1964 (March 27, 5:36 p.m.)

Richter magnitude: 9.2

Mercali intensity: XI

Number of people affected: 125 killed

Property damage: $300–$400 million

---

10 Facts FYI

Here's everything you wanted to know but were afraid to ask about the great Alaska quake, according to Jim Berkland, the USGS, and other organizations..

1 ⟿ The ground shook approximately four minutes; effects were large in many towns, including Anchorage, Chitina, Glennallen, Homer, Hope, Kasilof, Kenai, Kodiak, Moose Pass, Portage, Seldovia, Seward, Sterling, Valdez, Wasilla, and Whittier.

2 ⟿ The epicenter was about 10 kilometers (6.2 miles) east of the mouth of College Fiord, approximately 90 kilometers west of Valdez, and 120 kilometers east of Anchorage.

3 ⟿ This quake is the second largest ever recorded. (The largest is the 9.5 earthquake in Chile in 1960.)

4 ⟿ As a result of the 1964 earthquake, the Latouche Island area moved about 18 meters to the southeast.

5 ⟿ The fault caused drastic earth changes extending from near the

epicenter in Prince William Sound to the southeast coast of Kodiak Island.

6 On the first day there were 11 aftershocks with magnitudes greater than 6.0; in the next three weeks, nine more followed.

7 Smaller aftershocks carried on for more than a year.

8 Damage and the majority of lives lost were due to the effect of water waves.

9 Of the deaths linked to the effects of the ocean, about 30 percent were linked to the open-ocean tsunami: 4 at Newport, Oregon; 12 at Crescent City, California; and about 21 in Alaska.

10 The great quake triggered many landslides and avalanches.

The Alaska Quake of 2002

Each and every year, Berkland mails his list of top seismic windows to all subscribers of *Syzygy*. In January 2002, he indeed had shown the 8-day windows as opening on September 5, October 4, November 3, and December 2. As luck would have it, Berkland typed in the November issue that the window was November 4–11, so he had some critics carp because he was one day off.

No matter. The meticulous geologist took care of the minutia in his December 2002 newsletter, pointing out that he did correctly state his prediction in his annual list of top seismic windows and on his website. "This is important for me to correct," he noted, "as my critics would otherwise claim a total miss for the largest earthquake in North America since the Mexico City disaster of 1985."

On November 3, 2002, central Alaska was violently shaken for more than a minute by a major-to-almost-great earthquake. The magnitude reported by the USGS was 7.9. Also, Berkland noted, "Within 17 hours of the Alaskan quake, more than 200 small earthquakes were triggered 2,000 miles away at Yellowstone Park. This was a turnabout, as Old Faithful at Yellowstone had slowed its eruption cycle prior to the Good Friday earthquake of 1964 in Alaska."

Cascadian Tsunami—A Threat?

Recently, scientists have put together a convincing picture that a superquake of about 9.0 hit the Cascadia Trench off the Washington coast hundreds of years ago. According to Indian legends, violent ground shaking, a massive flood, and earth changes happened. Geologists have also found evidence for sinking of forests beneath the water and uplift elsewhere. Tree rings focus on a time near the year 1700.

Plus, says Berkland, "Written reports in Japan describe an unannounced killer wave that killed hundreds of people along the west shore of the islands. Knowing that a tsunami travels about 500 miles per hour, and tracing it back to the east, it would have originated off the coast of North America on January 26, 1700. That is most fitting in terms of tidal forces, as the date was in the secondary seismic window, midway between two extreme perigean spring tides. On January 5, the full moon and a close perigee were only nine hours apart, and on February 3, they were 11 hours apart." Thus, the coastal conditions were favorable to triggering an earthquake, and most likely that's what happened.

Adds Berkland, "It would have been interesting at that time to look for beachings of marine mammals, bear and deer fleeing inland, rodents scurrying around in broad daylight, and seabirds leaving the coast. With the next megaquake in the area, we are likely to hear of such phenomena. Let us hope that people will be aware of what it means." (See Chapter 13, "The Great Quake-Tsunami of 2004.")

Now that we've discussed Berkland's seismic windows in the Pacific Northwest, let's talk quakes in the Midwest and South.

EARTHSHAKING FACTS
TO DOG-EAR

- Don't discount abnormal animal behavior, white noise, or ear tones as potential precursors for an oncoming earthquake.

- Learn your body signals to help you get prepared for a potential earthquake.

- If you're in a high-rise building when a quake strikes, don't panic. Duck and cover.

- Consider turning to solar flares as another earthquake precursor.

- If you're in a West Coast region such as Alaska, British Columbia, Washington, or Oregon, when you hear a tsunami warning, don't ignore it. Head for higher ground.

10 ⟋⟍ Midwest Movements, Southern Shakes

Not many states can boast of major quakes and major hurricanes.
—Jim Berkland

EARTHQUAKES AREN'T JUST A WEST COAST THING. JIM BERKLAND, THE MAN WHO continues to predict earthquakes despite opposition from high science and skeptics, is aware of microquakes and great quakes in other regions of America, too. And yes, his seismic windows do apply to the Midwest and Southern states, too.

Since Berkland is just one individual, it's up to people who live in the Midwestern states and the deep South to pay attention to earthquake precursors (i.e., abnormal animal behavior; lost pets; changes in groundwater elevation, quality, and temperature, etc.), and decide if a quake warning is warranted. So, if a full moon or new moon is nearing and snakes are awakening on February's snow-covered ground in Nebraska, or a flock of birds are flying around disoriented in Arkansas, it might be a clue to store bottled water and find the emergency earthquake kit or create one, if you don't have one already.

New Madrid Earthquakes

"It is well known that Midwestern (and Eastern earthquakes) are much more efficient because of the older, less broken bedrock east of the Rockies," notes Berkland. And some people and scientists who live in this region do indeed have earthquakes, not just tornadoes and hurricanes, on the brain. After all, significant historical earthquakes such as the New Madrid quakes did happen and could happen again.

Among Berkland's topics of interest are past and potential quakes of the New Madrid seismic zone (a source of quakes that occurred along the Mississippi River, where devastating tremors hit in 1811 and 1812). According to the U.S. Geological Survey, several deaths were reported.

"On December 16, 1811, the area made itself known throughout the eastern United States as the site of perhaps the largest historic quake in North America. This is the epicenter of the great quake that 'rang bells in Boston' and caused the Missouri River to flow backwards for a time. The course of the river was changed, and the 20-mile-long meander was cut off to become 'Reel Foot Lake.' There were waterfalls where fractures crossed the river, and boats and [rafts] tipped over. The ground was seldom still until after the third great quake in the series struck on February 7, 1812," explains Berkland.

Early in Berkland's studies of lunar tidal effects, he noted that the first of the great 1811–12 New Madrid quakes happened on the day after a new moon syzygy, and was in a seismic window. What's more, Berkland says, "The strongest Midwest quake after 1812 occurred on Halloween night, 1895, and was felt in 23 states and Canada. It was centered near Charleston, Missouri, and caused extensive damage, with a maximum intensity of modified Mercalli VIII, and a magnitude of 6.0. It occurred hours before the full moon, at the opening of the secondary window of November 1–8, 1895." But whether Berkland's primary and secondary seismic windows can usefully predict an oncoming quake is still an open debate.

4.0-Plus Quakes Since 1900

If you're rethinking whether Berkland's seismic windows do apply to the Midwest and South, take a look at these numbers:

MISSISSIPPI VALLEY QUAKES AND SYZYGY

Date (Year/Mo/Day)	Mag	Place	Syzygy/ Perigee	(Synchron)
2005/02/10	4.1	Blytheville, AR	N + 2/P + 3	(24 hours) hit
2001/05/04	4.4	Enola, AR	F - 3/P + 3	(5days, 10 hours) miss
1996/11/29	4.3	Blytheville, AR	F + 5/Ap - 2	Secondary window
1989/04/27	4.3	New Madrid, MO	F + 6/P - 6	Secondary window
1982/01/24	4.1	Enola, AR	N + 0/Ap + 4	Secondary window
1982/01/21	4.5	Enola, AR	N - 3/Ap + 1	Miss, 2 days early
1977/06/02	4.6	Hatfield, AR	F + 1/P + 1	(5 hours) hit
1076/02/15	4.2	NE Arkansas	F + 1/P + 1	(5 hours)
1974/02/15	4.2	Arkadelphia, AR	F + 9/Ap - 2	Miss, 3 days late
1972/02/01	4.1	Warm Spgs., AR	F + 2/P + 10	Secondary window
1971/10/01	4.1	Jonesboro, AR	F - 3/P - 3	(2 hours) 5-year hit
1970/11/16	4.4	Fernvale, AR	F + 4/P + 7	(82 hours) hit
1970/11/16	4.4	Keiser/Manila, AR	F + 4/P + 7	(82 hours) hit
1969/01/01	4.5	Little Rock, AR	F - 2/Ap + 0	Miss, 1 day early
1966/02/11	4.3	Blytheville, AR	F + 6/P + 6	(6 hours) hit
1956/01/28	4.1	Tennessee border	F + 1/P + 2	(25 hours) hit
1955/04/25	4	4 states felt	N + 2/P - 2	(117 hours) hit
1939/06/19	4	Arkadelphia, AR	N + 2/P + 0	(55 hours) hit
1937/05/16	4	Blytheville, AR	F + 6/P + 6	(3 hours) hit
1927/05/07	4.8	N. Jonesboro, AR	N + 6/P + 8	(29 hours) hit
1923/10/28	4.5	Marked Tree, AR	F - 1/P + 0	(37 hours) hit
1911/03/31	4.7	Rison, AR	N + 1/P - 2	(68 hours) hit

Results of seismic windows:

- 17/22 (77.3 percent) of these were in a standard seismic window (chance allows 52 percent).

- 13/22 (59.0 percent) were in a predictable primary window (chance allows 26 percent).

- 5/22 (22.7 percent) weren't in a seismic window, but the 1969 Little Rock quake was one day early for a secondary window. The 1976 northeast Arkansas quake was three days late for a rare perigean spring tide window.

The "Brownian Movement"

It's no secret that folks in the Midwest do fear potential earthquakes, and for good reason. As Berkland points out, many people remember the "ill-fated 'Brownian movement' that failed on December 3, 1990." It was a time in history when earthquake predictor Iben Browning had publicized an imminent shaker to rumble through the Midwest. While he roused the media and public, his prediction fizzled—it didn't pan out.

Berkland says, "Although it was a time of extreme perigean spring tides, I had earlier rejected Browning's prediction during an extensive interview with *Unsolved Mysteries*. I gave the possibility of a major Midwest quake less than one-half of one percent for the entire month of December."

But since scientists and other wannabe quake predictors aren't able to reliably predict earthquakes, is it really so far-fetched for people who live in Arkansas, Missouri, Tennessee, Kentucky, and Illinois to monitor seismic windows?

From Perks to Predictions

An earthquake in southern Illinois in spring 1969 started one young man on his career in journalism. He had been studying journalism at Southern Illinois University and wanted to become a newspaper reporter. But he couldn't land a slot on the school paper, *The Daily Egyptian*. "A paying job there would be great on my resume, but the slots were filled," recalls Jim Hodl.

"The earthquake hit on a Saturday morning. Just enough to make the ground tremble a little. Students poured from the dorms, and a festive mood erupted. But I decided to get a story from it. I interviewed assorted students about what they were doing when the quake hit and how they reacted to it. Some were quite good. I typed up my story and dropped it off the following Monday at the *Egyptian* offices. On Tuesday afternoon, I was told that the faculty manager, Harry Hix of the *Egyptian* wanted to see me. Hix promptly gave me an *Egyptian* slot that I held until I graduated in September 1970. I later heard that at an editorial meeting that Monday morning, Hix asked the paid student reporters where their earthquake articles were. But they had all joined the post-quake party. So Hix waved my article and growled, 'Maybe the *Egyptian* has the wrong reporters!'" Being on the paper helped Hodl get many post-graduation offers, and he is still a working writer today.

So some people like Hodl can find the silver lining for earthquakes, but quake warnings in this area haven't had a good track record, thanks to Browning. While Berkland doesn't provide monthly predictions for the Midwest, like he does for the West Coast and the Ring of Fire, his monthly seismic windows announced both in *Syzygy—An Earthquake Newsletter* and on his website can and do work for this region.

Says Hodl, "I'd pay attention to Jim Berkland's earthquake warning system if it could be proved reliable. If it is only as reliable as weather forecasting, maybe not. Living in the Chicago area, I've gone through predictions of heavy snow accumulation that produced hardly an inch. On two occasions, I had to leave my car at work because the predictions of 'a dusting of snow' and 'sunny all day' produced 9 and 13 inches of snow.

"If the earthquake prediction were reliable, it would be hard to predict what I'd do. A tremendous tremor could damage your home, making you not want to stay there. But the highway could crack up (like I've seen in Alaska and Japan), so you wouldn't want to be there either. At least with predictions of heavy snow, you can stay home safe and sound," he adds.

Super Tremors in Yellowstone

In his book A *Short History of Nearly Everything*, Bill Bryson reports, "Yellowstone is America's restless supervolcano and it is due for another eruption. The power of a supervolcano is 1,000 times greater than an 'ordinary' volcano, as it explodes in a single mighty rupture. The explosion would be beyond the scale of anything known to humans."

Says Berkland, "As for Yellowstone, it is essentially a geologic park, with abundant signs of past volcanism and continuing hydrothermal and seismic activity. It is very likely to experience renewed volcanic activity, but should not approach the mega-eruption of mid-Pleistocene time."

In May 2005, I was told that some nearby residents noticed that animals were reacting to strange earth changes, whereas both scientists and authorities were well aware of the activity and keeping it quiet. "I would hope that the public will be kept informed in a timely fashion about the latest developments. It is not sufficient for authorities merely to block access from certain areas because of reported high heat flow, abnormally high release of gases, and unusual animal behavior. In the absence of forthright discussion of these matters by qualified investigators, we can only expect the continuation of half-truths, speculations, and conspiracy theories by the public," adds Berkland. (See Part 5, "Politics and Quakes.")

Getting Peace of Mind

While scientifically accepted earthquake warning systems aren't available yet, a 62-year-old family man in Nebraska turns to earthquake insurance for both of his houses to feel safe. Charles Kuchar has heard of quakes in Nebraska, he says, but he's more concerned about what may be coming rather than what has happened in the past.

"Reading about the quakes on Berkland's website caused me to inquire about coverage on my Kansas City home. It was inexpensive, so when we bought our retirement home in Nebraska, I included it in my policy up there also." Kuchar adds, "Yes, it gives me peace of mind, but all in all, if a major earthquake such as the New Madrid shakes again, I will probably not be able to collect." But, of course, Kuchar, being in the Midwest where earthquakes aren't as active as they are in California, Japan, China, and Alaska, is getting "cheap peace of mind." (See Chapter 19, "Don't Be Scared—Be Prepared!")

Southern Shakes

Back in the winter of 1973, Jim Berkland visited Florida when he was an assistant professor of geology at Appalachian State University in North Carolina. One job was to lead a student field trip to the Florida Keys—his interest was in oceanography rather than seismology at that time. Later, on October 27, 1973, central Florida was hit by one of its strongest quakes (a 4.2 on the day after syzygy). Not only does the South get its hurricanes and tornadoes, on occasion earthquakes visit, too.

While neither Berkland nor I experienced the Floridian earthquake of '73, we know that while southern Florida is almost immune to shakers, central Florida isn't. Berkland recalls that back in 1967, research showed that earthquakes reported for Florida happened between October and January, indicating the possibility of an "earthquake season" for the state where hurricanes hit. And three quakes of Intensity IV or V in the Sunshine State—October 27, 1973; January 12, 1977; and November 6, 1977—seem to fit the pattern. Plus, points out Berkland, other earthquakes in Florida hit in his seismic windows:

- December 22, 1945—Primary window

- October 27, 1973—Secondary window

- January 12, 1977—Primary window

And speaking of seismic windows, the East Coast isn't immune to earthquakes.

EARTHSHAKING FACTS
TO DOG-EAR

- Don't exclude the possibility of earthquakes happening in the Midwest and South, because they can and do strike these regions, too.

- Remember, the great New Madrid quakes did occur during one of Jim Berkland's seismic windows, as did the major Charleston, South Carolina, earthquake of August 31, 1886, during the second most extreme tidal period for the year.

- If you live in the Midwestern or Southern states, you might want to consider purchasing earthquake insurance, because it is relatively inexpensive and can give you peace of mind.

11 ⋙ The East Coast Rocks

When the East Coast rocks and rolls, everybody knows it.

—Jim Berkland

JIM BERKLAND REMINISCES ABOUT AN UNDOGMATIC GEOLOGY PROFESSOR AT THE University of New Brunswick in Canada who explained the details of their 5.9, the strongest quake in 126 years, which hit on January 9, 1980. "There was a total eclipse of the Moon that day, and the tides in the Bay of Fundy were over 50 feet. We think that the extra stress triggered the earthquake." Without hesitation, Berkland told him, "That's my idea. Would you come back to California with me and explain that to my colleagues?"

While the debate over the link between tides and earthquakes continues to shake up mainstream West Coast scientists in both Northern and Southern California, earthquakes continue to rock the Eastern seaboard from time to time—and tidal flows may be a factor, according to Berkland. People in the northeastern United States have noticed that for months it can be quiet, but then states such as New Hampshire get a lot of small quakes. Also, it's been reported that in New York City a fault line runs across 125th Street. And Berkland knows all too well that other potential quake-producing activity up and down the East Coast and past and present earthquakes show that the East Coast isn't immune.

Charleston, South Carolina, Earthquake

During the summertime on August 31, 1886, at 9:51 p.m., a 7.3 quake shook for more than a half minute; which could seem like forever, especially when it hit X on the Mercalli intensity scale. According to the U.S. Geological Survey, this is the most damaging quake to happen in the southeast United States and one of the largest historic shocks in eastern North America. Many buildings in Charleston were damaged, and the quake killed 60 people. Structural damage also affected Alabama, central Ohio, eastern Kentucky, southern Virginia, and western West Virginia.

So, was this quake in the nineteenth century predictable? Yes, says Berkland. "It would have been impossible to ignore the extreme perigean spring tides at the time, because the new moon and close perigee were only four hours apart on August 29, 1886, creating the second most quake-prone period of the year," he notes.

Virginia Quakes

On February 23, 2004, the USGS felt a small temblor that was said to have "excited" seismologists, said Berkland. "Not surprising to me, but somewhat exciting is the fact that it was the day of the full moon, following the perigean spring tide of the new moon two weeks earlier, which was my primary seismic window for the month, when syzygy and perigee were on the same day."

Take a look at four East Coast quakes:

- February 23, 2005 (2.0), Baltimore, Maryland, 24-hour synchroneity, one of the four perigean tides of the year

- December 8, 2003 (4.5), Richmond, Virginia, 0-hour synchroneity, one of the maximum possible five perigean spring tides for the year

- May 31, 1897 (5.9/VII intensity), 7-hour synchroneity, one of only four perigean spring tides for the year

- May 8, 1897 (VI intensity), Pulaski, Virginia, 4-hour synchroneity, one of only four perigean spring tides for the year

Berkland notes that all four of those quakes happened two weeks after a rare perigean spring tide at the opening of a secondary seismic window. What's more, this was a repeat of the situation for the 7.4 Eureka quake of November 8, 1980; the 6.8 Kobe quake of January 16,

1995; the 6.0 Parkfield quake of September 28, 2003; and the 9.0 Sumatra quake of December 26, 2004; and many others. (See Chapter 13, "The Great Quake-Tsunami of 2004.")

This history of earthquakes on the East Cost shows the significance of the secondary seismic window following perigean spring tides. While Berkland is intrigued by how Virginia area quakes follow such a pattern, he wasn't surprised that following the perigean spring tide of August 29, 1886, only two days later, the strongest quake in the history of the eastern United States happened at Charleston, South Carolina.

The Blue Mountain Lake, New York, Quake

If you think New Yorkers don't worry about earthquakes, think again. Just ask Laura Dauphine. She still remembers the Blue Mountain Lake 5.1 quake in New York on October 7, 1983, at 5:19 a.m. She was living off campus in Saratoga Springs, completing her education. She had two pugs who were snoozing in their gated areas in the early morning. "I had a tiny wind chime hanging from a floor lamp behind my bed. As I figured, when it chimed, I'd know the pugs were up to no good. The gentle and persistent tinkling of that tiny chime on the floor lamp woke me that morning. The dogs were still gated in another room, whining, using a vocabulary that I hadn't heard before," she recalls.

"Soon after I woke," Dauphine continues, "my bed started dancing sideways across the floor in mini-hops. Having never experienced an earthquake before, my brain flipped through known possible causes like garbage trucks or blasting, before settling on 'earthquake.' Just as I started to panic, the earthquake stopped abruptly, and I think it was only a 3.0 or 4.0, but I remember my heart, like a passenger in a stopped car, kept going for quite some time." She and her dogs survived without a scratch.

While this temblor caused only minor damage, Dauphine wasn't the only person who got a wake-up call. According to the USGS, two provinces in Canada and 12 states felt the New York quake, too. Also, landslides were reported and light damage happened in other towns in the Blue Mountain Lake area.

Hudson Valley, New York, Temblor

On October 14, 2004, I received an email from my literary agent, Jim Cypher, who resides in Beacon, New York. The subject read: "We Get Earthquakes, Too!" A 2.7 earthquake hit the Hudson Highlands and was felt in Beacon, 60 miles north of New York City, on Thursday at 5:36 a.m.

I read in one news report, since the eastern United States lies at the center of a huge tectonic plate spreading from the center of the Atlantic Ocean to the West Coast, tremors in New York and other East Coast states aren't usually as intense as they can be in California, where our two tectonic plates collide.

"Scientists understand that where crustal rocks are more discontinuous, more faulted, and not so dense, the seismic waves are weakened more quickly. Thus, a magnitude 4.0 quake may be felt only for 40 miles on the Pacific Coast, but more than 100 miles in the Rockies," explains Berkland. Thus, when a 4.5 quake hits east of the Rockies, you can bet that it will be felt over four or more states. "Many thousands of people will be highly concerned, whereas Californians might well sleep through it or shrug off an event."

Meanwhile, the Hudson Highlands minor quake, which probably rattled a lot of nerves, hadn't surprised Berkland. In his October 2004 *Syzygy*, he noted that October 13 to 20 was a primary seismic window period. "It fit the theory nicely—the day after the new moon, and two days before perigee," says Berkland.

Ironically, on the day before the quake rattled the Hudson Highlands, I received a rejection from a New York editor. She thanked my agent for submitting the proposal for *The Man Who Predicts Earthquakes*. Not only didn't it suit their publishing program at that time, the editor pointed out that their company tends to focus on practical, how-to books rather than general nonfiction topics. I couldn't help ponder, *Isn't a book that includes quake warnings to save lives practical?* Sadly, it took a bigger jolt for earthquake awareness to be seen as a practical, how-to part of self-preservation. (See Part 4, "The Big Wave.")

The Manhattan Quake Vision

In Berkland's September 2001 *Syzygy*, he wrote the following: "On my website *syzygyjob.com* Daniel Perez of Michigan had posted on August 2, 2001, about his premonition dream of an earthquake hitting New York. He 'saw' Katie Couric on the *Today* show, when the TV signal blacked out. He wrote, 'She was talking about 10,000 people dying in a building. Either she was talking about the Empire State Building or the World Trade Center. In the dream the quake was very devastating because she could barely hold her emotions together on the air, and in the background of the TV image, I could see huge open spaces where tall skyscrapers once stood, and one tall skyscraper was billowing smoke from all of its broken windows. While Katie was interviewing some survivors, more aftershocks hit the city and knocked out the TV transmissions once more. I usually don't write about dreams and I usually don't dream about far away places, but this dream stuck out because it scared me.'"

Berkland notes that five weeks later, Perez's vision of the collapsed World Trade Center in New York became an unforgettable national disaster. Adds Berkland, "I then owed him an apology for my post, which had chided him for posting about an impossible quake on my website, and possibly frightening people who might have taken it to heart. Daniel's psychic vision was another indication that science does not have all of the answers. (See Chapter 6, "Dreams and Visions.")

An Atlantic Ocean Quake-Tsunami?

After the Indian Ocean great quake-tsunami happened on December 26, 2004, people on the West Coast and East Coast wondered, "Are we next?" Berkland answers, "The threat of a giant tsunami more than 100 foot high to the Atlantic Coast is much less than we are led to believe, since it depends upon a submarine avalanche in the Canary Islands, and not necessarily upon an earthquake. Also, there is no reported history of such an event."

But Berkland cautions, that doesn't mean that the Eastern Seaboard has been free of tsunamis. He recalls a deadly seismic sea wave that happened off Newfoundland in 1929. It accompanied the 7.1 Grand Banks earthquake, he reports, which caused a great current that severed several Atlantic cables and covered them with debris far out into the Atlantic on November 18, 1929. The natural disaster occurred on the day of perigee and two days after the full moon. "It came at the time of near-record tides that reached two feet higher than the expected 11 feet at Boston Harbor, because of onshore winds abetted by a small tsunami. Closer to the epicenter, the tsunami was more than 10 feet high, and 27 people died from the inundation around Placentia Harbor, Newfoundland," recalls Berkland.

Whether you live on the East Coast, West Coast, in the Midwest, or the South, I know that for 30 years, Berkland has been urging everyone who would listen to monitor every aspect of precursory phenomena prior to times of maximum tides. He concludes, "Putting the pieces of the puzzle together can save many thousands of lives, and economic/political factors should take a secondary role." (See Chapter 14, "Where Are the Quake Warnings?")

Now that we've put quakes on the American table, let's talk about earthquakes worldwide.

EARTHSHAKING FACTS
TO DOG-EAR

-⋙ Stay aware of lunar changes and tidal flows, especially if you live on the West Coast, East Coast, or any coastal area in the world.

-⋙ Know that quakes do happen on the East Coast (such as in Maryland, Virginia, and New York).

-⋙ And note, while a killer wave to the Atlantic Coast is possible, it's less likely to happen—and the threat doesn't totally depend on an earthquake.

12 ~ What's Shakin' Around the World?

Many people think that there are more quakes than there used to be. However, in reality, it's that more people are thinking about quakes than used to.

—Jim Berkland

BACK IN 1994, JIM BERKLAND PREDICTED A 5.5 EGYPT QUAKE. AS THE STORY GOES, an Egyptian was reading *Al-Ahram*, an Arab newsletter. "I mentioned that I was a geologist who predicted quakes and that I expected one in Egypt during my tour of the country. He had just read the front page and knew that it had happened on the previous day, on the day I had arrived." Then, the fascinated native's eyes opened wide, and he pointed to the Arabic headline about the unusual jolt in northeast Egypt.

"That was one of my 50 MOSS predictions (monthly outright seismic speculations) that I published in my monthly newsletter. It was one of only four hits, however, so I stopped after 50, because I recognized that my intuition was not that good," admits Berkland.

Not only does Berkland make earthquake predictions for the San Francisco Bay Area, California, the West Coast, he also provides monthly seismic window predictions for earthquakes that can and do occur in the Pacific Ring of Fire region. It's in this seismically prone arc where intense earthquake and volcanic activity happens. This region covers New Zealand, along the northern edge of Asia, north across the Aleutian Islands of Alaska, and south along the coast of North and South America. And the historic record shows that about 80 percent of the 6.0-plus quakes occur within the Ring of Fire, notes Berkland.

Super Seismic Window Hits

On September 13, 1999, the strongest aftershock of the 7.8 Turkey quake struck and caused 59 more deaths. It measured 5.8, but Berkland said he was relieved that it didn't exceed 6.0, because via email, he had reassured several concerned residents of northwest Turkey that he didn't expect a 7–8 follow-up to the mainshock. In fact, he had responded that he didn't expect any aftershocks for the rest of the year to reach 6.0. "The mainshock hit during the August window, five days after the solar eclipse passed over Turkey. Then the strongest aftershock to date came a month later during the September window."

Also, within this particular seismic window of pre-fall, around the Ring of Fire, the strongest earthquake measured 6.4 and was centered in Bolivia on September 14. "The terrible Taiwan quake of 7.6 and a series of six aftershocks that began on September 20 weren't in a normal window, but eight out of 11 major 1999 quakes in the world up until then were within the seismic window," explains Berkland.

The earthquake in Taiwan brings to mind a friend of mine from Taiwan and her animated reaction to the Loma Prieta earthquake. As a Californian, I agree, this monster scared me, too, but she was *really* scared. She told me that the big quakes in Taiwan can be ugly. I didn't have a clue. According to Berkland, the Taiwanese are used to their big quakes being centered offshore, especially east of the island, where they don't get the severest shaking. "The on-land quakes in 1999 were much more violent and damaging than usually experienced in Taiwan," he says. "However, their modern building codes are similar to those in California, so the seismic devastation is much less than what is commonly seen in the Near East, North Africa, India, or South America."

The Niigata Earthquake of 1964

As Berkland puts it, the month of June is high on the list for good timing of past bad earthquakes. He recalls that the June 16, 1964,

Niigata, Japan, earthquake was a learning tool to structural engineers, as well as to geologists, regarding the phenomenon of liquefaction. "It is remarkable that this quake came less than three months after the great Alaskan quake of March 28, 1964, which also taught us much about liquefaction phenomena," he says.

I pointed out earlier that the Alaskan quake happened on the day of the full moon. It also struck at the time of extremely low tides in southern Alaska. "The Niigata quake hit during the top seismic window in four years, just six days after a solar eclipse and six days after the second closest approach of the Moon for the year," notes Berkland. He says, "The two astronomical events were less than two hours apart, the closest synchroneity between 1962 and 1972." A potential contributing factor? "The Sun was almost as high in the sky as it could get in Japan, within a week of the summer solstice," adds Berkland, who is aware that his earthquake theories were working overtime.

"As typical of postwar Japanese construction, large buildings were built with high seismic resistance, but one large apartment house had inadequate foundations for the sandy and saturated soils. The multistoried building settled and rotated 80 degrees, so that occupants could scramble out of windows and walk down the outside of the building to safety," explains Berkland, who adds that some of the most hazardous secondary effects of earthquakes were seen in the Niigata quake. Thirty-six people died in the Niigata quake, and 447 people were injured.

Haicheng, China, Earthquake of 1975

In 1975, Berkland had hit his predicted seismic window during the period of January 27–February 3, 1975. On February 3, a 7. 3 earthquake rocked and devastated the city of Haicheng, China. It occurred during perigean spring tides generated when perigee and syzygy occurred on the same day, notes Berkland.

"The Chinese had expected a 5.5-to-6.0 event in that area by June, and had issued its first warning on January 13, 1975," says Berkland, who adds that the warning was based on a variety of factors, including ground tilting, seismicity patterns, and strange animal behavior. "Its peasant network reported thousands of unusual bioseismic reactions [term coined by Berkland for animal/quake connections] over a radius of 155 miles from the epicenter, including birds, cats, cows, crows, deer, dogs, fish, frogs, hens, horses, rabbits, sheep, and tigers," says Berkland.

He adds that reports of odd animal behavior soared a few days before the earthquake. Then, after an eerie seismic silence, a swarm of small quakes caused the authorities to order the city to be evacuated. Many lives were saved; however, at least 10,000 people died, according to the U.S. Geological Survey.

Mexico City, Mexico, 1985 Earthquake

As Berkland tells it, "Mexico City was an eye-opener. It was in my ninth best published seismic window for 1985, but I had only officially predicted eight of them. It fit my theory, but I didn't officially predict it. There was a huge cover-up of deaths there." On September 19, this massive 8.1 earthquake that shook southern Mexico killed at least 9,500 people, according to the Pacific Disaster Center, but Berkland reports that he had eyewitness reports that the death toll was at least twice as great.

Gil Martinez was in Mexico City during the devastating earthquake of 1985 and remembers much of it vividly. He admits that he grew up in a region where tremors were not uncommon. So the initial quake wasn't the worst part—it was the aftermath that affected Martinez. The day after, he remembers, he went to school as usual. But during the blackout was when he started to find out what happened.

We learned that much of the downtown area had fallen down. That night, there was an aftershock, and my brother, father, and I all ran outside of the house. My mother stayed in, refusing to get out. I don't know if it was foolish or bravery, a death wish, or just a stupid decision. I do know my father was absolutely upset, and he decided to show us all what the city looked like. That's when reality hit me.

We drove around the areas that had been hit the hardest. I

had never seen something like that—buildings had pancaked. You could see beds, dressers, and other items of furniture sandwiched between layers of concrete. There were piles of rubble where before there had been factories, and what shocked my parents the most was that their favorite movie theater had fallen down. That weekend, we were glued to the news. My uncles and other adult relatives started to help. They drove their cars and had their fleet of trucks (they own a large business) at the disposal of authorities. They were used to carry bodies. I did not see this (I was too young), but they described what they saw. Some people had been cut up in half; others had exploded. And many had been burned beyond recognition (almost everyone cooks with propane in Mexico, and tanks ignited when the buildings collapsed).

The next Monday and for about a year, we went to school with name tags sewn to all our clothing, in case the school crumbled and more bodies had to be recovered. That's when the city began to stink and people started to get sick. Many sewers and water mainlines broke, and decaying bodies started to seep into the ground. At home we always boiled our water for an hour before drinking it, and now when we did this, a thick brown greasy crust collected on the top of the pot. We started drinking milk and bottled soft drinks. One of my uncles owned a textile factory, and he gave us about 100 blankets to distribute in the provisional camps. I was amazed by the amount of people who were left homeless.

One of the more horrible stories concerns the seamstresses who worked in the sweatshops. I have friends who worked there during this period, and they are haunted by the screams of the poor women buried under the rubble. The government considered them to be a low priority, and never sent equipment to get them out.

So that's my experience. I only have one question, but I don't think your expert will be able to answer it. The Mexican government's official tally is about 15,000 dead, but there are several hundred thousand who disappeared. I'd like to know exactly how many people lost their lives that day." [See Chapter 16, "The Frisco Quake Cover-up."]

Berkland notes that his unofficial seismic window was October 13 to 20, 1985, and the great Mexican earthquake of 8.1 was the strongest in North America since the great 1964 Alaska earthquake, 21 years earlier. "Ironically," he adds, "many more lives were lost in the 7.2 aftershock that followed the great Mexican quake, just as had happened on the day following the 8.1 in Tangshan, China, in 1976. This became an additional life risk for rescuing parties." According to the Chinese government, the two earthquakes in Tangshan killed over 240,000 people, although some estimates of the death toll are as high as 655,000.

Earthquake Near Coast of Peru

Berkland noted in his June 2001 *Syzygy* that it was a time for an "extremely favorable seismic window for June 20–27, based upon some extraordinary and converging astronomical events." Here, take a close-up look at what was to take place during this period:

- Early on June 21, the Sun will be as high as it can get in the Northern Hemisphere as the summer solstice occurs.

- Almost simultaneously there will be a 5-minute total solar eclipse passing from Angola to Zanzibar across central Africa and over Madagascar.

- Within two days there will also be the closest perigee and the highest Golden Gate tides (8.4 feet) since last February, which was a month of high seismicity.

- In addition, the planet Mars will be at its minimum distance to Earth on June 21, which will certainly attract the attention of both astronomers and astrologers.

As usual, Berkland made his four predictions for Central California, Southern California, Seattle, and the Ring of Fire. On June 23, 2001, two days after the solar eclipse, in the Ring of Fire, an 8.4 earthquake struck near the coast of southern Peru. It killed more than 150 people and caused widespread damage, according to a "Seismo-Watch Significant Earthquake Report."

The Greece Quake of 1993

In Berkland's July 1993 *Syzygy*, he reported that his primary window was July 1–8, with the highest Golden Gate tides of 7.3 feet on July 2–3. He had 75 percent confidence in his predictions for San Jose, Los Angeles, and Seattle, with a major global event. Plus, Berkland included an uncanny and out of the ordinary earthquake prediction. He wrote, "Also, the Mediterranean area seems much overdue, and I would not be surprised by a 6-plus in Greece or Italy during the window."

So what happened? On July 1, a 3.0 struck near San Juan Bautista, California. Two quakes hit on July 8: a 3.9 at Yucca Valley and a 3.6 near Barstow—both in California. The Oregon coast was rocked by two tremors, a 3.4 and a 4.1 on July 4–5. A 6.4 hit Easter Island on July 6, and a 7.8 rumbled through Japan on July 12—the strongest earthquake to hit that country in a quarter of a century, killing more than 200 people, with an 80-foot tsunami, notes Berkland.

And yes, the Greek earthquake did hit after Berkland's seismic window closed. I still can't help thinking of the adage, "Better late than never." And perhaps if people knew about Berkland's prediction, the late quake wouldn't have been such an eye-opener for some, and others may have protected valuables for the uncontrollable event that did occur six days late.

George Georgakilas of Sao Paulo, Brazil, remembers July 14, 1993. "The Patras region was rocked by a 5.4, which produced quite a lot of damage. I was traveling from Athens to Pyrgos, which, by the way, had been damaged by a quake a couple of months before. At about 3:00 p.m., we were on the bus. I had this feeling that something with the engine was going wrong, kind of like feeling that there was a flat tire. No one paid attention to that, but I do recall a few surprised faces. Some minutes later, we reached Patras, and things were chaotic there: sirens, alarms going off, people running, some panicking, some others absolutely calm."

Georgakilas continues, "I saw two men running out of a building and looking upwards. So I figured, 'There's been an earthquake.' Sometime later, we saw some people gathering around someone apparently injured, a woman weeping outside her car, and when the bus stopped, someone two seats ahead of me opened the window and asked, 'What happened?' And a lady shouted back 'Seismos!' [earthquake in Greek]."

While Georgakilas is from Brazil, he claims it is nonseismic, and he felt a bit cheated because he didn't feel that moderate earthquake, and just thought the bus had been bouncing around for a few seconds for some other reasons. He points out, "We tried to visit Olympia's museum, but the guard calmly said it was closed. Okay, then. In the next morning's paper, we learned that the reason why it had closed was that in at the moment of the quake, there was a big noise, and some big piece of art had been knocked down."

Greek earthquakes are nothing new, according to Berkland. He notes the Greek city of Salonika as the site for periodic destructive quakes since ancient times, with at least 12 exceeding 6.0 in the twentieth century. On June 20, 1978, a 6.5 quake killed at least 50 people. Says Berkland, "The quake occurred only 15 minutes before the moment of the full moon and the day before perigee and the summer solstice. Thus, it was in a classic seismic window."

The Bam, Iran, Quake of 2003

On December 26, 2003, a killer quake hit Bam, Iran. This unforgettable disaster hit in Berkland's seismic windows linked with the full moon. This was a classic prediction for Berkland. All year long in 2003, he had warned of the record tides coming in December, with a 9.2-foot Golden Gate tide being the highest possible, he reports. "My December 21–28, 2003, seismic window was based on the new moon syzygy of December 23, the close perigee on December 22 (just 22 hours earlier), the winter solstice tides of December 22, and the closest approach of Earth and the Sun 10 days later," recalls Berkland. On December 26, a 6.8 deadly quake flattened the adobe city, killed at least 30,000 people, and injured 30,000, according to the USGS.

Take a look at Berkland's strong warning for his December 2003 Syzygy:

As I have warned you for several months, we will experience a "super-syzygy" in December. On the 23rd of this month, the Golden Gate tides will attain a range of 9.2 feet in a 6-hour period. This has not happened since December 1986, when it was accompanied by a predicted San Jose quake of 4.6 and South Pacific 6.8. Such tides will occur only seven times in the century, the next two times on January 8, 2005, and then not again until December 24, 2026. It is important to visualize what happens during such occasions, specifically in San Francisco Bay, where more than 400 square miles experience huge fluctuations in tides in just six hours between high and low. The local crust has adjusted to normal tide ranges of 4.0–4.5 feet, and then the load is piled twice as high. Each cubic foot of saltwater over one square mile adds about one million tons to the crustal load. Such considerations also apply to the 17-foot ranges at Puget Sound and 35 feet in southern Alaska where the great geologist G.K. Gilbert wrote in 1909, "The ocean tides are sufficient to trigger earthquakes."

It must be recognized that only faults on the verge of failure can be stimulated into movement by the tides, and that the maximum tides do not necessarily trigger maximum earthquakes. However, the potential for earthquakes increases during such extreme conditions as we will undergo during the last 10 days of the year 2003.

Speaking of warnings, in the next chapter, "The Great Quake-Tsunami of 2004," Berkland sent out quake warnings throughout 2004 about record high tides in December and their potential harm globally.

EARTHSHAKING FACTS
TO DOG-EAR

⌇ Use Jim Berkland's seismic window theory monthly to help you to know the periods when an earthquake is more apt to happen.

⌇ And note, once a seismic window is over, don't get caught off guard. An imminent quake may come a bit later. It's fairly common to find that large quakes happen in the secondary windows that open halfway between two extreme primary windows. (The super-windows were December 21 to 28, 2003; December 10 to 17, 2004; and January 8 to 15, 2005.)

⌇ To help understand how large the magnitude will be, tune into the past seismic patterns and strange animal behavior as did the people in Haicheng, China.

⌇ Be sure to store bottled water so you'll be prepared if an earthquake hits and it affects the water supply in your region.

⌇ If your water supply has been affected, do boil it before using.

⌇ Calm yourself. Try not to panic before, during, or after an earthquake. Your life may depend on staying cool. (See Chapter 19, "Don't Be Scared—Be Prepared!")

Part Four

The Big Wave

13 ᴡ The Great Quake-Tsunami of 2004

Animals interpret for us when the earth speaks.

—Jim Berkland

Do Animals Have a Sixth Sense?

Animals have such amazing senses that it seems they can predict quakes and tsunamis. No *way*, you're thinking. But it's true—they can, and for a variety of reasons. Here, Jim Berkland and other experts offer possible theories to explain animal behavior, and maybe your pet's mysterious insights.

On December 26, 2004, on the day of the full moon, a 9.0 earthquake hit off the west coast of northern Sumatra, and a big wave of destruction followed. According to media reports, before the killer waves hit Sri Lanka—an island south of India—and India coastal areas, elephants headed for higher ground, dogs wouldn't go outside, and zoo animals fled into their shelters and wouldn't budge. Wildlife officials reported that at Yala National Park— near the area of mass destruction—elephants, leopards, and deer miraculously survived. Unlike humans, few animal carcasses have been found after the killer tsunami hit the wildlife sanctuary.

Berkland is not surprised by the post-tsunami disaster reports of animals and their sixth sense. After all, both he and I have been creating a buzz about our friendly "seismic sentries" for more than 20 years.

So what gives? Diana L. Guerrero, author and animal disaster behavior expert in Big Bear Lake, California, says, "Animals appear to exhibit an awareness of impending disaster. Changes are common in both wild and domestic animals prior to seismic activity. So I would suspect that animals vacated the area prior to the tsunami based on their survival instincts."

How do animals do that? It's just another astounding act that makes animals seem psychic. But do they really have a supernatural sixth sense?

Clairvoyant Cues

Animal experts claim there doesn't seem to be any other explanation. Animals possess super-senses that are beyond the scope of normal sensory perception. Ever notice how pets often seem to know something we don't? They wake up before the alarm rings or recognize their owner is ill. Some experts think they have ESP. And some things animals know are unsolved mysteries—or are they?

Do animals really have a sixth sense? "Anecdotal accounts seem to indicate that they appear to. A common example would be the survival response in groups of animals in response to predators—they avoid the hunters and ignore those that are not on the prowl. I would hypothesize that the same adaptations relate to geological and related threats," explains Guerrero.

In my book 202 Pets' Peeves, I discuss animals' sixth sense. "Pet Peeve #70," from the viewpoint of a cat, is: "Cataclysmic Events: Before, during, and after a terrible disaster—tornado, hurricane, fire, or earthquake—we behave strangely. Some people say it's ESP, or a sixth sense. Personally, I can't tolerate it when narrow-minded humans roll their eyes when I start to act chatty, or clingy, or hide under the bed. It bothers me a lot, too, when humans think our sensitivity to change is a laughing matter."

Perhaps animals don't sense danger, says Georgia-based certified animal behaviorist Dr. John Wright, but they do sense and react to a change in routine or the environment. And sometimes animals such as caged wildlife will act out or make a noise to get outdoors or free themselves.

"I don't think the bonds between people and domestic animals are particularly important in saving lives, because many wild animals also show premonitions," says British author Rupert Sheldrake. And post–Indian Ocean quake media reports show that the undomesticated animals indeed sensed danger. "The ability to feel an impending earthquake is part of animals' nature. Of course, if they have bonds with people, it may make it easier to notice their fear or anxiety before a catastrophe strikes."

Animal Warnings

So we know that both domestic and undomesticated animals may be so sensitive to the movements of the earth's crust that they can actually predict earthquakes, too.

Remember, Berkland predicted the 1989 World Series earthquake and the 1994 Northridge quake in Southern California. What led this geologist to make these predictions? Missing cats and dogs! As I mentioned in previous chapters, he's found that the numbers of lost pet ads peak before an earthquake hits. Evidently, our pets will often disappear, heading for safer ground. And apparently, the wildlife in Sri Lanka did just that.

Odd animal behavior has been reported elsewhere. There were unexplained beachings of almost 200 whales and dolphins hundreds of miles to the north at Tasmania, New Zealand, and Australia. Three weeks after the strange animal happenings began, an 8.1 earthquake struck south of New Zealand off Macquarie Island on December 23, 2004. At that time, it was the strongest quake in the world in three years, and it was preceded by the most widespread example of marine mammal strandings in history, notes Berkland.

Turning to Mother Nature

But there is more to Berkland's theory than just missing pets and strange animal behavior. As I've noted in previous chapters, he also predicts quakes by using information on the tidal flows, and the positions of the Moon, Sun, and Earth. Plus, the Moon in the full or new phase with fluctuation of both extreme low and high tides can cause significant earthquakes. And not only "was the great 9.0 Indian Ocean underwater earthquake and tsunami on the day of the full moon," points out Berkland, "the last 9-plus earthquake and tsunami was in Alaska on March 27, 1964, also the day of the full moon."

Berkland says, "All year I have been warning of the record tides coming in early December. I have said that if a great quake was going to occur, December was the most likely time. And now we have two separate great earthquakes within one week, which may be unprecedented." Keep in mind that the 8.1 monster quake hit off Macquarie Island on December 23, 2004. Interestingly, it has been reported that penguins, like the Sri Lanka animals, escaped harm, too.

How Did They Know?

Some scientists believe that animals earlier sensed the underwater earthquake and the devastating tsunami of December 26, 2004. There is abundant evidence that magnetic crystals in the bodies of many creatures (perhaps even people) enable them to detect changes in the magnetic field that precede earthqakes. Berkland is confident that this magnetic mechanism provides clues to phenominal animal navigation, such as is exhibited by honeybees, butterflies, salmon, whales, and dolphins.

We do know animals sense hurricanes. While scientists use wind patterns, barometric pressure, sea surface temperature, and other climate factors to predict hurricanes, fishermen watch their cats. In fact, cats have long been considered good luck on ships for their ability to ward off storms, sea monsters, and ghosts. Europeans of the past centuries believed cats knew the way home and would reveal the direction by sleeping on the side of the ship that was closest to port.

Gail Beecher, a veteran cat breeder from Needville, Texas, got a special warning before Tropical Storm Frances hit the Texas coast on September 9, 1998. Some of Beecher's pregnant cats began to go into early labor. "When the barometer shifts during bad weather, my cats always go into early labor," she says. "I knew the storm was coming this way." Wind speeds reached a maximum of 65 miles per hour, and one person died due to the intense flooding of the Gulf Coast.

We also know cats are extraordinarily sensitive to minute changes in the weather. In fact, some cat experts believe cats are more reliable weather predictors than weather forecasters on television.

Sound silly? Perhaps not, say scientists who are aware that dozens of reports came in after the December 26 quake-tsunami. The animals sensed disaster was coming and simply headed for higher ground, and few animal bodies were found. But people were killed by the killer waves, and countless bodies were found.

"It is known that whales have the mineral magnetite in their upper sinus passages, and dolphins have formed it in the protective membrane (dura) around the brain, with the largest grains of magnetite enclosed in tiny nerve endings. This is no accident, but relates to their navigational abilities, which may be confounded by magnetic field changes prior to earthquakes," explains Berkland.

What Were the Sensitives Doing?

While animal warnings were happening before the great quake-tsunami of December 2004, human earthquake sensitives were also affected—but in subtle ways—before the "big wave." Often, humans are busy with everyday life and tune out nature's changes, whereas animals are more in tune with Mother Earth.

Still, while the Sumatra quake-tsunami struck many countries, it also affected people worldwide both physically and psychologically, some before and some after. Just ask visionary Clarisa Bernhardt. She'll tell you, "Everyone on the planet is affected by atmospheric shock waves from earthquake energy activity, not just the epicenter of the area hit by the quake. This can cause an increase in binge eating and drinking or excess of anything."

Bernhardt explains, "I have found the energy of earthquakes can be far more disruptive to people in general than they realize, and being so sensitive to these energies, I find they can affect one's health. Many people who have insomnia on some nights, do not realize that it may be an approaching energy frequency that is actually keeping them awake. I sometimes wake up for no apparent reason to later learn that is when the quake had occurred or it awakened me by the atmospheric change of the shock wave arriving from the occurrence of the quake."

Says *Anxiety, Phobias & Panic* author Reneau Peurifoy, "You already have read about the various theories of how animals might sense an earthquake due to things such as magnetic variation, high-pitched sounds from cracking bedrock, or radon emissions. A person with a very sensitive body may also have some subtle reactions to whatever animals react to. When a person with a history of panic attacks experiences these unusual sensations, they simply react in the old patterns characteristic of their panic disorder. They would have the same reaction to any body reaction that is unusual or strange."

So the question remains unanswered: Were the earthquake sensitives' predictive dreams that I noted in Chapter 6, "Dreams and Visions," a coincidence?

The Wave of Destruction

Rick Von Feldt, a 42-year-old Singapore-based American tourist on vacation, vividly recollects his experience on Phuket Beach, Thailand. The deadly tsunami hit around 10:15 a.m. He can't forget how the ocean receded and seemed as if "a god pulled a giant plug on the bathtub." Feldt noticed people walking out toward the sea to look at "the new landscape." Little did families, seniors, and fishermen know that this was the big wave that would change their lives forever.

At first, you saw it. The horizon began to be blocked out, and you saw a blue-black wall spring to life. You could tell the water was coming back. And soon, all of your newly discovered play areas would be back to normal, covered once again by water. Sure, it felt odd. And you wondered, "Why is this happening?" But no logical reason came to mind. It was a full moon last night. So perhaps the moon was creating an abnormal tide. Most of us didn't live by oceans, and so we had no clue as to how the ocean was really supposed to work. Many locals stood up at the retaining wall, in awe, looking at their backyard sea of water that was no more. But they knew the power of the ocean—and were fearful to get any closer.

But then we saw the wall. At first, way out to sea. If you blinked your eyes, it changes positions really fast. And then we could see it was moving too fast. For a few seconds, everyone was mesmerized by the wall. And the sound. And then, people started to walk. Fast. And then run. And soon, everyone started to scream. "Get up on the wall!" The water filled up the beach like a gorging bathtub. Water came at the people at 150 miles per hour, and no matter how hard you tried, unless you were close to the wall, you couldn't outrun it. The water came in fast. Some people stumbled. Some held their ground or were swept with the water toward the wall. People sputtered and coughed. The water spilled over the road.

The second and most deadly swell came. Taller by 10 feet, this one came so strongly and pushed everything it its path toward the town. The water weaved its way for four blocks inland, getting caught like a guided stream between banks of buildings. The force pushed between buildings, rising as high as 10 feet down perpendicular roads to the beach, again washing out everything. And the people? If you were lucky enough to get away from the first wave, and you ran upstairs to tops of buildings, you might have been lucky, but on Phuket Beach, nearly 500 people who were on the beach never made it.

People talk of two waves. But once the water from the second wave pulled back, everything floating in that water had to fall. Half of it flowed back to sea, like a hand of a monster grabbing—and not letting go.

And Von Feldt is just one of countless observers who saw, and survived, nature's wrath.

"There Were No Dogs"

While a vast majority of the wildlife survived the disaster, some animals, like humans, didn't make it either. Von Feldt tells what he witnessed at Phuket Beach on Thursday, December 30, 2004.

One of the memories I had of Phuket were all the dogs. In many of the beach resorts, there are a lot of stray dogs... Each morning, you could see packs of dogs playing down on the beach. They would run around chasing each other, playing doggy versions of tag and king on the hill. In the morning, they would run along the beach road, looking for scraps of food or handouts from willing tourists. Many looked the same, a kind of mongrel breed that, over time, looks like a mix between many medium-size dogs.

But now, there are no more dogs. Each morning, with the bodies of people also come bodies of dogs. As they clean up the destruction and bring out body bags of people, they also bring out dogs. They are placed in plastic bags and thrown into special vehicles. They can't exactly haul them away with the garbage, as the rotting flesh will also cause disease. But they also don't have a morgue for the mongrels.

On the morning of the wave, they most likely were able to keep their heads above the water when the first swell came in. Dogs have a way of being able to swim. But when the second, more churning wave came, they also would have been thrashed about—and eventually all dragged back into the ocean. [*www.phukettsunami.blogspot.com*]

While many dogs died on Phuket Beach, other animals lived. Still, mainstream geologists and seismologists believe animals are unreliable earthquake sensors. But, because more animals survived than perished after the Indian Ocean catastrophe, is it really so silly to monitor our sensitive animal friends?

Berkland advises people to do just that. Prepare. In the meantime, he'll be noting the moons and tides, and listening to reports from people worldwide who observe changes in animal behavior.

Your Seismic Sentries

Looking for a beacon to the next earthquake? Here are some animal clues gleaned from Diana L. Guerrero's animal disaster preparedness booklet, *Animal Disaster Preparedness for Pet Owners & Pet Professionals*:

Wild animals: Animals vacate areas, gather in groups, or enter into human inhabited areas prior to incidents. Wild animals that normally avoid humans will come in close contact with them, sometimes entering into dwellings or barns. Fishing improves in the local area. Zoo and oceanarium animals will try to escape, refuse to be confined, and more! Remember, behavioral changes can occur for a variety of other reasons.

Cats: You may see warning signs such as hiding, running around frantically trying to escape outdoors, and meowing. Many times, they will be aggressive, or will want to be "Velcro" pets and stay close to you. Pacing, hissing, or growling can also be symptoms. Most cats will hide, so check their favorite hiding places and behind cupboards, refrigerators, sofas, and beds; in closets and shelves; and behind the water heater.

Dogs: Dogs will usually hide. Behavior before a quake includes howling, whining, barking, restlessness, aggression, and increased devotion to animal guardians. They will often run around, and can bolt through gates, windows, or doors, or stick to you like glue. Some dogs will become more protective or aggressive, while others will be fearful or act dejected. Drastic differences in the number of advertised lost dogs and the animal shelter loads can precede quake activity in a specific area. Large increases in these numbers could give you a clue to upcoming earth activity. (You'll find advertised lost cats, too.)

Horses and livestock: Hoofed animals often refuse to enter their barns or pens and often refuse to tie. They tend to group together in open areas, act nervous, or pace.

Other animals: Caged birds will often hang on their cage; sometimes they will flap frantically, or they can be abnormally quiet. Breeding birds will often abandon their eggs or discard them from the nest. Other animals will show abnormal behavior. Some of the unusual changes include actions such as hibernating animals will emerge early (snakes, bears, etc.); spiders and ants will move indoors; rodents will invade the house, or if they are in residence will disappear; wild birds become quiet or aren't visible.

But note, not all animals can and do predict earthquakes.

The World Was Spinning

While animal reports amazed humans, there were also amazing media reports that the earth was still vibrating from the undersea quake off Indonesia that triggered the big waves. But this wasn't the first time seismic waves wreaked havoc on the globe. According to a report by the USGS, following the great Alaska earthquake of 1964, long-period seismic waves traveled around the earth for weeks. In fact, the earth vibrated like a church bell.

According to some seismologists, the December 26, 2004, Sumatra-Andaman earthquake created the longest lasting time of faulting ever witnessed. Media reports point out that some experts believe this mighty underwater temblor lasted up to 10 minutes. Berkland, however, says that too much was made of the 9.0 Sumatra quake's changing the earth's rotation and making it smaller. He believes that the 24-hour day is less than one millionth of a second shorter now and that the globe knocked two inches off its 8,000-mile diameter.

"These phenomena resulted from the underthrusting of the oceanic plate beneath the Sunda plate. This subduction process repeated all around the earth could result in the globe becoming smaller were it not for the oceanic ridges, where new crust is being created almost continuously. That is the beautiful balance of plate tectonics," adds Berkland. But the beauty of Mother Earth's ocean sometimes shows its ugly nature after movement.

SHOCKING EFFECTS

Quake: Sumatra-Andaman Islands earthquake (December 26, 2004)

Off the coast of northern Sumatra

Richter magnitude: 9.0

Mercali intensity: at least X

Number of people affected: More than 283,100 dead, 14,100 missing, 1,126,900 displaced by the quake and tsunami in 10 countries in South Asia and East Africa.

---

10 Facts FYI

Here's everything you wanted to know but were afraid to ask about the earthquake off the west coast of northern Sumatra. These facts were gleaned from a variety of sources: Jim Berkland, the USGS, and other organizations..

1 ➝ This is the fourth largest quake in the world since 1900 and is the largest since the 1964 Prince William Sound, Alaska, earthquake.

2 ➝ The earthquake itself caused severe damage and casualties in northern Sumatra, Indonesia, and the Nicobar Islands, India.

3 ➝ It was felt (Modified Mercalli Intensity IX) at Banda Aceh; (VIII) at Meulaboh; and (IV) at Medan, Sumatra; (VII) at Port Blair, Andaman Islands, India; (III–V) in parts of Bangladesh, mainland India, Malaysia, Maldives, Myanmar, Singapore, Sri Lanka, and Thailand.

4 ➝ The tsunami caused more casualties than any other in recorded history and was recorded nearly worldwide on tide gauges in the Indian, Pacific, and Atlantic Oceans.

5 ➝ At least 108,100 people were killed, and 127,700 are missing and presumed killed by the earthquake and tsunami in Indonesia.

6 ➝ Tsunamis killed at least 30,900 people in Sri Lanka; 10,700 in India; 5,300 in Thailand; 150 in Somalia; 90 in Myanmar; 82 in Maldives; 68 in Malaysia; 10 in Tanzania; three in Seychelles; two

in Bangladesh; and one in Kenya.

7 —⁣⁣ Tsunamis caused damage in Madagascar and Mauritius, and caused minor damage at two places on the west coast of Australia.

8 —⁣⁣ Seiches (water oscillations) were observed in India, and water level fluctuations occurred in wells in parts of the United States.

9 —⁣⁣ Landslides were observed in Sumatra.

10 —⁣⁣ A mud volcano near the Andaman Islands became active on December 28, and gas emissions were reported in Arakan, Myanmar.

A Modern-Day Disaster

In the twenty-first century, people like you and me turned on their TVs and saw the Indian Ocean tsunami wreak havoc on countless lives, both humans and animals. I remember on December 26 that message boards on the Internet were jammed. Posters were asking, "Why?" As I was in the process of writing this book, it's no surprise that I received dozens of emails that contained a variety of opinions about why this disaster happened. Some folks said it was the beginning of the end of the world; some said that deadly earthquakes are linked to human's disobedience of God; others insisted that the quake-tsunami was linked to aliens from another planet or military explosions. I felt dazed and confused. I didn't know whom to believe.

Like countless people, I was trying to digest the modern-day disaster in between graphic footage on CNN. I also tuned into messages on Berkland's website; scientists, earthquake sensitives, and animal experts tried to provide answers to why it happened.

Bernhardt, who has a fascinating theory, says that if you want to predict an earthquake, pick a holiday. She points to her vision on Thanksgiving Day 1974. "That's a very emotional time for a lot of people because they realize their families are gone, and their friends are gone." She feels intense energies have a lot to do with earthquakes. What's more, she doesn't discount the fact that the great Alaska quake-tsunami of 1964 and the Indian Ocean quake-tsunami of 2004 happened on a full moon—a time when people's emotions are often out of whack.

Catastrophe!: The 100 Greatest Disasters of All Time's author Stephen Spignesi says, "The death toll alone would have warranted ranking this horrible disaster in the top 20. If I had been writing the book now, and we used the 300,000 figure (which will almost certainly climb), the tsunami would have been ranked at number 17, between the 1891–92 Russian famine (407,000 dead) and the 542 Plague of Justinian (approximately 300,000 dead). (Disasters in modern times were ranked higher, even if the death tolls were similar, because of the financial impact on the technological infrastructure.)"

Spignesi adds, "Life on earth is a staggeringly fragile event. Almost 80 percent of everything alive on the planet was wiped out from the great comet that killed dinosaurs and yet life returned and flourished. We are at the mercy of nature, and we are astoundingly vulnerable to natural disasters. We can monitor, and sometimes forecast, but we cannot prevent." But there's more…

Sneak Preview, Sumatra Aftershock

The night before the northern Sumatra, Indonesia, earthquake hit on March 28, 2005, I was reading the last of my research papers to input information into this book. I came across my notes on Australia-based Harry Mason, a geologist/geophysicist. He warned of more seismic activity in the Indonesia area. Also, I had put his tape out by the computer to transcribe the following morning. On the same day, a Singapore-based man, Rick Von Feldt, emailed me anecdotes of his tsunami experiences on December 26 in Thailand on Phuket Beach. So, was it a coincidence—or a fascinating phenomenon?

Here are some pre–March 28, 2005, posts I found:

Date: March 22, 2005, at 19:27:48
From: Bonnie
Subject: sick and shaky
The dizziness and nausea are increasing, along with feelings of

sadness. I think that there will also be a larger event Indian Ocean/Indonesia area.

Date: March 24, 2005, at 19:58:41
From: (anonymous for privacy)
Subject:. . .out of my solar plexus! This started last night and is really a pain!! Although I haven't had any "ear-splitting" tones to back this up…with this solar plexus thingy and the fact that I'm eating everything in sight…I'd say there's a pretty good chance of a 7-plus EQ within the next week!!!!!

Predicted Semi-Sequel Quake

On March 28, 2005, an 8.7 aftershock hit Indonesia's island of Sumatra. It happened three days after the full moon during Jim Berkland's secondary window. According to media reports, panic hit as thousands fled to higher ground, fearing a sequel of the killer waves that came after the 9.0 Indian Ocean earthquake on December 26. Keep in mind that the December 26, 2004, mainshock happened on a full moon. And don't forget, the great Alaska earthquake in 1964 struck on a full moon, too.

What's more, all three of these major quakes struck both during a full moon and near or on a holiday: Christmas, Good Friday, and Easter. Remember, I mentioned Bernhardt's full moon and holiday earthquake theory? While I definitely recalled her theory, she reminded me after the aftershock hit: "So it was a full moon on Friday…and Good Friday and yesterday Easter and this morning the 'significant' quake in Indonesia. Fits right into my timeline." Plus she reiterated her theory in her Thursday March 24, 2005, online column on *www.shirleymaclaine.com*.: "It has been my observation that sometimes earthquakes frequently occur during this period of three days before or three days after the full moon and with Good Friday approaching it is something to casually observe what may or may not occur."

Somewhere in between Bernhardt's nonscientific holiday theory, Berkland's secondary seismic window, and other experts in the next chapter, "Where Are the Quake Warnings?," the earthquake did hit Indonesia's Nias island, a surfing area off Sumatra island's west coast and near the epicenter. According to reports, the death toll is at least 1,000. According to the USGS, extensive property damage occurred on Nias and Simeulue. The earthquake was felt in Indonesia, Malaysia, Singapore, and Bangkok.

Interestingly, however, is that no post-quake tsunami hit like it did on December 26. I remember on March 28 as I watched CNN, I called Berkland and asked the question: "What are the odds a tsunami will strike like before?" He answered, "About 90 percent." Thus, the big waves didn't happen this time.

Why? Why not? Says Berkland, "Like almost everyone else, I had no doubt that an 8.5-to-8.7 quake in a subduction zone would cause at least a 20-foot tsunami. Yet the highest known wave so far reported was 10 feet, not 80 feet like on December 26, 2004." Berkland, like other scientists worldwide, was puzzled but thankful that there was the lack of the big wave. He adds, "The consensus narrows down to four factors: (1) The water depth was much shallower for the 8.7; (2) the quake was only one-eighth as strong; (3) the plate movements were much less; and (4) the sea wave was blocked by the island west of the epicenter."

So, two questions remain: (1) Why wasn't anyone warned about the great quake-tsunami of 2004—or were they? And (2) Were there earthquake warnings from experts who gave repeated alerts of more to come after the Sumatra earthquake that it wasn't over? In the following chapter, you'll discover the answers that lie behind the scenes.

EARTHSHAKING FACTS
TO DOG-EAR

-⚡ Yes, animals (both domesticated and wild) do have a sixth sense and you can tune into it for a warning sign of disaster.

-⚡ If your pets or wild animals act strangely, consider it a potential quake warning, especially if you are in a foreign land.

-⚡ If there's a full moon, tidal flows are extremely high or low, and animals are behaving strangely, prepare yourself for a potential quake.

-⚡ Avoid collecting shells and flopping fish, if you're by the sea and it suddenly recedes. Instead, head for high ground as fast as possible to avoid the inevitable returning seismic sea wave that follows.

14 ⟶ Where Are the Quake Warnings?

When animals warn of an earthquake, it is not the time for men to form a committee.

—Jim Berkland

WHILE EARTHQUAKE PREDICTOR JIM BERKLAND CAN'T TELL PEOPLE THE EXACT HOUR, day, and place where the next big one will hit, his quake warnings, like weather forecasts, are helpful—especially when scientists' high-tech black boxes aren't providing timely alerts for people who live on or near faults in California and Japan.

Berkland admits that he wishes he could pin down where in the Ring of Fire quakes will be most likely to happen, but he is merely one man who predicts earthquakes, not a seer. "With the total eclipse of the Sun on August 11, 1999—[which] passed over the Atlantic Ocean, Great Britain, France, Turkey, and India—I did warn that Turkey and India were especially susceptible to shaking between August 10 and 17, 1999," he recalls. On August 17, 1999, the Izmit, Turkey, earthquake killed at least 14,000 people, according to the Pacific Disaster Center.

Berkland is hardly alone. In fact, quake warnings have been ignored in the past and present and will continue to be ignored in the future. The great Sumatra earthquake-tsunami that hit the Indian Ocean on December 26, 2004, is no exception; neither is the aftershock that hit off the Indonesian island on March 28, 2005.

One Scientist Gave Warning(s)

Kerry Sieh, professor of geology at the California Institute of

Technology, for one, gave repeated quake-tsunami warnings to Indonesian officials. Not unlike Berkland, he, too, was ignored. As the story goes, for more than 10 years, Sieh has been studying the area. In fact, he installed monitors on islands off Sumatra.

In the summer of 2004, he believed so strongly in the likelihood of loss of lives that he passed out 5,000 posters and brochures around some of the regions later struck by the monster Indian Ocean quake on Boxing Day. His warning was for people to avoid shorelines. But his meeting with Indonesian officials in December didn't take place, because the officials said they lacked money.

In mid-December of 2004, Sieh boosted his warning efforts. As Berkland reported, "He expressed his fear that a big earthquake and tsunami were overdue in the region at a conference in San Francisco. Sieh said this weekend: 'No one can predict exactly when an earthquake will happen, but it was clear that this area was at relatively high risk and such an event would happen one day. We told them it would kill people, wreck infrastructure, and destroy livelihoods; but our warnings were falling on deaf ears. My team and I decided to bypass the national and local government and start warning people directly. I hope our efforts saved some lives.'

"Sieh pointed out the tendency for large quakes to occur in clusters, and he 'believes that another quake could be on the way. There is some evidence that the stresses on the tectonic plates south of the epicenter may now have increased and raised the chances of another major earthquake.'"

Berkland agreed in his January 2005 Syzygy. "If Kerry Sieh suggests such a possibility, we should pay attention. I sense a kindred spirit in Kerry, and I recall my own efforts to alert Bay Area residents to large local earthquakes in 1984 and 1989. I spoke in churches and schools, service clubs, and local agencies. Many media outlets interviewed me, and I know that some people responded to my advice. Just as Kerry has discovered, the struggle for credibility is unending." Three months after the 9.0 quake hit, the unprecedented aftershock of 8.7 struck about 100 miles south of the mainshock, just as Sieh had forecast.

United States Geological Survey geophysicist Andrew Michael adds that he doesn't believe Sieh would tell you that he knew the earthquake was coming on a certain date. However, through his geologic studies, he had looked at sudden uplifts of the ground on coral reefs in the Sumatra region. Plus, when he saw that very large earthquakes happened in this area, he pointed out the fact that it could happen again, and that a tsunami would be a likely result. "I would say what Kerry was doing was much more on the end of hazard assessment. It was knowing that this was a hazardous region and working very hard to get that message out," points out Michael.

Sieh is hardly alone. After the quake-tsunami on December 26, 2004, I interviewed Harry Mason, geologist/geophysicist, a resident in Perth, Western Australia. He, too, pointed to more earthquakes to come in this region. In his article "Sumatra Continuing Seismic Noise—Danger Continues," written on January 1, 2005, he reported: "It is early yet but I do not believe that the danger from this Boxing Day Sumatra event has passed. The locality off NW Sumatra has now demonstrated unprecedented seismic instability over a duration of several days and the region has a very violent and well-documented quake-tsunamis-volcanic eruption history. Whatever precipitated this disastrous event, it is highly unlikely that it is over and therefore danger remains...Keep your wits about you since yet more massive quakes and explosive volcanic eruptions and tsunamis may well occur over the next few months (or years)—these may not be limited to the Indian Ocean region."

Four months later, the USGS "List of Latest Worldwide Earthquakes" included these major quakes since December 26, 2004: 6.5, Sulawesi, Indonesia, February 19, 2005; 6.7, Simeulue, Indonesia, February 26, 2005; 8.7, northern Sumatra, Indonesia, March 28, 2005; 6.8, Nias region, Indonesia, May 14, 2005; 6.7, Simeulue, Indonesia, May 19, 2005; and 5.1 northern Sumatra, May 31, 2005; and 6.7, Nias Region, Indonesia, July 5., 2005 So were Mason's predictions on target, or were they just another coincidence?

On May 4, 2005, he sent me an email, which included these warnings: "I am reasonably certain that this scenario will go the whole hog to serious explosive volcanism over the next few months, possibly few years. Either this Indonesian Arc thing will slowly die off, or you will see more seismic episodes, usually around the full moon each month, and increased signs of volcanic activity over the next few months…Volcanic activity should go explosive around August, if previous Krakatoa-style time tables are adhered to." Also, Mason notes that a "nuclear winter" may be the end result. (This cooling and darkening of the atmosphere happened in 1815 after the Tambora volcano in Indonesia erupted. There was no summer throughout the world.) Mason warns "it is a wise move" to be prepared. (See Chapter 19, "Don't Be Scared—Be Prepared!")

Tsunami Warnings

Meanwhile, as of the spring of 2005, the Indian Ocean still doesn't have a system for tsunami detection. No doubt a warning system would have been useful prior to the Christmas week 2004 quake-tsunami disaster and helped to save many lives. There's a tsunami warning system in the Pacific, but there isn't one yet in the Indian Ocean. Reportedly, Japan and the United States had planned to create starter tsunami warning systems for countries surrounding the Indian Ocean in early 2005, until the area can develop its own system.

As Mason wrote in his "Danger Continues" article, "If a new major quake-tsunami happened today or tomorrow, is there any system in place to warn the relevant populations and get them out of harm's way? Even here in Perth, Western Australia, no such warning system exists yet. Sure, radio, etc., could give warnings, but there are no evacuation plans, sirens, nor established disaster alert procedures—certainly none that 99 percent of the population are aware of. We need to educate the public now and set up an immediate warning system. If nothing is in place here in a relatively developed society, what about the rest of the largely third-world Indian Ocean? A seismic event warning system is an absolute must for the Indian Ocean. It should be mandatory for the entire planet.

"It will not cost much to develop, install, and operate such a system. It should be rushed into operation now. We are at continued major risk over the next few months from possible developments resulting from the Boxing Day Sumatra seismic event. Such events will happen again—most likely over long time intervals—but the cost is so high we must install insurance procedures now," stresses Mason. "This is something our governments and the UN should initiate immediately," he concludes.

Many scientists, like Mason, agree that tsunamis, unlike earthquakes, can be measured and take minutes to hours before they hit the coasts and cause devastation. Therefore, "It is very easy to warn people and save their lives, at least at the larger distances from the earthquake source," says Dr. Max Wyss, director of the Switzerland-based World Agency of Planetary Monitoring and Earthquake Risk Reduction (WAPMERR). But it's not that simple, because it takes humans to put these warning systems together. And it hasn't been done yet.

Earthquake Sensors Can Feel It

Meanwhile, is a do-it-yourself earthquake sensor available now to help protect yourself? Well, some folks are turning to homemade earthquake sensors. For one, Berkland recalls a prototype that was enclosed in a housing. He explains, "The tapering plumb bob hangs within a hole in tin or steel, so that any sideways or up-and-down sway makes contact, and an electric circuit is closed. Mine had a flashing red light and a loud buzzer, and it worked, giving me precious seconds to react."

There's also QuakeGuard™ from Seismic Warning Systems, Inc., which provides that early warning through advanced, patented P-wave technology. This pricey product provides "earthquake intelligence" to commercial, residential, industrial, and government markets. What's more, it might provide a warning time of 20 seconds, according to its website (*www.seismicwarning.com*).

Initially, I was excited. I thought, *Hey, this is just the beginning of sophisticated seismic warning systems*. So I asked retired USGS "evaluator" Roger Hunter for his opinion. He says, "It's nothing new. It's a seismometer that detects the quake and sounds a warning before the larger surface waves arrive. Yes, it's useful in some cases. The improvements are in filtering out noise to avoid false alarms and the ability to handle a variety of tasks once it's been triggered." He adds, "I'd want to see how accurate it was at weeding out noise since a lot of noise looks very much like a quake. Even the automatic equipment at NEIC [National Earthquake Information Center, Golden, Colorado] gets fooled, which is why humans review everything."

Meanwhile, if you're saving your money to be able to purchase QuakeGuard™, you might want to be practical and use more innovative methods. Glen Larson in Ramona, California, boasts that he has one of the best earthquake sensors on the planet. "It is my house," he says. "Built around 1946, during the postwar housing boom, it is constructed of wood, with a number of windows that face northeast, southeast, southwest, and northwest. The corners of the house face north, east, south, and west right on. When there is an earthquake, the portion of the house facing in that direction reacts, such as windowpanes that rattle, and a number of pops in the wooden joists. So, no fancy pendulums for me. Just a chandelier and this old house. Price is right, too."

Or try what another creative, budget-minded individual does. Simply put, attach a stone to a string and hang it so it's touching the glass on a window in a room in which you spend a lot of time. Each time the rock rattles, you'll get a cheap heads up. But if human warning systems aren't for you, perhaps animals are.

Animal-Based Warning Systems

Okay, so many animals escaped the great Asian earthquake-tsunami on Boxing Day 2004. Since there isn't an earthquake warning system in certain countries, is it absurd to have the masses pay attention to unusual animal behavior? Rupert Sheldrake doesn't think so. He believes pet lovers and farmers in earthquake-prone regions could participate in such a project through the media. "If people noticed these signs or any other unusual behavior, they would immediately call a telephone hotline with a memorable number—in California, say, 1-800-PET QUAKE. Or they could send a message on the Internet."

Adds Sheldrake, "A computer system would analyze the places of origin of the incoming calls. If there were an unusual number of calls, it would sound an alarm and display on a map of the places from which calls were coming." He points out that there would most likely be swarms of false alarms and hoax calls. But if there were a quick rise in calls from a particular region, this might give a heads up regarding an oncoming quake or tsunami.

"To explore the potential for animal-based warning systems would cost a small fraction of current earthquake and tsunami research. By doing this research, we would be sure to learn something, and could probably save many lives," points out Sheldrake. At present, he adds that a lot of money is being allocated for setting up tsunami warning systems. Like many of us, he hopes that those people responsible for spending this money will not tune out what animals can tell us.

As I sit here looking at my bulletin board that has my tacked-on published article, "What Kitty Knows" (complete with Jim Berkland's website address), I'm wondering if I've missed something. Isn't this idea of a phone line and computer-based animal program what Berkland had created years ago? Berkland tells me he did have a 900 line from 1990 to 2000, where he would post his regular seismic windows, and add to them, such as when he warned of the potential for a large quake in Turkey or India after a total solar eclipse passed over those countries on August 11, 1999. The Izmit, Turkey, massive killer temblor followed on August 17. He also made special predictions based on animals or earthquake sensitives. People would pay $1.49 a minute. The name of his 900 line, Quakeline, created static, so to speak, with a company back east, which had the same name but didn't make predictions. So the progressive animal-based warning system went belly up, partly because of the rapid growth of Berkland's website, *www.syzygyjob.com*, which he introduced in March 1997 and which, he reports, had received more than 100 million hits by 2002. Yet high science has ignored Berkland's efforts to inform the public about earthquakes and earthquake safety. (See Chapter 15, "High Science vs. Four-Leggers.")

Still, five days after the December 26, 2004, quake-tsunami, Berkland did get attention for his past and present work from talk show host Jeff Rense.

Quake Animal Warnings Validate Geologist Berkland

Rense told his audience:

Brilliant California geologist Jim Berkland discovered how to predict most earthquakes in the 1970s (80-plus percent accuracy) as being factors of the moon's gravity and tidal flows. He also discovered and has been discussing pre-earthquake animal warnings for over 20 years.

Jim was the first to observe that in virtually every case of a substantial earthquake in the U.S., the number of classified newspaper ads for missing dogs and cats skyrocketed. The building up of hydrostatic and geologic pressure along fault lines somehow disturbs the magnetic fields in the area of the quake days in advance...and the animal world reads those changes clearly. Dogs and cats will often vanish, heading to safer ground, in the days before a quake. If organized geology had spent less time being jealous of Berkland's achievements and ridiculing him for decades, regular earthquake warnings could have been instituted years ago.

Berkland isn't surprised that animal warnings were finally validated, but he, like myself, is frustrated that people listened later rather than sooner. He says, "It is somewhat satisfying to see the increasing acceptance about the topic of animal behavior as a clue to quakes. But it is painful in the way the current discussion originated. It took the strongest quake in 40 years and the greatest tsunami disaster in history to bring the topic alive in the midst of death." As many people know, both the Internet and newspaper articles contrasted the lack of dead animals with the dead bodies of people throughout the tsunami zone. The answer? The animals' sixth sense offered advance warning, and they fled to higher ground.

Australia-based Mason adds, "The night of the big event up north, a lot of dingoes here all howled their heads off. They went berserk. They were unruly, upset, and not happy with life." But even if scientists at the USGS believed geologists such as both Mason and Berkland, who have witnessed animals sensing oncoming quakes, would they have provided the public earthquake warnings based on animal-related behavior? Probably not.

Keeping Mum to Prevent Panic

In natural disaster films, the government is cautious about providing earthquake warnings, whether they come from strange animal behavior or human predictions. Why? It can create panic and chaos with evacuations that go nowhere, and wreak havoc on a booming real estate market or the tourist trade. In other words, quake warnings that do or don't deliver a hit can and do affect the economy.

Real life isn't much different, according to some experts. Says seismologist Roger Musson of the British Geological Survey in Edinburgh, "The effects of a long-term prediction, in depressing property values and discouraging investment, could be worse (at least economically) than the earthquake itself. Most seismologists see greater benefits to society in protecting communities by assessing the overall hazard and strengthening buildings accordingly. If buildings don't collapse when an unpredicted earthquake occurs, casualties will be few."

Some mainstream scientists and earthquake prediction skeptics will tell you that since earthquake predictions and forecasts aren't 100 percent reliable, it just doesn't make sense to create panic and chaos. Indeed, short-term earthquake predictions and warnings can have their downfall. Back in 1980, bad PR resulted from the USGS warnings for Mammoth Lakes, California, following several quakes and hundreds of smaller ones, says Berkland. He says, "This was right after the Mount St. Helens catastrophic eruption, and I certainly support the right to warn." But history shows that tourism plummeted and the real estate market suffered.

Iben Browning's 1990 earthquake prediction for New Madrid, Missouri, caused unwarranted concern. Reports show that countless lives were disrupted; schools were shut down for a few days; seismologists were distracted from their regular earthquake monitoring work; state emergency preparedness agencies spent tens of thousands of dollars regarding the prediction; and people were afraid as panic set in. The result: no earthquake.

But I can't help remember from the film *Jaws* how it was more important to keep the tourists happy than to evacuate for safety's sake. Plus, panic forces people to take action, like in the film *The Trigger Effect*, which shows how fast society loses control during a blackout— without power, phones, and computers. The message is, it's key to be self-reliant because when bad things happen you're on your own.

Dr. Wyss adds, "In my opinion, it is unacceptable for an individual or a government, who had information on potential risk due to natural disasters, not to warn the public. All of Japan and California lives with the economic disadvantages of living in a known earthquake area. And look where it has gotten them. They are doing very well economically. There is no comparison of the importance of the greed of a local chamber of commerce versus the lives of people in an endangered community." In addition, Berkland reminds me of the several occasions when scientists have informed us of near-misses by asteroids after a close encounter rather than before. "Who makes that decision?" he asks.

Californians Log On for Forecasts

Surprise! On May 18, 2005, I, like other people, noticed that the USGS began publishing a public website (*pasadena.wr.usgs.gov/step/*) that shows the odds of a modest quake happening in the Golden State within the next 24 hours. However, the real-time forecasts don't provide predictions or warnings of forthcoming big earthquakes.

Explains USGS's Michael, "The main use of these maps is for aftershock sequences. We have issued warnings about the likelihood of aftershocks for almost 20 years and it is very useful for evaluating the safety of already damaged structures. These new maps are a very nice way of automating this process and displaying it along with the long-term background probabilities. So far, it is only available in California."

Says Berkland, "I think it is a step in the right direction in admitting that earthquakes can be predicted. However, their main hope at this point seems to be forecasting aftershocks after a strong event occurs." So the USGS won't be creating panic by displaying these real-time maps.

How do people avoid panic when they hear a tornado or hurricane warning? "They have a plan. They have received clear advice as to what can and cannot happen. The same must become routine for people living in earthquake country, and this colorful map is a positive step toward that end," adds Berkland.

Meanwhile, as earthquakes and other frightening natural disasters continue to happen around the world, politics often set the pace of where, when, and who gets earthquake and tsunami warnings—as you'll see in Part 5, "Politics and Quakes."

EARTHSHAKING FACTS
TO DOG-EAR

-⑪- Do realize that quake warnings, like Jim Berkland provides, can't tell you the exact time and place an earthquake will strike, but his warnings can give you a heads up to an imminent quake, and stimulate awareness and preparedness.

-⑪- Listen up when reputable scientists provide warnings for people to avoid shorelines. It can't hurt to pay attention for safety's sake—and prepare yourself, your family, and pets.

-⑪- Remember, wild animals can and do listen to their sixth sense. If you observe any strange animal behavior, proceed with caution.

-⑪- Don't forget to check out other odd changes in the earth and use them as potential quake warnings. Springs and groundwater may have unusual smells, tastes, or temperature.

-⑪- Follow your heart. If you feel animal behavior or earth changes are giving you a warning but the authorities are ignoring Mother Nature, take action. Prepare yourself just to be safe.

Part Five

Politics
and Quakes

15 ⚓ High Science vs. Four-Leggers

If you conform, you can't create.

—Jim Berkland

IN THE SUMMER OF 2004, JIM BERKLAND ATTENDED AN OAKLAND, CALIFORNIA-based meeting titled, "Have We Turned a Corner in Earthquake Prediction?" He spoke up and admitted that he was delighted about the meeting but he didn't "need to turn a corner," as he had been "on a straightaway since 1974." His colleagues weren't amused. But the man who has predicted earthquakes for more than 30 years continued to show and tell.

He had brought with him 20 copies of his earthquake predictions posted in *Syzygy* early in the months of September and December 2003. He had tangible evidence of his predictions of the 8.1 quake in Hokkaido, Japan, of September 25, 2003 (the day of the new moon), and the deadly San Simeon quake of December 22, 2003, the day of perigee and record tides accompanying the full moon. Berkland recalls, "I offered the proof of my predictions to the group, but no one approached me. When I went to individuals, several shied away as if I were offering them hemlock."

But this negative response is nothing new for Berkland. After all, "high scientists" (*high science* is a term used by Dr. Arnold Lieber in his book *The Lunar Effect*) have called Berkland unforgettable names, which include a "clown," a "crackpot," an "earthquake buff," an "enthusiast, not a scientist," a "reader of tea leaves," and "a self-proclaimed earthquake guru." So the 2004 meeting was a minor glitch but not a major shake-up for Berkland.

Still Ignoring the Four-Leggers

While it seems as if earthquake prediction may be in vogue these days, the scientific community continues to put down the man who turns to tidal flows, moon phases, and cats and dogs as means to predicting earthquakes. Simply put, short-term quake predictions aren't taken seriously by the no-nonsense scientists.

As I began this book, and before I interviewed U.S. Geological Survey scientists (who still don't believe animals are reliable earthquake predictors), I checked out the USGS website's response to the question: "Can you predict earthquakes?" It reads: "No. Neither the USGS nor Caltech nor any other scientists have ever predicted a major earthquake. They do not know how, and they do not expect to know how any time in the foreseeable future." Actually, its focus is on the long-term mitigation of earthquake hazards. In other words, its mission is to help improve the safety of buildings, rather than try to accomplish short-term predictions.

USGS geophysicist Andy Michael told me, "What we do is prepare information—statistical models of how likely different levels of shaking are in different places. This is what's called earthquake hazard assessment." Michael admits earthquake prediction can be "emotionally compelling." Why? Why does it stir emotions and rattle egos? "People want control over their environment and knowledge of what's going to come next." But the fact remains, as prediction was a difficult thing to do, the scientists at the USGS began to focus on hazard assessment.

Meanwhile, as an earthquake enthusiast, it's difficult to sit back and ignore dedicated earthquake predictors like Berkland, who often get accurate hits. Is anyone doing any better?" "Well, it's not a question if anyone is doing any better," answers Michael. "The question is, 'Is he doing something that's useful? Would following his predictions give people more safety than simply ignoring all predictions?'"

Barking at Berkland's Theories

Mainstream scientists continue to reject Berkland, who insists on monitoring Mother Nature. He has heard for years that mainstream scientists are unable to show a link between tidal forces and quakes. But then, Berkland sees worldwide studies that tie tides and quakes together.

So, what gives? "I've looked at the tidal effects," says Michael. "I was unable to find the effects he says are there. And there also has been a lot of literature about the influence of tides on earthquakes. The effect appears to be very small."

The interview reminded me of my discussion with UCLA seismologist John Vidale, the anti-syzygy scientist with whom Berkland made an earthquake prediction bet. When I interviewed Vidale, I must admit I got lost in his scientific "technicalese." I'm not sure if it was before or after he began talking about 2-millimeter measurements of tides, but I wasn't keeping up. However, it was clear that he, like Michael, doesn't believe that earthquakes strike when the tides are larger than usual.

Now, I figured he was off base after the 9.0 Sumatra earthquake-tsunami disaster hit on December 26, the day of the full moon—like the previous 9-plus quake in Alaska on March 27, 1964. Ironically, extreme tides also happened between December 7 and 15, 2004, in the month Dr. Vidale and Berkland made the $500 wager that California would experience a shaker of at least 4.5 during the eight-day seismic window. And a 4.5 earthquake did strike near Eureka on December 12, 2004. Is it all just coincidence?

Berkland Goes to the Cats and Dogs

In 1989, Jim Berkland told me, "I'm a real threat to the USGS because they've been unable to accurately predict earthquakes. I've hit all these 5 point magnitude quakes, and they haven't hit one. They're being paid millions of dollars, have all this expensive equipment, and they haven't made it. I've gone to the Menlo Park USGS several times, and they just turn me away. 'Don't have time, Jim,' they say." And more than 15 years later, things haven't changed—at all.

Despite Berkland's published World Series earthquake prediction in the *Gilroy Dispatch* on October 13, 1989, after the quake in 1989, scientists at the USGS told me (and still tell me) that you can't predict earthquakes.

I remember as I wrote an article for *Cats* magazine, I quoted Berkland saying to me, "Since the Loma Prieta quake, my modem connection with the USGS computer in Golden, Colorado, hangs up on me every time it receives my number. I can go into the USGS library in Menlo Park, California now, but I can't check out a book like I could for 16 years as a county geologist." When asked why he thought he was being treated this way, Berkland said, "They said at a public meeting that they were going to come down hard on these pseudo-scientists out there who were predicting quakes. I think that's a very unscientific attitude. We certainly can't advance science if we wear that kind of bureaucratic blinders where they just adopt an answer and won't listen to the new data."

And don't forget, after making another prediction for a 3.5-to-6.0 quake to hit from November 11 to 17 in 1989, Berkland ran into big trouble. Making this controversial earthquake prediction led his bosses to suspend him from his Santa Clara County job before they checked with him. Yet county officials say they suspended Berkland because he was causing panic. He says that he had called for a 3.5-to-5.5 quake during the November seismic window, but noted that an 8.7-foot Golden Gate tide would occur on November 17 to 18, 1989. Then, a supervising geologist misconstrued this information and thought he said that an 8.0 quake would follow in November, according to Berkland, who found a memo dated October 24, 1989. Berkland admits to predicting the devastating earthquake that struck Northern California on October 17 (and the missing four-leggers helped him to predict this 7.1 monster) but denied reports that he projected an equally violent quake in November.

Often tagged as a "maverick geologist," Jim Berkland didn't want to alarm people back in 1989, or today or tomorrow, but he tries to be honest about what he believes. The quake of '89 was big, and it was terrifying for many people, but it wasn't the big one. And Berkland continues to predict earthquakes.

Berkland's Biggest Pet Peeve

After the Boxing Day earthquake on December 26, 2004, mass reports came out pointing to the animals' sixth sense. While hundreds of thousands of humans were reported dead, animals headed for higher ground and survived. Did this mean that what Berkland and I had been talking about for years—an animals' sixth sense—was finally validated? Yes and no.

Early in January 2005, I went straight to the USGS website to check out its new answer for a frequently asked question: "Question: Can animals predict earthquakes?" "Answer: Changes in animal behavior can not be used to predict earthquakes. Even though there have been documented cases of unusual animal behavior prior to earthquakes, a reproducible connection between a specific behavior and the occurrence of an earthquake has not been made. Animals change their behavior for many reasons, and given that an earthquake can shake millions of people, it is likely that a few pets will, by chance, be acting strangely before an earthquake."

I thought, *Wait, this can't be right. They've been too busy to change their statement.* Thus I decided to contact Waverly Person, chief of the National Earthquake Information Center at USGS in Golden, Colorado, for the answers.

"There's not anything to modify. If this happened again, how can we use it to save lives? There's not enough time to evacuate people when the animals start to react. The research shows the animals react just before an event. There's not enough time," says Person.

I thought, *But countless animals lived, countless people died in the December 26 great Indian Ocean quake-tsunami.* I asked Person, "What would it take to prove that animals can sense earthquakes?"

He replied, "I don't think anyone is trying to disprove it. They're just saying that animals don't react in time to evacuate. If you're going to do something, you want the time to get the people out, and if you don't have that time, it doesn't do any good."

Michael adds, "There's a difference between predicting an earthquake and sensing a traveling wave. It may be that the animals sensed the tsunami, but we don't know if they sensed the underwater quake."

So I brought up my cat Ashley, the feline who on August 8, 1989, moved out of the house until October 17, 1989. "Another coincidence?" I asked.

"Who knows?" answered Michael. "The problem is that animals are very noisy sensors. They do lots of strange things at different times and it makes it very difficult to get a statistically significant result." Then Michael went on to say that the thing to do, would be to gather data from veterinarians who could input reports of all the animals in their offices that are acting strangely and see if it correlates. "In the scientific community people tried things like that back in the '70s and '80s and got such negative results." But this is the twenty-first century, and animals sensed the Indian Ocean disaster. Doesn't it count?

Evidently, anecdotal evidence isn't as strong as peer-review studies in the earthquake world. To me, as a health journalist who has written about groundbreaking natural remedies—from the benefits of soy to antioxidants, which are now accepted in the mainstream of science—this is a familiar scenario. Rupert Sheldrake, author and scientist, says, "There is a general suspicion of anecdotal evidence within science, but in fact all science begins from personal experience, and much of medicine relies on anecdotes—except when they're published, they are promoted to the rank of case histories."

He adds, "Wherever possible, however, anecdotal evidence should be backed up by surveys and experimental tests. The problem with earthquakes, of course, is that one cannot do experiments. No one can create an earthquake in the laboratory on demand, nor, fortunately, can they create one in the real world either."

Berkland's Pet Critic

While working scientists, for the most part, don't validate earthquake prediction or Jim Berkland, neither does Roger Hunter, a retired seismologist/programmer formerly with the USGS. In fact, Hunter goes out of his way to find holes in Berkland's earthquake predictions. For example, this friendly skeptic with a capital "S" created a table for me that covers 30 years of Berkland's predictions.

Hunter notes Berkland's predictions for four regions: Mount Diablo in the San Francisco Bay area, Los Angeles, the Washington-Oregon area, and major quakes globally. As a man who pays attention to detail, he painstakingly explained his meticulous work to me, the girl who flunked math: "He uses the same time window for each of these but insists on an archery target system for near misses. The table has a column for each area divided into four sections, one for each ring of his target. The bull's-eye is his standard 8-day window. Each ring adds a day on either end, so ring one is 10 days, ring two is 12 days, and ring three is 14 days. These lengths multiplied by the number of predictions he has made (293) give the amount of time covered by his predictions. That number divided by the total days from 1974 through 2004 (11,323) gives the probability of success for chance for each ring."

He adds, "Number of quakes is the number that fits his location and magnitude ranges for each ring. This increases as the rings get bigger; number of hits is the count of quakes within the ring. This also increases as the rings get bigger; hit ratio is hits divided by total number of quakes, converted to a percent."

So, what is Hunter's goal? He wants to show that Berkland's quake predictions compared to probability shows they aren't much better than chance. Berkland reviewed the Hunter table and said that his critic should have obtained a license for his hunting game. What Hunter did, should have caught the attention of a game warden, as the game played fast and loose with Berkland's theory and predictions.

Playing the Odds
by Roger Hunter

		Global 7+	L.A.	Mt. Diablo	WA-OR
Bull's-eye: 8 days	Number of days	11,323	11,323	11,323	11,323
	Number of predictions	293	293	293	293
	Probability (%)	20.70	20.70	20.70	20.70
	Number of quakes	447	1,755	849	1,014
	Number of hits	98	329	184	161
	Hit ratio (%)	21.92	18.75	21.67	15.88
Ring 1: 10 days	Number of days	11,323	11,323	11,323	11,323
	Number of predictions	293	293	293	293
	Probability (%)	25.87	25.87	25.87	25.87
	Number of quakes	559	2,498	1,277	1,144
	Number of hits	163	714	378	242
	Hit ratio (%)	29.16	28.58	29.60	21.15
Ring 2: 12 days	Number of days	11,323	11,323	11,323	11,323
	Number of predictions	293	293	293	293
	Probability (%)	31.05	31.05	31.05	31.05
	Number of quakes	863	4,058	2,287	1,431
	Number of hits	279	1,447	745	375
	Hit ratio (%)	32.33	35.36	32.58	26.21
Ring 3: 14 days	Number of days	11,323	11,323	11,323	11,323
	Number of predictions	293	293	293	293
	Probability (%)	36.22	6.22	36.22	36.22
	Number of quakes	1,630	4,247	3,715	1,431
	Number of hits	589	1,752	1,243	429
	Hit ratio (%)	36.13	41.25	33.46	29.98

As I input these statistics, it reminded me of when I was a temp-for-hire statistical typist. Plus, as I examined the second batch (third and fourth) of successful hit numbers, I couldn't help pointing out to Hunter, "Hey, if those were my odds at state-line casinos, I'd be there right now playing the slots. The USGS isn't doing any better, is it?"

"No," Hunter replied, "but they don't try to make short-term predictions. Jim's results are too close to chance to be taken seriously and are actually less than chance in some cases." And, I'm thinking, *If I heard that there was a nearly 36 percent chance that it was going to snow, I'd cover my wood. So if Berkland provides quake predictions with the same odds, I'd say it's not silly to stock the pantry, make sure the earthquake kit is up to par, and monitor the cat and dog.*

As I mentioned before, every month Berkland predicts a global quake of 7-plus, and he points out that it most likely will hit within the Ring of Fire, where 80 percent of the noteworthy earthquakes shook the earth in the past. "With my eight-day window and the fact that a major quake happens about every 25 days, it can be seen that I have about 32 percent chance of a hit randomly," Berkland explains. "My critics pooh-pooh the value of such a prediction, but I try to emphasize that a worldwide window puts scientists and laypersons alike on notice to look for confirmatory signals during specified windows."

Speaking of critics, in the table "Is It a Silly Rigged Game?" Hunter, a master of earthquake evaluation, shows percentages of Berkland's predictions that were on the money. "When his hit ratio is about the same as probability of success, it means that the hits are no more than expected. In other words, just luck," says Hunter. "It's important to note the probabilities; otherwise you see that three-fourths of the predictions are correct and think Berkland's good when the chance odds are 80 percent. It's like rolling a die and getting a seven every time. It helps to know that seven is the only number on that die," says Hunter. "Jim claims a 75 percent average and you can see that the ring three probabilities will average out around 75 percent. He's getting no more hits than expected by chance."

Is It a Silly Rigged Game?
by Roger Hunter

		Global 7+	L.A.	Mt. Diablo	WA-OR
Bull's-eye: 8 days	Number of predictions	293	293	293	293
	Number of hits	81	115	105	82
	Hit ratio (%)	27.65	39.25	35.84	27.99
	Total number of windows	1,416	1416	1416	1416
	Number of hit windows	368	638	492	369
	Probability of success (%)	26.01	45.09	34.77	26.08
Ring 1: 10 days	Number of predictions	293	293	293	293
	Number of hits	119	196	169	109
	Hit ratio (%)	40.61	66.89	57.68	37.20
	Total number of windows	1,133	1,133	1,133	1,133
	Number of hit windows	417	736	595	397
	Probability of success (%)	36.84	65.02	52.56	36.07
Ring 2: 12 days	Number of predictions	293	293	293	293
	Number of hits	172	252	240	147
	Hit ratio (%)	58.70	86.01	81.91	50.17
	Total number of windows	944	944	944	944
	Number of hit windows	545	803	736	445
	Probability of success (%)	57.79	85.15	78.05	47.19
Ring 3: 14 days	Number of predictions	293	293	293	293
	Number of hits	245	270	265	160
	Hit ratio (%)	83.62	92.15	90.44	54.61
	Total number of windows	809	809	809	809
	Number of hit windows	665	741	713	422
	Probability of success (%)	82.30	91.71	88.24	52.23

After I input Hunter's table "Is It a Rigged Game?" I contacted Berkland. "Roger is driving me insane!" I exclaimed. And then, it hit me like a nun reprimanding me in catechism class when I was a kid. Roger Hunter is the same guy who flip-flopped like a rabbit with his prediction evaluation back about 25 years ago.

Berkland reminds me that back in 1979, Hunter gave him some good news. Evidently, his computer gave the geologist a 5-year evaluation of earthquake predictions from 1974 through 1979. Hunter had shown that there was one chance in a hundred that Berkland's record was coincidental. Despite this amazing finding, Hunter shrugged it off to luck, and told Berkland if he disclosed these results to the media, he would deny it. I remembered during the research of this book I was curious about this past event and asked Hunter, "Why would you deny it?"

His response was that he had no recollection of the conversation, but he could imagine why he might have said it. "That would have been the beginning of the program, before the math was fully developed. Jim didn't have that many predictions at that time, so anything I said would have been premature. My comment would have been a humorous way of stressing that fact. And time showed that I was correct in saying his results at that point were just luck."

Berkland further explains, "I kept his secret until I read his final written summary of his four-year story in which he indicated that, 'As yet no one had met the statistical test for valid predictions," and "No scientist had even bothered to submit any predictions."

I pushed further and asked Hunter, "Why did you state 'no one'? Why didn't you mention Mr. Berkland?"

Hunter replied, "By 'scientist,' I meant a seismologist working on the prediction problem. Jim was a county geologist working on his own, outside his field, and not getting any results at that time. He just didn't come to mind as a scientist." Keep in mind, Berkland is listed as a scientist in six different *Who Who*'s, and notes he is a member of six other scientific organizations. It appears that again, Hunter didn't do his homework.

I quickly became confused. Hunter's words didn't add up. Berkland was getting results at that time, according to Hunter back in 1979. Plus, it seemed as if Hunter and I were drowning in a sea of semantics. I grabbed *The American Heritage Dictionary* and looked up two words—scientist and geology:

Scientist: A person having expert knowledge of one or more sciences, especially a natural or physical science.

Geology: The scientific study of the origin, history, and structure of the earth. [Geologist is part of the definition.]

Then I went back to Berkland's newsletters and found a comment that settled the score, as far as I'm concerned.

Berkland wrote, "A summary given to me by the USGS of all of the 2.5-plus quakes occurring between 1963 and 1977, and centered within a 70-mile radius of San Jose, showed one 3.0-plus event every 18 days and one 3.5-plus every 35 days. Thus my seismic window of only eight days has less than one-in-four random chance of happening for a minimum 3.5 quake." Plus, the first year of his earthquake predictions, he scored six out of eight (that's a 75 percent success rate). And he's held onto that accuracy ratio for local quakes.

As for Hunter's tabular evaluation of Berkland's history of predictions, it was full of false assumptions and erroneous data. Hunter conveniently forgot that two main concepts are involved with seismic windows. The first concept is the theory of eight-day windows associated with syzygy, of which there are two per month—a primary window and a secondary window. Only one is utilized routinely for predictions. Second, the actual predictions involve the primary windows, which have the higher levels of confidence because of the higher tidal forces. The only question should be how many predicted windows contained quakes meeting the predicted magnitudes within the predicted areas. Hunter's data looks at the total quakes versus how many were in a window.

Plus, Hunter ignores the fact that for many years Berkland didn't predict for every primary window, or for all four of the areas evaluated.

Thus, Hunter's summary of 293 supposed predictions included many windows and several areas for which no predictions were made. Also, the "dartboard method" of scoring wasn't even proposed until 1999, so Hunter's use of it was merely of academic interest.

Berkland called for a 3.5-plus quake within 140 miles of Los Angeles in July 2005, during the rare perigean spring tide window of July 19-26. "This is especially likely because of the near-record rainfall this past season in Southern California," he said. Hunter had determined that there was less than 40 percent chance of such a quake and was betting against it. If it doesn't happen I pay him 50 dollars. If it does, Roger has agreed to abandon my website and never darken my door (or my windows) forevermore," noted Berkland.

On July 24, 2005, Berkland's Southern California prediction was fulfilled by a 4.2 quake in the Channel Islands, 95 miles west of Los Angeles. "This event came nine days after the most missing dog ads (23) in more than a year in the Los Angeles Times, and two days after the second highest L.A. tides of the year," explains Berkland.

He adds, "This July seismic window contained the third of only three perigean tides for 2005, and it was particularly satisfying to me because not only did I hit a grand slam with my four successful predictions, but I eliminated an annoying critic from my site, who consistently maintained that earthquakes can't be predicted, and that syzygy had nothing to do with their timing."

Hunter's parting words to Berkland on July 28 were sent in a brief but to-the-point email:

> The 4.2 was 107 miles from L.A. If the parameters hold up, it's a clear hit for the bet and your L.A. window. I concede. Congratulations. I will post no more.
>
> —Roger

The Pesky Pizza Problem

Time after time, Berkland has been informed by high science that if an earthquake is a few minutes or miles off the predicted value, the entire prediction is valueless. Michael remembers taking a peek at Berkland's predictions for the Bay Area. "If the earthquake was 70 miles from San Jose instead of 60 miles from San Jose, that's what I refer to as the 'pizza problem.'" In other words, Michael says Berkland makes the circle a little bigger and it covers a lot more area.

Berkland finds this pizza problem aggravating, "especially with the magnitude level, which often varies from observer to observer, from station to station, and from time to time. Sometimes the magnitude is revised significantly by a seismologist—often months or years after the event," he points out. Also, the pizza problem is nonexistent, says Berkland. He adds, "The radius for the area of concern is clearly defined and marks a bull's-eye. For one, two, and three rings out, the probability is somewhat greater, so the score is lowered to 90, 80, or 70 percent. Beyond that it is off the board. This permits evaluation beyond hit or miss and allows meaningful comparisons with predictions for various years and various predictors."

In a nutshell, if Berkland predicts a 3.5-to-5.5 quake for a 140-mile radius and an eight-day window, he might get a hit of 3.4, 14 miles beyond the given circumference, and one day late. His total score would be 72.9 percent, he says. If the confidence had been assigned 70 percent in an area where there was historically a 30 percent chance for the prediction to be correct, it should be useful, he insists, and not ignored by experts.

"I maintain that," adds Berkland, "despite their facade of fairness, the earthquake experts of high science are most happy to cast another near-hit into the junk heap of failed predictions, rather than to consider that miss as meaningful, when it is just one ring off from a bull's-eye!"

What Do the USGS Two-Leggers Do?

It's no secret that the USGS doesn't believe animals or humans can predict earthquakes. So its mode of operation has been to focus on providing long-range forecasts of the likely locations and impacts of damaging earthquakes. For instance, scientists estimate that over the next 30 years, the probability of a major earthquake occurring in the

San Francisco Bay Area is 62 percent. (These numbers helped me to make my move to Lake Tahoe rather than live in San Francisco, so I can't put down long-range forecasting even though I prefer something a bit more timely and useful.)

Also, scientists are able to predict the type of ground motion to expect based on the geology and the history of earthquake activity in the region. Engineers and building code developers use these models of site response to improve the safety of structures, thereby reducing the ultimate earthquake risk. (See Chapter 19, "Don't Be Scared—Be Prepared!")

So why does the layperson gravitate toward Berkland's earthquake theories—such as monitoring lunar cycles and counting lost cats and dogs—rather than pay attention to hazard preparedness? "It's intriguing," says Michael. "It's easier to understand. If I try to tell you that we can give you the ground motion that will be exceeded over 2 percent of the time over 100 years—that's a mouthful. That's a more complicated concept than there's going to be an earthquake tomorrow."

Cat-and-Mouse Government Games

Meanwhile, I do respect the USGS for its useful website, which offers post-quake data. I go to its California/Nevada earthquakes link often to see if my headaches make a hit, and to see if scientists have had a change of heart about animals and earthquake prediction. However, I'm troubled by Berkland, who can't forget an alleged past USGS occurrence. Do you remember the missing earthquake prediction tape I discussed in Chapter 9, "West Coast Vibrations"? It makes me think of the times when editors told me my check was in the mail—and it wasn't. I get flashbacks of my favorite films, *Three Days of the Condor* and *The Pelican Brief*. Perhaps Berkland wasn't being paranoid, I thought to myself when he told me this story time after time.

Then, on March 17, 2005, an eye-opening article in the *San Francisco Chronicle* caught Berkland's attention—and mine. The headline reads, "Yucca nuclear dump papers appear to have been faked." The lead reads, "Government employees may have falsified documents related to the Yucca Mountain nuclear waste project in Nevada, the Energy Department said Wednesday. The disclosure could jeopardize the project's ability to get a federal permit to operate the dump."

Okay, comparing nuclear dump sites and earthquake predictions is like comparing apples to oranges, right? Not necessarily. The common denominator here is that the government is linked to both events, Berkland's missing tape and the dump site. And both events hit home, since I'm writing about Berkland and I live two miles from Nevada. I asked Berkland why this dump ordeal that is linked to the geological survey is relevant to this book. His response: "That is how hidden agendas work, and makes the recent disclosures about a fraudulent USGS report on Yucca Mountain especially revealing." And I sit here, a math dummy, wondering if Berkland may have a point by putting two and two together.

Meanwhile, for more than 25 years, Berkland systematically accumulated data about sensitive animals and people, lunar cycles, and tidal flows to make his earthquake predictions. He's confident that his correlations will withstand scrutiny. And he's also aware that his early efforts to publish on his work were mostly rejected by peer review. Following his success of predicting and naming the World Series earthquake, four days before it occurred on October 17, 1989, it appears, Berkland says, "that high science has attempted to turn me into a nonperson."

Speaking of the government and forgotten people, the next chapter, "The Frisco Quake Cover-up," will show you that for more than a quarter of a century, Berkland insisted year after year that there was indeed a cover-up of thousands of deaths from the great San Francisco earthquake-fire of 1906; now after 100 years, it's being revealed.

EARTHSHAKING FACTS TO DOG-EAR

-⊪ Don't ignore short-term earthquake precursors, despite what mainstream science says.

-⊪ If you see a link between quakes and tidal flows, moon phases, odd animal behavior, or earth changes, continue to monitor these quake warnings and stay prepared for your safety's sake.

-⊪ Check out statistics that prove unconventional quake warnings to be no better than chance; but when hits continue to hit, forget the numbers game. Put your safety first and get prepared.

-⊪ If an earthquake prediction is made, don't panic. Keep an open mind; be prepared (physically and mentally); and know what to do before, during, and after a quake hits. Then, go about your daily life. (See Chapter 19, "Don't Be Scared—Be Prepared!")

16 ~ The Frisco Quake Cover-up

In great disasters, too often the greatest casualty is the truth.
—Jim Berkland

IMAGINE: IT'S EASTER VACATION...APRIL 18, 1906. SAN FRANCISCO IS A BREATH-taking place to be. The weather is perfect. The hotels and rooming houses are packed with locals and tourists. Then, at 5:12 a.m., a fore-shock hits the San Francisco Bay Area. Twenty seconds later, a violent earthquake shakes the ground for 45 to 60 seconds. History is made in one minute as the great San Francisco earthquake devastates the city. Fewer than 500 died.

Is there something wrong with this picture? Some people, such as Jim Berkland, insist there's something dead wrong about the 1906 San Francisco earthquake-fire death toll. For more than 25 years, Berkland believed the number of deaths was much larger, although until 1979, he accepted *The World Almanac* toll of 452. He publicly announced in the *San Jose Mercury News*, Sunday, December 9, 1979, that there was a cover-up of the 1906 quake death toll. "I was the first one to disclose the now widely accepted fact that not mere hundreds died in the 1906 quake, but more like 5,000 to 10,000," he notes.

He adds that if people had access to the Internet in 1906, we would have known that thousands of people had died in San Francisco's great earthquake, not the few hundred that the Army, city, and American press reported. "Many foreign reports recognized that thousands had perished. This fact has only recently gained wide-spread, but not universal acceptance," says Berkland, who came across the truth in 1979. However, his several attempts to convince governmental agencies about the "Seismic Watergate" were denied, along with his efforts to publish his findings.

Gladys Hansen, city historian, had also questioned the death toll count. Back in the sixties, the San Franciscan librarian began to match names to the numbers, she says. Like Berkland, she was discovering that the death toll, one by one, was growing and growing. In fact, early in the 1980s, Berkland met with Hansen on different occasions, and she reinforced his convictions that a huge and successful cover-up had been achieved.

Here's a fascinating look at old and new data that provide an original and retrospective, up close, and very personal look at the aftermath in the city and counties the earthquake affected when it hit 100 years ago.

The 1906 San Francisco Earthquake

Not until 1979 did Berkland become well aware of the likely odds that there was "an attempted distortion of history" by playing down the role of the San Francisco earthquake. But then he found references that made him think otherwise. In the December 9, 1979, *San Jose Mercury News* article, Berkland pointed out that he had searched newspapers for the time period following the great quake and discovered that the first statements of governmental officials and firsthand observers indicated that thousands, not hundreds, of people had been killed in the earthquake.

According to Berkland, efforts to get an accurate account encountered difficulties because the Army was burying bodies in common graves. Plus, the post-quake fire flames were so hot that other people were most likely consumed without proof. Cast-iron radiators melted, which required temperatures in excess of 2,500 degrees Fahrenheit. Berkland checked with two San Jose crematories and learned that they needed only 1,800 degrees for less than two hours to reduce a human body to ashes.

It was San Francisco's Coroner William Walsh's job to tally the death toll, and in the first few days he and General Frederick Funston were confident that at least 1,000 people had perished. However, as Berkland puts it, "Somewhere between the 24th and the 26th of April, there was a cover put on the facts, and it came from as high up as the White House of Teddy Roosevelt."

Berkland points out that numbers from south of Market Street and Chinatown weren't accessible when the first estimates were tallied, and that included collapsed and burned hotels and rooming houses.

"I did become aware of the strong likelihood that there was an attempted distortion of history by downgrading the role of the San Francisco earthquake in destroying much of the city. Accompanying this travesty was the official suppression of the true number of deaths that resulted from the catastrophe," says Berkland. He adds, "There is abundant evidence that shows that the death toll was numbered in many thousands, rather than a few hundred, in San Francisco, and that similar cover-ups were attempted in Santa Rosa, Agnews State Hospital, and, to a lesser degree, in San Jose."

These days, in the twenty-first century, we know that the quake caused significant damage and it was concealed. The 1906 quake is number 45 in Stephen Spignesi's book *Catastrophe! The 100 Greatest Disasters of All Time*. "I list it as the 1906 San Francisco earthquake because the precipitating cause for the death and devastation was the earthquake. The quake caused the fires, so the quake is the primary disaster. My chapter provides more information on the damage done by the quake. It is ranked at number 45 because that's where it fell in terms of deaths and financial toll," he says.

Until 1979, Berkland hadn't given a second thought about the low casualty list in the San Francisco earthquake. His way of thinking was that back in 1906, building materials, design, and workmanship in the United States were superior to those of other countries. Plus, he notes, the photos of devastation linked with the quake were due to the fires, not the earthquake. But, he points out, some of the old photos were doctored to show insurance companies that the buildings were still intact—before the fires ravaged them. "The insurers had insisted that they would pay for no earthquake damage, so the early estimate quickly changed from 50 percent earthquake destruction to only 5 percent, with the remainder strictly from the fire," he explains.

But there's a lot more to masking the numbers than earthquake insurance. City Historian Hansen says, "The fire did cover up a lot of the damage created by the earthquake. Most large cities that suffered fires had come back from them. It's all economics. It's money. If you have a big earthquake and something that can happen again, people might think twice about actually investing in a city." So if the earthquake was played up, real estate investors might look down on San Francisco as a great investment.

Tallying Up the Numbers

In one "instant book" from 1906, Berkland discovered a map of the burned area in San Francisco that noted that 452 city blocks had been destroyed. According to Berkland, this figure explained why the number of deaths had been listed for many years in The World Almanac as 452. "This would be only one death per block, or only one per thousand in a city of 450,000 inhabitants. It was important to have acceptable numbers, even if they were totally fallacious," he says. But Berkland dug deeper and found more information that led to a miscalculation of deaths in various regions.

For example, from his own research, which included study of back issues of about 20 newspapers and review of data from the Sonoma county recorder's office, he found 106 dead, not including the missing persons in Santa Rosa. Five major hotels in the downtown area collapsed and burned, and survivors spoke of how few had emerged from them. In the April 19th newspapers, it was widely reported that there had been 58 deaths in Santa Rosa, and somehow that number persisted for decades.

The third area of deaths was in Santa Clara County, notes Berkland, where even as a county geologist, he encountered resistance to being allowed to see the death records for 1906. "Eventually, I was informed that I could examine the books, as the information was more than 50 years old. I was surprised to learn that the county coroner's records indicated that everyone who died in 1906 had perished in alphabetical order. There were April 18th deaths from 'diabetes,' 'hemorrhage,' and 'terminal melancholy.' It was obvious that there was an official agenda," points out Berkland.

Berkland notes that there were more than 1,100 patients in Agnews State Hospital. He claims that various sources listed the number of deaths as 90, 103, and 119, including 12 of the hospital staff. And other sources that Berkland had studied were suspicious or showed confusion. "The question is, how much was the confusion used to play down the death toll?" he asks.

In late 1979, Berkland started a one-man campaign to lecture publicly about the governmental cover-up of the true death toll of the 1906 earthquake—without support from the federal, state, or county government. "I was criticized roundly about my not accepting history as it was written," he says, adding he was told that there was no reason to try to change historic facts.

Meanwhile, Berkland collected information and talked to people who endured the 1906 earthquake. As Shelley Cothran, the 90-year-old survivor he interviewed in 1979, told him, "I agree with your hypothesis that thousands upon thousands died in that earthquake and fire, and I do know that the word *earthquake* became an anathema." And other people were also questioning the validity of the official death count of a devastating earthquake and coming up with different and shocking facts and numbers.

Like Berkland, Historian Hansen believes that the original toll in the 400s is off. Hansen told me it's closer to 3,400 and still climbing. So, did the tally overlook single women, and Chinese, Japanese, and Irish workers because they were immigrants? "I don't know that they were overlooked. They probably were in their beds at the time, and the buildings fell and took them in the fire. There's no evidence," she says (*www.sfmuseum.org*). "How can you say they were overlooked? This is a very difficult situation where I have to depend now on family to provide me information."

Berkland reported that as a graduate student at UC- Davis, one of his classmates was Alvin Joe, who established a geotechnical firm in Chinatown. When they both became officers in the Association of Engineering Geologists in San Francisco, Berkland told Alvin Joe of his suspicions about the death toll and asked him to find out what he could from his friends and family in Chinatown, as that was a key area in which to establish the truth. Weeks later Alvin Joe admitted to Berkland, "Jim, I have never seen such a stone wall in my life. They tell me, 'Do not disturb the dust!'" Apparently, they didn't want new regulations and controls on construction, and were content to let "the dead past bury its dead."

Hansen presented evidence to newspapers in 1986, on the occasion of the 80th anniversary of the big one, that more than 2,000 deaths occurred at the time of the catastrophe in San Francisco, notes Berkland. He also points out that in her 1989 book, *Denial of Disaster*, her estimate had risen to more than 3,000, and in 2004, she was quoted in several news items as believing that the correct total was much higher. "I could not agree more," says Berkland.

Opening Pandora's Quake Box

Hansen recalls that back in the 1960s when she was city librarian, there was a request from the public for a list of those who died in 1906. "When I found that there was not an accurate list, I decided I would put it together. Reading the board of supervisors designation of 478 as the official toll, I thought that all I had to find was 478 people. My first run through the papers brought a lot more than 478. When you find something wrong you just keep going," she says, adding that one-fourth of the city was destroyed in the quake-fire. It's been said again and again, that nobody will ever really know exactly how many people were killed by the earthquake and fire. "It all comes down to believing people's stories," says Hansen.

So did the city suppress the death toll? "I really don't know if they suppressed it. The city had to move on, had to become a progressive city again, had to lure money back into the city," explains Hansen. "So many of the people in San Francisco died in the flames, the building went down, the building caught on fire, and they died right where that building fell. There was apparently very little search made for anybody. There wouldn't be bodies; there would be bones," explains Hansen, who adds that these bones appeared in the debris boxes that were used in a variety of places, such as to fill problem areas such as Mission Bay.

Did any people die from the earthquake itself outside of San Francisco? Hansen points out that people also died in Santa Rosa and San Jose from the buildings coming down. In other words, it was like the Loma Prieta earthquake, where the epicenter was in the Santa Cruz Mountains but damage was widespread in a variety of regions throughout the San Francisco Bay Area.

These days, Hansen says the total death toll is at 3,000. She has received a grant so she can continue inputting data to find out what the last count is. "It may be an open entry because there'll never be a way of finding out just who died in San Francisco." And when Hansen heard about the 2004 Indian Ocean quake-tsunami, she thought, *It's almost the same thing. They're facing water; we faced fire.*

Unprepared Then and Now

Berkland agrees that a common thread links the San Francisco 1906 earthquake-fire and the Indian Ocean 2004 earthquake-tsunami. "To anyone who has studied the historic record, it is obvious that there has been great lethargy on the part of the government, as well as the public, to take positive action against natural hazards until after the threatening event has occurred. The great Sumatra earthquake and tsunami of December 26, 2004, provides another classic example. Only after 300,000 people were lost were there serious moves to establish a network of tsunami detection buoys across the Indian Ocean. We need a steady-state system of preparedness, not the feast and famine patterns that prevail."

And the fact is, San Francisco wasn't prepared for earthquake damage in 1906—or in 1989. "The city's problem is primarily that of ground shaking, which is multiplied for locations on filled ground and marshlands, and these areas were mapped and proved to concentrate the damage from the next major quake in the Bay Area, the Loma Prieta earthquake of October 17, 1989," points out Berkland.

He concludes, "In 1906, it was in such areas that critical failures of the San Francisco water conduits occurred, resulting in the inability to control the conflagration from the waterfront to beyond Van Ness Avenue. Even without the earthquake, the fire hazards in San Francisco were very real. From 1849 to 1900, the city had been wrecked by fires on numerous occasions." In other words, San Francisco wasn't prepared for the firestorm.

But as Hansen will tell you, technical talk about safer buildings and better building codes isn't what everyday people want to hear about, today or yesterday; that is the job for geologists, engineers, and disaster preparedness experts. The interest lies in the many lives that were lost. People want to know about the people who died and the people who lived. Family members desperately try to find their loved ones so they can have peace of mind.

A Twist of Fate

Berkland found an article in the April 28, 1906, issue of *The Saturday Bee* (Sacramento, California). The staff correspondent wrote that he had a chance to talk to John Justus, a man who had lived at the Brunswick Hotel, at the corner of Sixth and Howard Streets, and who had his hands swathed in bandages.

Justus was quoted as saying, "The hotel was five stories high. There must have been nearly 300 people in it at the time. So far as I know, only three escaped, and I am one of the three…I am sure most of the people in that hotel lost their lives, and I think this is true of most of the frame hotels that went down." Evidently, Justus had leaped naked out of his fifth-story window and grabbed the fire escape of an adjacent four-story structure as they swayed close together. He cut his hands severely on the rusty stairway, but made his way down to the lower landing, where he was trapped.

Later, in 1982, Berkland met another San Franciscan quake survivor, 89-year-old Walter Harmon, who told him about his own 1906 experience, when he was a 10-year-old boy. "After the quake, he and his father loaded up his handcart with their meager possessions and headed for the Ferry Building. Their way was blocked by debris on Market Street, so they took a detour around Mission Street. There he saw ruins of the collapsed Brunswick Hotel, with a woman in a tattered robe sitting in the debris. He saw the smoke of the fire rising up behind her and asked his father to help her out into the street, which he did. He also gave her one of his blankets to wrap around her. Walter also remembered an odd sight on the adjacent building, where a naked man was standing helplessly on the fire escape. Walter believed that at least 500 had died in the wreckage of that one hotel (with 300 rooms, each most likely averaging more than one occupant)."

Then, on Valentine's Day 1985, Berkland interviewed Samuel Faix, a 101-year-old man at his San Francisco home. Faix told Berkland that he was 22 years old when the quake hit his apartment near the waterfront on Second Street. The wood-framed building was tilted so that it was difficult to get downstairs, but it did not collapse. He made his way through the Tenderloin and noticed many destroyed brick buildings. Berkland asked if he had heard any cries for help but was told, "No, it looked like a steamroller had gone over it; anyone in there was dead. He saw smoke rising south of Market Street and headed toward it when he saw the ruins of the Brunswick Hotel, which was a mass of kindling. He saw only two survivors, one of whom was coming down the fire escape of the adjacent building. The man was naked and appeared dazed as he reached the lower landing. Sam pointed the man out to a fireman, who helped him down to the street where a woman came over and gave him a blanket to cover himself. Sam was surprised that I knew that the man's name was John Justus."

These stories, like other indicators, show that "the official death lists of only a few hundred persons were grossly in error, and certainly there was a deliberate governmental cover-up of the facts," Berkland says. And the real-life survivors are other signals that the quake and fire caused more damage than what people were told.

A Post-Frisco Quake Letter

On the 75th anniversary of the big one, Berkland had been given this heartfelt letter from a sister to her brother.

April 21, 1906
2104 232nd St.
San Francisco, CA

Dear Brother,

I heard a while ago that it was possible to send mail out, so I though [sic] it best to let you know that all [are] all right here, having come through the earthquake very lucky, and not being near the fire zone [Mission District from 19th St. out]... escaped from the flames by a lucky change of wind we had last night.

The shack stood the shocks well and we scarcely lost a dish, but there isn't a whole chimney in place hereabouts. We got mother away from McWirthers about noon on Wednesday and it was a good thing we did, as the fire burned itself out around the German hospital early this morning. How the patients fared I don't know, as it is impossible to get any news that can be depended upon, but I guess Mrs. McWirther and the children are all right, as young Jack and McManon were saying by them.

All the downtown district is burned or shot down [by cannon fire] and thousands of people are living out on the bare hills all around here. All of the stone-cutters who lived down that way escaped with their lives, but little else; McGrills are staying at the policeman's house [Campbell's], McConville is staying with us, Gillies is at Pollack's, and others in odd corners that (are) too numerous to mention.

We ain't crowded and if any of them turn up, we'll do our

best for them as long as we have everything. We have been very lucky ourselves and are not wanting for anything much. As Mother says, we can fall back on the chickens when the rest runs out. I have been joshing the Old Lady about her flitting habit and she says she admits that Frisco people can beat her for quick flitting, and big flitting and every kind of flitting. But it was a terrible sight to see old and young of all ages and sizes, pulling trunks with all their stuff, carts with men in the shafts, and women, too, with goods of all kinds; wagons with horses in shafts cost from twenty-five to one-hundred dollars a load, and short hauls at that. Moving vans are not to be got at any price.

I seen some of the funniest sights and some of the most pitiful that I ever care to see. At the first shock woke up and threw off the bed clothes, then laid still until I thought it was over; then hopped out, but I hadn't touched the floor when the Big One came, and I was afraid for a little while that the house would topple over, but I told Floss to stay in bed as I knew the springs would save her from most of the jolts. After it steadied again we dressed and went into the hall and got the door open, ready to jump down the steps if it started again; but aside from a little swaying, it was over for a while. While we looked out, people were flying from their houses, some in night clothes and some in their good looks only, and, of course Flossie and I stood on the steps and laughed ourselves sore; but it was too comical to watch and not laugh.

We were the only ones that had our clothes on in the whole place as far as we could see. People forgot their modesty for an hour after it was over and stood around in their shirttails waiting for more shakes. One woman on DeHavo Street was out in the field with her pants in her hand, and it was fifteen minutes before she could steady herself and put them on, but she didn't care, and put them on where she stood.

Most of the houses around here are frame ones so they stood, while the brick ones nearly all fell and buried lots of people in ruins. There is no way of learning the amount of the dead, but it's being guessed at as up in the thousands. There are hundreds of bodies buried in the ruins, and I hear that there is a part of Golden Gate park covered with them.

Susie and Mary just came in, and they say that they can see McWirthers from the distance and that is still standing, so I guess it is all right over there, too. Anyway, I got some snap-shots and I am sending a couple along, but as I had only some worn-out developer, they are very poor prints, but the films will be all right for future use, and I'll send you some better ones later.

You can rest easy about Mother, as she is here with us and taking it easy. She is over her fright and is only worrying over you two, as she thinks you will believe that the entire city is wiped out. But it's bad enough from the ferries to 29th Street, where it is all ruined, and from about Brannan Street clear over to North Beach, Chinatown, and the Barbara Coast; and all of the swells on Nob Hill are burned and shot down, so you see it would be hard to recognize Frisco.

The snaps were taken on Valencia Street, and one is the remains of the Valencia Street hotel. Three storry [sic] high, but the earth opened and swallowed two storries,[sic] and all in the rooms buried. It looks now like a one storry [sic] house…As you see, the other is a crack on 19th Street about ten feet deep and fifteen across.

Keep your mind easy, brother, for we are all right…KRC

This letter was typed by Jim Berkland, July 8, 1981, from a copy of the original letter written in longhand; Berkland retained the author's misspellings. "I had transcribed 'flitting' as flirting, but it didn't really seem appropriate. In 2004, I checked the big dictionary and found that 'flitting' is a Scotch-English term for changing address. Now it makes sense," notes Berkland.

Other Sidelights

While people like KRC were coping with the aftermath of the big one, other folks were reported to have missed it all. Chicago-based journalist Jim Hodl tells the story: "Opera singer Enrico Caruso was performing in Frisco when the quake hit early in the morning. Caruso was staying in the penthouse suite of the Palace Hotel. Scared by the quake's rumbling, Caruso reportedly panicked and ran down the stairs of the hotel, screaming at the top of his lungs and knocking other hotel guests out of his way. Caruso's aide knew that if this story hit the papers, Caruso's reputation would take a hit, and he might lose high-priced engagements. So the aide reported to each paper in Frisco that Caruso had actually been singing to calm the other guests. Also left out of this report was that Caruso, still unnerved later that morning, fired his pistol at Palace Hotel employees sent to retrieve his baggage from his suite, thinking they were stealing his property."

Hodl adds, "There was also a report that actor John Barrymore was in Frisco on the morning of the quake, but having spent much of the night imbibing in local taverns, was unaware of the quake until someone told him about it the following evening."

But statistics show that the 1906 San Francisco earthquake-fire did indeed happen, and it left its imprint on the city forever.

SHOCKING EFFECTS

Quake: The great 1906 San Francisco earthquake (April 18, 5:12 a.m.)

Richter magnitude: 8.3

Mercalli intensity: VII to IX (Berkland believes the 1906 quake definitely reached XII.)

Number of people affected: at least 3,000 deaths; 225,000 homeless

Property damage: $400 million in 1906 dollars from earthquake and fire, $80 million from the earthquake alone.

10 Facts FYI

Here's everything you wanted to know but were afraid to ask about the great 1906 San Francisco earthquake. These facts were gleaned from a variety of sources: Jim Berkland, the USGS, and other organizations.

1 ⊸ɭ⊢ At 5.12 a.m., a foreshock happened and was felt throughout the San Francisco Bay Area. The great earthquake hit 20 to 25 seconds later, with an epicenter near San Francisco.

2 ⊸ɭ⊢ The strong shaking lasted about 45 to 60 seconds.

3 ⊸ɭ⊢ The quake was felt from southern Oregon to south of Los Angeles, and inland as far as central Nevada.

4 ⊸ɭ⊢ It ruptured the northernmost 430 kilometers (according to Berkland, it was 486 kilometers, 270 miles) of the San Andreas fault from northwest of San Juan Bautista to the triple junction of Cape Mendocino.

5 ⊸ɭ⊢ Liquefaction caused severe damage to buildings in San Francisco's Marina district as well as along the coastal areas of Oakland and Alameda in the east San Francisco Bay shore area. Liquefaction also contributed significantly to the property damage in the Santa Cruz and Monterey Bay areas, which lie near the epicentral zone.

6 ⊸ɭ⊢ Gladys Hansen and Emmet Condon estimated that over 3,000 deaths were caused directly or indirectly by the disaster. Berkland believes that the total was closer to 10,000 in accordance with several early estimates. The population of San Francisco in 1906 was about 400,000.

7 ⊸ɭ⊢ The fire lasted for three days, which caused more damage than did the earthquake. "The early estimates were 50:50 until insurers said they would pay for fire damage but not for losses from the earthquake," says Berkland.

8 ⊸ɭ⊢ The burned district covered a 4.7-square-mile area.

9 ⊸ɭ⊢ At least 28,000 building were destroyed.

10 —◆ The San Francisco quake ranks as one of the most significant earthquakes of all time.

One hundred years later, there are new data about the death toll cover-up of the 1906 San Francisco earthquake, which didn't strike in Berkland's standard seismic window; it did hit just after the end of a perigean spring tide seismic window, notes Berkland. The best news is that we, the people, are finally getting closer to the correct death toll. It has been upgraded to 3,000 and will continue to climb as Hansen continues to dig—because as Berkland knows in his heart and Hansen says with conviction, "It may even be higher."

EARTHSHAKING FACTS
TO DOG-EAR

- ⫸ Consider the new, improved death toll for the great San Francisco 1906 earthquake.

- ⫸ Note that the total death toll for the 1906 San Francisco earthquake-fire will never be known.

- ⫸ Do understand that earthquakes, not just fires, can cause massive damage to buildings.

- ⫸ If you're hesitant to believe that the government would cover up the death toll, go back in history and think about other cover-ups—from the Watergate fiasco to the long-term physical and psychological effects of Agent Orange on people who served in the Vietnam war.

- ⫸ Get involved and find out if your home, work, and other buildings are earthquake safe and up to building codes.

Part Six

Bracing for the Big One

17 —⊸—⊸ Good-bye, California?

California goes into the Pacific right after the Eastern states slide into the Atlantic.

—Jim Berkland

MORE THAN 30 YEARS AGO, JIM BERKLAND FIRST HEARD ABOUT CALIFORNIA'S SLIDing into the sea when he was working on his doctorate at Cal Davis. The "infamous book," *Last Days of the Late, Great State of California* by Curt Gentry, published in 1968, created a furor at the U.S. Geological Survey. "Its public contacts suddenly went off-scale. I think it hired a PR person to handle the incredible interest. It began to refer to 'The Book,' and compare activities 'pre-Book' and 'post-Book,'" recalls Berkland. Ironically, he adds, "I was above all that back in academia and firmly convinced that California was secure, as well as 'knowing' that earthquakes could not be predicted."

He adds, "When I spent my one year at Appalachian State University and was preparing to return to California after the spring 1973 session, several of my North Carolina colleagues and students were surprised that I was returning to my native state, as there was a common feeling that California was doomed." And the myth spun out of control.

Beachfront Property in Nevada?

Richard Ely, a geologist in Sonoma, California, remembers the geomyth all too well:

I first heard this myth in 1969 when I was working for the California Division of Mines and Geology. In those days, the division was located in San Francisco in the Ferry Building, right at the foot of Market Street. Along with the offices of the geologists, there was a huge, somewhat decrepit, display of minerals and an information desk where the public could buy publications and ask questions of the staff.

One day they were shorthanded, and I was keeping an eye on the desk during lunchtime, when an ethereal young man floated through the doors. He was a type that we saw frequently in those days: Jesus-style hair and beard, with megawatt eyes that had been through far, far too many 500-microgram doses of LSD. He was nervous, but I made him feel welcome, and he shared with me his concern. He had it on good authority that atomic-powered submarines had dived 1,000 feet deep 50 miles offshore in the Pacific Ocean, and then sailed below the continental shelf, eventually to emerge through a hole in the shelf into San Francisco Bay. His friend had told him that the next time there was a great earthquake, the shelf was going to break off, and all of coastal California was going to sink into the sea. What he wanted to know was, how far did he have to go inland to be inside the break-off zone?

I gently explained to him that the continental shelf was not constructed like a bookshelf, but in fact was a very flat landform (also called the continental terrace), and that below it there was rock all the way to the center of the earth with no big holes. I told him that rocks are very weak when placed under tension, and that in nature, a cliff with an overhang of 100 feet was rare, being found only in areas with exceptionally strong and sparsely fractured rock. It was physically impossible for the weak, sedimentary rocks of the continental shelf to overhang 100 yards, let alone 50 miles.

My words seemed to reverberate inside the man's addled brains as he took in the information. He clearly was torn, and part of him wanted to believe me, but at the deep level, he knew that California was going to fall into the sea, even if the scientific facts said otherwise. He thanked me in a vague sort of way and departed, planning, I suspect, to move far inland.

Berkland agrees with Ely. "If the public can be made aware that a continental shelf is not at all shelflike, they would not ask about California's sliding into the sea. The edge of the continent very gradually descends into the deep sea, and there are no fish and submarines to be found under the state. The Pacific plate is sliding past California as North America drifts westward. The pressures of the plates are more than sufficient to hold us in place."

Slip-Sliding Away...

What's more, the U.S. Geological Survey confirms that no, the Golden State won't eventually fall off into the ocean. Evidently, the Pacific Ocean isn't a huge hole into which California can fall, but it is itself land at somewhat lower elevation with water above it. It's simply impossible that California will be swept out to sea, insist the scientists.

Instead, remember the song "North to Alaska"? Well, USGS scientists claim southwestern California is moving horizontally northward toward Alaska as it slides past central and eastern California. The dividing point is the San Andreas fault system, which extends from the Salton Sea in the south to Cape Mendocino in the north. This 800-mile-long fault is the boundary between the Pacific plate and North American plate. The Pacific plate is moving to the northwest with respect to the North American plate at approximately two inches per year. At this rate, Los Angeles and San Francisco will be next-door neighbors about 15 million years from now, and in an additional 70 million years, Los Angeles residents will find themselves with an Alaska zip code!

More Quirky Quake Myths—Or Not?

Ever think if it's humid that an earthquake is due? Wondering if quakes can swallow you up? Are we having more quakes in the twenty-first century, or not? Read on, and find out.

Does earthquake weather exist?

"Twenty years ago," remembers Berkland, "I would have scoffed at it. Then I heard of several instances of warm, humid, deathly quiet conditions that were followed by significant earthquakes. A special moment was when exactly those conditions existed in Santa Clara County on October 16, 1989. As I walked by two women on the way to the parking lot, one said to the other, 'This feels like earthquake weather.' I agreed with her and gave them each a copy of my prediction for a World Series earthquake, which hit the next day."

Eleven years later, Berkland experienced the same type of weather, and three hours later, a 4.2 quake shook the area. Those were two isolated incidents when Berkland experienced such phenomena. "Some people consider earthquake weather to be hot, dry, and still, which is far more common in the California Coast Ranges, which seldom are hot and humid. If there is such a thing as 'earthquake weather,' I vote for the humid definition," he says.

Do big earthquakes happen only at the crack of dawn?

Berkland notes that there is a widespread belief that large quakes tend to strike in the early morning. History points to the following early morning hits: Fort Tejon, 1857; Charleston, 1886; San Francisco, 1906; San Fernando, 1971; and Idaho, 1983. But earthquakes also happen during the middle of the day or night.

"In a July 1983 article in *Nature* by astronomer Steven Kilston and seismologist Leon Knopff, they successfully predicted a 6-plus on the San Andreas fault of Southern California around November 1987. They actually were doubly correct, when a 6.3 and 6.7 quake struck northwest of the Salton Sea on November 23and 24, 1987. More amazingly to me is the fact that they had expected the quake within two hours of dawn or dusk, and the first one was recorded at dusk by my office pendulum in San Jose, and the second one struck near dawn the next morning," recalls Berkland.

Thus, because of that event and his own experiences, Berkland generally expects earthquakes to hit within two hours of dawn or dusk, which amounts to an eight-hour window, or one-third of the time available each day, he says.

Do earthquakes swallow cities or cows?

These myths follow a close second to California's sliding into the sea, says Berkland. "Fault lines or ground shaking or liquefaction can create crevasses and scarps measuring tens of feet high, but there is no opening wide of the ground and gulping down large structures or animals." In fact, he notes that the classic case of the cow's tail in the 1906 Trace in Marin County was a hoax. As the story goes, a nephew of a dairy rancher 'fessed up to the swallowed-cow episode decades later. Evidently, the rancher knew geologists were coming and decided to play a prank, says Berkland. "He took the tail of a recently slaughtered cow and stuck it into a narrow crack along the fault. The geologists accepted the story without digging deeper, and the phenomenon received such widespread attention that the rancher was too embarrassed to explain the true story. The myth of the swallowed cow still persists."

Is under a doorway the safest place to be in an earthquake?

Surprise. The doorway may not be the ideal place for you to duck and cover, for a variety of reasons. For one, if the dominant shaking is parallel to your extended arms, you can support yourself, but if it's at 90 degrees, you'll most likely be knocked down by a strong quake, says Berkland. Plus, not only can a swinging door crush your fingers, but it's difficult for more than one person to stand in a doorway. Your best bet is to get under a sturdy desk or table, and stay clear of a chimney or plate glass window.

"Also," adds Berkland, "recent evidence favors seeking shelter on the floor next to a bed or stairway, which can support collapsed roofs." P.S. Forget rushing outdoors. It's a common mistake, but you'll be vulnerable because tile roofs, broken chimneys, falling walls, and electric wires all become deadly.

Are earthquakes happening more these days?

Quakes aren't any more frequent than they were a century ago, or even 10 years ago, for that matter, says Berkland. "It is just that we have more sensitive instruments, more seismographic stations, more incentive to analyze earthquakes, and there is more public awareness and interest in seismic activity. We still expect and measure an annual average of about one great quake (8.0), 15 major quakes (7–7.9), 129 strong quakes (6.0–6.9), and 900 moderate quakes (5.0–5.9)."

Earthquake or Earthquack Films

Speaking of geo-myths, ever watch natural disaster films and ponder, "Gee, could this *really* happen?" Here's the lowdown on popular quake films. Berkland provides his grounded geologist's point of view. He rates each one on a one to ten magnitude scale, with ten being a super quake film.

- 1965, *Crack in the World*: Scientists drop a bomb inside a borehole in the earth, hoping to create a new, improved energy source. As the crack circles the globe, cracks open and lava shoots upward, and quakes and tsunamis cause world destruction. Berkland's POV: "I never saw it and barely heard of it. I think Superman had a better solution when he saved Lois by back-spinning the earth." (NR)

- 1982, *St. Helens*: Volcanic eruption of Mount St. Helens. Based on a real-life story, Harry Truman won't leave Spirit Lodge, and 59 people, including a geologist, lose their lives. Footage of actual eruption. Berkland's POV: "I was impressed with this docudrama, and I was personally involved with the 1980 eruption cycle. An educational TV director asked me on March 27, 1980, what I thought about Mount St. Helens. I said, 'I think that volcano means business, and I give it a 50:50 chance to erupt this year.' The director responded, 'I hope you're right, Jim. We are going to fly around it this afternoon.' Shortly after they dropped me off at my office, I learned that St. Helens had begun to erupt, while we were filming on an overlook of the Calaveras fault.

  "One week later, I was flying around it myself in a chartered plane, with a couple of other geologists. St. Helens was socked in, and we dropped below the clouds to see brown stripes of volcanic mudflows marking the snow; also, there was ice-covered Spirit Lake. With time running out, we headed back above the clouds just in time to witness a spectacular eruption with black clouds rolling up to 40,000 feet and chunks of glacial ice with steam trails accenting the picture." The big eruption on May 18, 1980, was still three months away. 10.0

- 1990, *The Big One: The Great Los Angeles Earthquake*: A seismologist warns superiors of an oncoming major quake after a swarm of small temblors. After a quake hits, she battles city officials to warn the public of potential disaster. Chaos and panic are frightening. Berkland's POV: "Pretty realistic for special effects, bureaucratic foot-dragging, and behind-the-scenes political maneuvering. It does feed the perception that warning the public can be worse than doing nothing. We just need to look at the results of the real-life lack of warning for the Sumatra tsunami to disprove that canard. Better public education and governmental warning networks are a must." 8.0 (See Chapter 14, "Where Are the Quake Warnings?")

- 1996, *Phenomenon*: George Malley (John Travolta), a likable guy, is knocked down by a flash of light, which gives him the power to sense phenomena such as pre-quake activity. Berkland's POV: "The acting was superb and the plot reasonable for someone who knows. There was much I can relate to. I know that psychic predictions are possible, because several quakes have been given to me by a psychic, days or weeks before the events. Even Travolta's reaction on crossing a straining fault line is real, and some people and some animals do share that gift (or curse?)." 10.0

- 1997, *Dante's Peak*: A dormant volcano comes to life while scientists dispute about when it should erupt. The film shows the fact that sleeping volcanoes like in the Mammoth Lakes, California, area can and do put people and property at risk. Berkland's POV: "Mostly shot around Mount St. Helens, and probably the best volcano disaster movie. I thoroughly enjoyed it, but there were a couple of problems: Bathers being instantly cooked in a hot spring; and alternating flows of acidic rhyolite and basic lavas. Also, from personal experience, I saw something that just doesn't happen: The aging head USGS volcanologist apologized to the young whistleblower (Pierce Brosnan) for not believing him about the impending disaster." 9.0

- 1997, *Volcano*: After a series of tremors, it becomes evident that Los Angeles could be sitting on top of a volcano ready to blow. A seismologist attempts to understand this event, while city services join forces to try to halt the flow of lava and destruction. Berkland's POV: "I had great expectations for this one, but it became almost comical, making me groan rather than laugh. Some of the political ramifications surrounding the disaster seemed real." 5.0

- 1998, *Armageddon*: A misfit oil drilling team is sent into space on a mission to zap an asteroid zooming toward Earth. As the rock nears, they overcome unanticipated problems and find solutions to save lives. Berkland's POV: "Good acting and special effects saved this one for me. Even the concept of blasting an asteroid before it can hit the earth has been studied by scientists. (How about being struck by 1,000 house-sized blocks versus one Great Pyramid?) Perhaps this will be tested during the 2029 scheduled close approach of an asteroid. Much better would be to attach rockets and divert the intruding body. Let's see, I'll be 99 years old when it arrives, so I guess I'll ignore it." 8.0

- 1999, *Aftershock: Earthquake in New York*: When a killer earthquake strikes New Yorkers, they're caught in a chilling quake-related disaster. Lives are lost and families are split up, while the mayor and former fire chief try to put together an emergency earthquake preparedness plan. Berkland's POV: "I guess it was the mainshock that was the problem here .I didn't see this movie, although I wanted to. From the reviews, I think it will be worthwhile to rent the video." (NR)

- 2003, *The Core*: What if the earth's electromagnetic field collapses? Birds go berserk and disaster occurs, prompting scientists—complete with nuclear bombs—to go on a journey into the earth's core, hoping to jump-start it back in gear. Berkland's POV: "I was impressed by the original special effects, but as the journey to the core proceeded, I felt, 'Was this trip really necessary?' Nuke the core. What a concept!" 7.0

- 2004, *10.5*: A trigger effect of hidden faults in the Pacific Northwest creates a succession of earthquakes, which lead up to a potential superquake that may hit Los Angeles. During the swarm of quakes, from Puget Sound to San Francisco, a seismologist tries to troubleshoot how to fix the fracture that threatens to change the geography of the West Coast as we know it. Berkland's POV: "I saw only part of this fiasco and went quickly back to real life. My fear is that many people accepted the plot as realistic." 2.0

Living in a Shaky State

In the spring, I picked up a copy of the *Tahoe Daily Tribune* and read the headline, "Future Looks Shaky: Large temblors, tsunami could occur in region." New research suggested that the earthquake danger at Lake Tahoe and in the Reno-Carson area is much higher than previous studies have shown. If a quake hit the basin, a 10-meter, tsunami-like wave, or seiche, could form in the lake.

Berkland says that it wouldn't be a tsunami from movement on the lake bottom, but a seiche wave from oscillations of a body of water (like carrying a dishpan full of water without spilling it). While I live two blocks away from Lake Tahoe, Berkland adds, "I see no way that your house would be in the path of a seiche. However, a huge avalanche into the lake could cause a big splash, although I never heard of one at Tahoe."

Meanwhile, I read in the local newspaper article "that the three Lake Tahoe faults—the West Tahoe, North Tahoe/Stateline, and Incline Village faults—are connected, and movement at one fault could trigger movement in another." And I can't forget the fact that Lake Tahoe is a very deep and cold lake. Still, Berkland insists that the San Francisco Bay Area, where I'm originally from, is in more danger of a future temblor than Lake Tahoe, where I currently live.

On April 26, 2005, I sent Berkland an email: "I think Kerouac is a budding seismically sensitive kitty." I had sent an email to myself on April 22 regarding a potential earthquake: "Told neighbor and hair stylist today intense sinus headache last night and today. Cat super clingy since last night/today. What's going on? I say within the next day." Then, one day after the full moon on Monday, April 25, 2005, a 2.7 quake hit Tahoe Vista, California, 22 miles from my home in South Lake Tahoe. So I wonder if my mixed-breed domestic longhaired cat has a sixth sense or is it just another coincidence?

Berkland continues, "In regard to earthquake potential, Northern California has three main provinces to consider."

- The Coast Ranges and the western San Andreas system of mostly strike-slip faults. This area has a potential for a repeat of the 1906 great quake.

- The eastern Sierra and Cascade mountains of block faulting and volcanism. This area has been historically limited to quakes of maximum of 6 to 7.0.

- The northwest subduction zone north of the Mendocino trench, where the San Andreas fault ends. This area has been the center of the most 6 and 7.0 quakes in Northern California, and shares some of the potential for a 9.0 from the oceanic trench extending south from Washington and Oregon.

Last but certainly not least on Berkland's earthquake prediction list is Southern California. In his May 2005 *Syzygy*, Berkland begins his newsletter by saying, "Based on the past near-record rainfall and the upcoming extreme tides, I have been warning about a strong summer quake in Southern California." He believes there's an 80 percent chance for a 6.0-plus earthquake in California and a 50 percent chance for a hit in Southern California—especially for June, July, or August. On June 12, he already came close with a 5.2 quake that was first reported as 5.6 near Anza in Southern California.

Since Berkland's earthquake prediction accuracy rate is 75 percent, if he doesn't get a hit, he says, "Just chalk it up to the 25 percent that I miss. But I have a strong feeling about this with the record precipitation and the extreme full moon tides this summer. The animals will be the clincher."

Kathleen Fjermedal in Santa Monica, California, has been sending Berkland lost pet reports from the *Los Angeles Times* for at least 20 years. It's her contribution to a man who has spent decades collecting data to support his earthquake predicting theories, she says, "with his intent being that of saving lives and property." As a California resident, she's gotten advance warnings many times from her own animals prior to the Sylmar, Northridge, and the Loma Prieta quakes. On July 11, she reported that 11 dogs and one missing cat were listed in the L.A. *Times'* pet ads.

After fireworks on Independence Day, during July 8–12, is the peak time for missing dog ads all around the country. "However, usually the cat ads don't climb so rapidly, as they're not as sound-oriented as dogs, which panic on the Fourth of July. The 11 cat ads may mean that a quake is imminent for the San Diego area," added Berkland on July 11, 2005.

California Jitters in June

As was predicted by Berkland, the month of June 2005 was seismically active in the Golden State. On June 15, two days after his secondary seismic window from June 6 to June 13, a 7.2 quake struck off the coast of California. "It was felt from central Oregon southward to the San Francisco Bay Area, and it triggered a tsunami warning up and down the coast. Fortunately, the maximum height at Crescent City was only 10 inches," he points out.

Reports showed that after the 7.2 earthquake happened, sirens sounded off in coastal towns from Eureka to Crescent City (remember, a killer tsunami hit Crescent City after the 1964 Alaskan earthquake). This time, more than 40 years later, 4,000 residents evacuated to safety. But it was also reported that San Francisco got a "tardy tsunami warning." In other words, if a tsunami had hit the city it would have been too late to head for the hills. "After two more days," adds Berkland, "a 6.7 aftershock rattled more California residents' nerves, and it was felt as far south as Santa Cruz. No tsunami alert was called, although people were much more prepared this time."

Berkland continues, "Southern Californians were equally agitated by a 5.2 quake at Anza on June 12 and a probable 4.9 aftershock at Yucaipa in the greater Los Angeles area two days later." Keep in mind that all of this activity was prior to his predicted primary seismic window of June 20 to 27, 2005, which was based on the full moon, first day of summer on June 21, followed 31 hours later by a very close encounter of the moon accompanied by near-record tidal ranges along the California coast.

On June 21, Berkland said, "I am 80 percent confident there will be a 3.5 to 6.5 magnitude quake in Northern California between June 20 and June 27, 2005." And this is the same month the swarm of tremors had California on edge. On June 18, after four significant quakes hit in less than a week, Californians were nervous, with some, such as myself, stocking up. I bought water and pet food, and got "quake cash."

Tahoe Animals Sense Quakes

Later, on June 22 at 1:40 a.m. in my South Lake Tahoe home, when the full moon was big and bright, coyotes woke me up. My two-year-old Brittany, Simon, barked at their eerie howling. Plus, for the next few mornings, Simon didn't eat breakfast; neither did Simon's pet pal, my neighbor's sensitive rat terrier, Zorro. This strange animal behavior reminded me of when Alex, my orange-and-white cat, didn't eat the morning of the 7.1 monster World Series quake.

On June 23, 2005, my cat Kerouac, who had sensed small quakes in the Tahoe region before, began acting clingy (his pre-quake clue). I also noted on the USGS Earthquake Hazards Program-Northern California website, *quake.wr.usgs.gov,* that a 1.1 quake hit Tahoe Vista, about 19 miles from South Lake Tahoe. (But nobody knows for sure if animals or humans can sense an oncoming microearthquake.) I sent an email to myself: "Wish cat would go away—it's making me think quake."

On June 26, when I was working in my study at approximately 11:30 a.m., Kerouac jumped up into my lap. He was too affectionate. Fifteen minutes later, my cabin shook hard. (It was a quick memory jolt of the loss of control I felt in the Loma Prieta quake.) According to a report from the U.S. Geological Survey, a 4.8 earthquake struck at 11: 45 a.m. five miles from Tahoe Vista, California. It was eerie and exciting to see the big red square on the USGS California-Nevada map. I quickly plopped K.C. into his crate and put Simon on his leash. I didn't know whether it was a foreshock, and I wanted to be ready if a mainshock or strong aftershock hit. (Five small aftershocks happened between 11:45 a.m. and 12:02 p.m.)

That day when I compared notes with Zorro's "mom," Carol Reck— an earthquake prediction skeptic—she told me that she didn't feel the jolt. However, when it hit, her two-year-old canine "ran around in circles in the living room and barked," she says. I believe her pooch sensed the P-wave (the fastest and first seismic wave that animals and humans often feel).

Meanwhile, Berkland isn't surprised at all that this temblor shook the North Shore. Nor is he surprised that two dogs and a cat sensed it coming. After all, he had called for a 3.5-to-6.5 event within 140 miles of Mount Diablo, and this was satisfied on June 26 by a 5.2 quake at Lake Tahoe, just 137 miles from Mount Diablo. (The quake was downgraded, but I can assure you it didn't feel like a light shaker.)

While the Tahoe quake in my own backyard wasn't the big one, I know that it's a good feeling to be proactive and get prepared for both you and your pet's safety's sake. For dozens of helpful animal-related items, log onto *www.hsus.org/search.jsp* and type in "disaster preparedness."

P.S. — On August 29, 2005, I posted my southern California quake prediction on Berkland's website. I wrote, "Vision: 5-plus earthquake in southern California desert in the next week." On August 31, Berkland posted his own savvy message on his website: "A rash of very shallow quakes up to 4.6 at Brawley on the San Andreas fault may culminate in a 5.0-plus. If it reaches 6.0-plus my long-standing prediction for SoCal for this year will be satisfied." The next day, a 5.1 hit Southern California, one mile from Obsidian Butte, California.

While you may think you've got a handle on future shakers, there's always more. In the next chapter, Berkland answers some earthquake-related questions that may open your eyes, wherever you live.

EARTHSHAKING FACTS
TO DOG-EAR

- ◂╫▸ If you live on the West Coast or are considering moving to the Golden State, experts will tell you that Californians won't be sliding into the Pacific Ocean.

- ◂╫▸ Don't believe that earthquake weather and early morning quakes are myths; they may very well be a reality, after all.

- ◂╫▸ You can relax if you're worried about the earth swallowing up those countryside cows, or your own cow.

- ◂╫▸ If an earthquake hits, heading for the doorway to be safe is history. The present-day survival strategy is to duck and cover under a table.

- ◂╫▸ Disaster films are fun to view and are entertaining, for sure. But be wary of fact and fiction, especially when this may involve child viewers.

18 ⎓ The Most Important Questions about Earth Changes

The questions raised regarding earthquakes deserve prompt and unflinching answers, not to be postponed for 30 years when the answers probably won't matter.

—Jim Berkland

DESPITE PEOPLE'S LACK OF TIME TO PAY ATTENTION, FEAR OF HEARING FRIGHTENING news, or simply putting earth changes low on the list of world problems, the fact is that people of all ages actually want to know the worst-case scenario. And when we do hear it, it's often right after a megaquake or tsunami, like the Indian Ocean quake-tsunami on December 26, 2004. However, taking precautions when you're feeling Mother Earth is "quiet" may just save your life in the long run.

Ever wonder what's up with the Hayward fault in the Golden State? Or do you think that a swarm of earthquakes might be the beginning of the end? Do you know which state in America has the most shakers? Here are the little questions that can have a big impact on your overall well-being, and Jim Berkland's responses to them.

Tremors and Tsunamis

Is a ripple effect possible?

Would the Indian Ocean earthquake trigger a ripple effect

around that tectonic plate or other plates in the world? In other words, could we see a 9.0-plus around Chile, the Los Angeles/San Francisco area, or Japan?

—Freedom Fighter

JB: FF, such a great ripple has never occurred in the past to my knowledge. A fault line can only yield up the energy stored in it no matter how strong the trigger. With a gun, pulling the trigger harder does not make the bullet faster or more explosive.

Should people reconsider Berkland's seismic windows?

Do you feel any responsibility for people in Asia who believed your prediction, avoided the beaches until the window closed and went surfing the 26th?

—Roger

JB: Roger, you are childishly trying to hang a guilt trip on me for picking an eight-day period with the greatest vulnerability to quakes. When did I ever say that the risk was over when the window closed? I have always said that there are two windows per month—one associated with the full moon and one with the new moon. The 9.0 Sumatra quake occurred on the day of the full moon just as did the last 9-plus quake (Alaska 3/27/1964). All this year I had warned that December would have the highest potential for large quakes in 2004.

Are earthquakes a sign of the end?

Everyone says that the earth has not had so many quakes or quakes as strong as they are now. Some even dare to say that the end of the world was coming by a disastrous events. Have you seen similar activity before? Have you seen as many quakes as recently?

—Jorge

JB: Jorge, the number of earthquakes is *not* increasing, although there is almost always a flurry of quakes following major events, such as we had in late December 2004. The earth's rotation sped up two millionths of a second. (Hold on!) Rumors run wild, speculations bloom, and fears multiply after every natural disaster. This last quake-tsunami was no exception. Cool it.

Do you know of any research on the use of abnormal animal behavior to predict tsunamis?

I know that the Sumatra 9.0 magnitude quake and tsunami caused a new evaluation of the need for worldwide tsunami warnings with proper instrumentation. I've been using animal behavior in my earthquake prediction methods since the 1970s and believe that the main mechanism utilized by animals is the known changes in the local magnetic field that precede significant quakes. If there is another mechanism detected by animals from tsunami action, I don't know of one. However, most tsunamis are preceded by large earthquakes and most large earthquakes are preceded by measurable magnetic field changes, so why would animals need a tsunami-alert mechanism? How could you separate the quake alert from the tsunami alert?

One test might be to look at the rare tsunami not preceded by earthquakes and see what the record shows. Also, check the history of animal reactions thousands of miles away from an epicenter, where the causative quake couldn't be felt and environmental warnings for the quake wouldn't be likely to have occurred locally. For example, the January 26, 1700, superquake near Washington caused a killer tsunami two days later in Japan. Was there any documentation in Japan for animal warnings?

What's the U.S. state with the most earthquakes?

I read in an interview you had with Mitch Battros (ECTV) that Hawaii is ranked first in the U.S. with the most earthquakes. Was this a misprint? You surely meant Alaska, which is ranked in the USGS website with 57 percent of U.S. earthquakes. Hawaii is third with 7 percent. Please clarify.

—Lisa

JB: I did the calculation for frequency of quakes divided by the area of the state. The most quakes per square mile are clearly in the state of Hawaii.

California Quakes

What are the tsunami effects in San Francisco Bay and Elliot Bay?

I have been wondering whether or how a tsunami crossing the Pacific Ocean toward the West Coast could have an effect on the inland bays of San Francisco and Seattle.

—Fran

JB: Fran, in a listing of U.S. tsunamis from 1690 through 1988, NOAA (National Oceanic and Atmospheric Administration) shows little effect within San Francisco Bay, which isn't surprising because of the relatively narrow entrance through the Golden Gate. I saw nothing higher than the 1.5 meters (5.0 feet) that was measured at San Rafael from the great Alaskan quake of 3/27/64. Most of the other heights were less than 0.1 meter. Even the 5/22/60 great Chile quake (9.6) created a maximum tsunami of 0.3–0.4 meters (1.3 feet) at Alameda and San Francisco.

Will there be a big California earthquake?

Mr. Berkland, I heard you predict a rather large earthquake for the state of California in 2028. Can you provide me more details about this? Thank you.

—Dave

JB: David, when did you hear that? I would be rather premature with such a prediction. I think you're confusing my predictions with the

USGS "forecast" that there is a 67 percent chance for a 6.7-plus quake by 2028 in the Bay Area. I do note that on 12/24/2026 there will be record tidal ranges at the Golden Gate.

What is the latest on the Hayward fault?

Jim, you were anticipating a ping-pong quake on the Hayward fault following the Loma Prieta earthquake, based on historical pairs of quakes. Fifteen years have passed—are you still expecting this quake, and if so, do you have any insight as to why the delay?

—Melanie

JB: Melanie, you have a good memory. Yes, my research certainly saw pairs of damaging quakes from East Bay/West Bay. Thus I expected a 5-plus in the East Bay within six years of the World Series quake. We did get the northwest 5.0 Bolinas quake in 1999 followed by the northeast 5.2 Napa quake in 2001. But the Hayward fault has produced no 5.0-plus since 1868. Interestingly, shortly after I predicted the East Bay quake in six years, USGS Alan Lindh said the same thing. He was supported by high science, while I was pooh-poohed for the same interpretation of the "ping pong" data (or "echo quake" as I called it).

Can snowpack and tides cause earthquakes?

Jim, with all the snow we had the past couple of days here in Tahoe and hearing you talk about tides, I was wondering if you ever considered the effects of a big snow pack, with the Sierra being so near an ocean and with a major fault in between. And one more thing: What about rain-soaked land? It seems that would be a lot of pressure.

—Charles

JB: Charles, we have reservoir-induced seismicity (RIS) and flood-induced seismicity, so perhaps snow-induced seismicity is appropriate. I have been looking at that possibility for many years. The strongest quake in California since 1906 was the 7.7 at Kern County in July 1952 (day of new moon). In the previous winter there had been a record snow pack. When that snow melted and filled the reservoirs, we were sitting ducks for a big earthquake. When the Wasatch Range was loaded with snow, I had predicted a quake for the Salt Lake area from the runoff. (I think it was 1982.) That May, a 5.4 quake was centered under the Salt Lake City airport.

Earthquake-Prone Regions

Is it possible for a big quake to happen in all places but Ontario, Canada?

For the place to be "right," there should be local clues such as rats and mice running in daylight, pets and other animals leaving their normal places of security, unusual spring activity, well water changes, etc. Ontario is one of the more stable places on the continent. But Lanark County, Ontario had a damaging quake on 2/10/1914; also several strong New York quakes caused damage in Ontario as well.

Do you predict earthquakes in Turkey?

Hi. I am a university student at Çukurova. Especially I would like to learn Turkey's fault lines. Are there lots of dangerous fault lines and does it cause danger every day? Turkey people don't know how they can live with earthquakes. What should we do for this? Thanks.

–Murat

JB: Murat, Turkey is one of the most dangerous earthquake countries, not only because of the many active faults, but because of the lack of earthquake-resistant designs and proper geologic locations. Looking all around the world, the fault that is most similar to the San Andreas is the North Anatolian fault, in type of strike-slip movement, activity, length, and hazard to the populace.

When the total eclipse of the Sun passed over Turkey on August 11,

1999, I warned people that Turkey and India were especially vulnerable to a big, tidally triggered earthquake. The terrible Izmit, Turkey, quake followed on August 16, 1999, and killed over 20,000 people.

Can the Ring of Fire set off earthquakes?

In looking at earthquake maps, it is evident that the western side of the Ring of Fire appears to have seismic events hitting in the Indonesia area and reverberating up through Japan and China/Russia and then over to Alaska. But the West Coast of the United States appears quiet. Do you see the shifting of the tectonic plates on the west side of the Ring of Fire eventually setting off quakes on the eastern side, or is that more or less solely dependent on syzygy and tides?

–Susan in Utah

JB: Susan, your observation is valid, and a number of people have suggested it in the past. Since 80 percent of the world's large quakes occur within the Ring of Fire, the pattern should have been established by now, but it has never been consistent. It was strange to me how, outside of the Indian Ocean tsunami area, 6-plus magnitude quakes almost shut down after December 26, 2004 (full moon and date of 9.0 magnitude quake at Sumatra). Rather than triggering distant quakes, it had the opposite effect (is there such a word as *un-triggering*)?

Quake Talk

Do quakes produce sights like a wave forming on the ground, as reported by a police officer during the great San Francisco earthquake of 1906?

I saw those waves with the very first quake I ever experienced. It was the Daly City, California quake of 5.3 on March 22, 1957. The P-wave hit my home about 60 miles north of the epicenter, and I felt and heard a boom. I headed outside and saw the neighbors' meadow undulating like a choppy sea with waves about 18 inches high. My seismology professor said he was "green with envy," as he had never seen the waves himself but had heard many others describe them. However, my colleagues at the USGS pooh-poohed the idea and said the ground waves would be almost too small to see. That was when I realized that the experts didn't know everything, and I would do better to trust my own eyes.

Do you know what is the origin of a subduction zone tremor?

Is it related to the motion of fluids (i.e., water and/or magma in relation to slow-slip events)?

–Linda Gibsons, B.C. (Canada)

JB: Linda, most of the largest quakes have been in subduction zones, where denser plates dive slowly beneath lighter ones (usually continental). The friction generates quakes. The longer since the last quake, the larger the magnitude potential for the next one. Usually increased fluid pressure reduces friction and allows a fault to slip more readily.

Also, under the continental plate, the friction from subduction melts rocks, creates magma chamber(s), and feeds volcanoes.

P.S. Almost all active volcanoes are over active subduction zones or over hot spots like Yellowstone or Hawaii.

Do planets have any effect on earthquakes?

Jim, I repeatedly hear from "scientists" that planetary alignments have very little to do with causal effects on earthquakes, merely because of the associated distances and gravitational effect. Is this actually the case, or is it more that while not a causal effect they are a contributing effect?

–Silver Eagle

JB: Silver Eagle, I have to go along with the scientific reaction to astrology. All such predictions sent to me have failed. Usually, I get reports *after* quakes as to how astrology predicted them. The combined force of all of the planets when aligned is far less than 1,000th the effect of the moon alone, as far as gravity is concerned. Many very bright people are convinced about the usefulness of astrology. I have yet to be shown it's true.

Are we entering the new Dark Age?

Do you see horrible chaos and devastating earth changes such as massive earthquakes and volcanic activity in 2006–07?

–Theresa

JB: Theresa, frankly, I'm not focusing on 2006–07. However, I'm intrigued by the Mayan calendar ending in December 2012. Is the world running out of time, or did the Mayans run out of rock for their inscriptions? The Aztec/Mayan calendar is the most prized artifact in the Mexican Museum. The large circular stone was found during sewer construction in Mexico City. It's carved in stone and indicates the landing of Columbus, the conquest of Cortez, and the end of the world following the new moon of December 12, 2012. Many futurists and psychics have focused on the year 2012 as marking the end of civilization. Perhaps I'm being overly optimistic in asserting that the Mayans simply ran out of rock.

Maybe I'm closer to the calendar than I could expect. After some debate, when our son was born on October 3, 1974, we named him Jay Olin, giving him the initials JOB, the same as my father and me. Ten years later, I saw a description of the images carved in the Aztec calendar. The second most powerful god was the god of earthquakes, Olin. Jay Olin Berkland was born on the day of the huge killer quake in Lima, Peru, the land of the Incas.

Is there any correlation between seismic activity and "mystery" hums?

There are many reports of sounds prior to quakes. A former miner heard noises "like blasts deep in a mine" before the 6.2 Morgan Hill quake in 1984. For a week prior to the World Series earthquake in 1989, people within about five miles of the epicenter heard deep booming noises before the 7.1 quake. They were reluctant to discuss it with neighbors until they had an "earthquake survivor party" a month after the quake and compared notes with each other. The most famous ground hums are called "Moodus noises" near East Haddam, Connecticut. The American Indians, colonists, and modern residents have been spooked by these hums, which sometimes accompany or precede shallow earthquakes. If you're in the mood for a seismic mystery, connect with East Haddam.

EARTHSHAKING FACTS
TO DOG-EAR

➤ Respond quickly to tsunami warnings, because they can help save your life.

➤ Do note that quake-prone regions include California, the Pacific Northwest, and the Pacific Ring of Fire. But while these places are more seismically active, no place is earthquake free. (Well, maybe North Dakota and southern Florida are close to being earthquake free.)

➤ Don't let your emotions fly off the handle when it comes to earth changes. Nobody has control of natural disasters.

➤ Educate yourself about natural disasters, and get prepared no matter where you live, since earthquakes, killer waves, volcanoes, and other events can affect infrastructure and lives.

➤ While you can't stop quakes from happening, you can heighten your quake preparedness strategies and be ready if and when the next big one hits.

19 ⌁ Don't Be Scared— Be Prepared!

Earthquake preparedness is like driving along a coastal highway. On one side is the rut of apathy, on the other the precipice of panic, and, in between, there are many potholes.

—Jim Berkland

I REMEMBER THE LOMA PRIETA EARTHQUAKE OF '89. AT 5:04 P.M., WHEN THE quake shook the San Francisco Bay Area, I grabbed my Lab, Carmella, and darted for the doorway. I didn't make it. I fell on the wood floor in the dining room and looked up in awe at rattling glass windows and French doors with too many windowpanes. It felt like my world was coming to an end.

As I'm a native Californian, and a journalist who has written several articles about Jim Berkland and earthquakes, you'd think I'd play it cool and have it under control. But this quake was different. It was big. It was bad. And I panicked. I desperately tried to make my way to the front door. After 15 seconds, I made it.

After the mainshock, I didn't know what to do. I knew it was bad when I turned on the TV—and it was out. I wondered about damage in other regions. Alone with my dog, I went outdoors to take a look. It was weird. Nobody was outside. With my pooch in tow, I walked on Laurel Street in San Carlos. I noticed some windows were broken on building structures; others weren't. I heard car alarms. Forty minutes later, when I was back inside my bungalow, a frightening aftershock hit. Then, when the TV came back on, I placed it on the floor and watched the news, hour by hour, day by day. I couldn't believe how the 7.1 quake wreaked havoc on the places I have lived and visited—Santa Cruz, San Francisco, Oakland. It was surreal.

Ever wonder what *you* would do when a spooky earthquake strikes? I went straight to the experts to find out about cutting-edge strategies for earthquake risk reduction—what scientists are doing to help save lives in future earthquakes. Also, there are things you can do yourself right now to help put earthquake preparedness into motion. In the following section you'll discover what is being done and what you can do to prepare for the next big one instead of acting like a victim in a horror movie.

Earthquake Risk Reduction

Who in the world is working hard to reduce the effect of natural disasters on people? Dr. Max Wyss, of course! He is the director of the World Agency of Planetary Monitoring and Earthquake Risk Reduction in Switzerland. WARMERR is a nonprofit organization, started by a group of philanthropic individuals, to reduce the effects of natural disasters on people.

Now the scientist has been put to the test. One day he answered my questions. It was a unique experience to be able to hear what this dedicated earthquake expert's plan is. After all, after the great Sumatra quake-tsunami, I couldn't help wondering, "What is risk reduction all about?" And now, this man, who uses a computer tool to estimate building damage and human losses due to earthquakes anywhere in the world, was ready to tell me how risk reduction works and answer other questions I just had to ask.

Q. *Why is there a "do nothing" attitude within the international community in the face of natural disasters?*

A. Seldom are countries hit by a major earthquake disaster more than once in a generation. So people forget. Developing countries have other problems that are very real, and perhaps more pressing—certainly more daily in the lives of people, such as hunger, poverty, illness. Elected officials are in office for limited periods. They figure the probability that an earthquake disaster hits their country during their watch is low. The international community seems to have no money to fund projects to mitigate natural disasters before they happen. They have plenty of money to discuss them after they happen.

Q. *Explain the concept of earthquake risk reduction.*

A. Reduction of earthquake risk can be achieved by educating people in what to do when an earthquake happens, and in how to make their home less deadly by simple means. Risk reduction can also be achieved by strengthening existing buildings of poor construction, especially schools. The risk can be greatly reduced by building the new buildings according to building codes. The additional cost is approximately 5 percent. I think my life would be worth this amount.

Q. *Explain the benefit of your project, refining the* QUAKELOSS *data bank. What is the importance of this work in progress?*

A. Immediately after disastrous earthquakes, injured people can be saved from underneath their collapsed buildings if one acts quickly. So within about one hour, we need to generate estimates of how bad and where an earthquake struck. Computers can immediately pick out the epicenter within a mile or so, as long as three or more seismographs detect the signals. If the quake is in the middle of the ocean, it is more difficult. If only one seismograph picks up the quake, all you have is a direction and a distance. You need three stations to create a "triangle of error," which is relatively large if the seismographs are at great distances. To make these calculations, we also need to know the population numbers and the quality of buildings everywhere in the world. This data bank is enormous, and not very detailed for many parts of the world. We need to improve the data bank to generate more reliable loss estimates for hypothetical future earthquakes and to rescue people in real time after earthquakes.

Q. *Explain the benefit of building inventory from satellite images.*

A. We have collected satellite images for 700 cities in earthquake-prone areas. On these images, we can see items as small as a bicycle. From the side view and the shadow of buildings, we can calculate their heights. In this way, we can count how many buildings in a city have 1, 5, 10, and 30 stories. This allows us to roughly classify the buildings by resistance to earthquake shaking. Together with some simple information on the building styles, generated by an engineer on the ground, we then can construct a pretty good inventory of building stock, in any city on the planet.

Q. *Explain why seismic risk analysis using QUAKELOSS is important. Why is it key to estimate losses that have to be expected in potential future quakes in the Himalayas and in the United Arab Emirates?*

A. QUAKELOSS has been calibrated to give the correct results of fatalities for about 1,000 earthquakes of the past that killed people. I have tested it using about 500 earthquakes of the past and about 100 in real time. So we know that QUAKELOSS gives approximately correct results for the seismically strongly active regions of the world. QUAKELOSS is the only program that can do this, at present and for the whole world. With our calculations, we offer a quantitative estimate of future losses, although approximate. We think our estimates are only accurate to an order of magnitude, that is, to a factor of 10.

Officials who could allocate the money necessary to reduce the earthquake risk usually don't listen to our warnings. The more quantitative these warnings are, the more likely that perhaps someone will follow our advice.

At a UNESCO [United Nations Educational, Scientific and Cultural Organization] conference in Paris in June 2001, we suggested that the Indian Ocean be instrumented with devices that measure tsunami and storm waves, so that people could be warned. According to our plan, the entire region affected by December 2004's killer tsunami would have been instrumented, and people would have been warned. Nobody came up with the money to implement that plan. Sadly, tens of thousands of lives could have been saved. Imagine that.

Q. *What can we do as citizens to help countries worldwide to be prepared, not scared?*

A. Good question; I wish I knew a good answer. For a wealthy citizen, a foundation, or a corporation, it is simple to help: Make a donation to us or another nonprofit organization with the expertise to reduce earthquake risk. We can work out, together with the donor, a specific plan, targeted at a certain problem, at a certain region to save lives in future earthquakes. Then we would sign a contract with the donor to achieve the targets set in return for the funds donated (*www.wapmerr.org/projects.html*).

Getting Prepared

After the Loma Prieta quake, like countless people, my friends and I got prepared for future aftershocks. But some people—like Berkland, who is a down-to-earth nature boy—are always ready for a natural disaster. "As to preparedness," he tells me, "I always have had camping equipment, Coleman lanterns and stoves, extra flashlights and batteries, multiple portable radios and a portable TV, first aid kits, water bottles, plenty of extra food, and always discussed disasters with the family. In preparing for Y2K, I also bought a 5,000-watt Honda generator."

While there are ever-ready survivalists in the world, sometimes it takes the big one or an impending Y2K disaster to get it all together. For example, before Y2K, I went overboard and went into mega survival mode. I stocked the pantry; withdrew cash from my bank account; got extra pet supplies, wood, and bottled water; and even upgraded my computer. (It crashed because the computer tech was working overtime, was sleep-deprived, and installed the wrong part.) The motto: It's more practical and easier to be prepared all of the time, rather than get it all together in a mad frenzy during a potential disaster.

In other words, as Berkland puts it, "strive for a steady state in earthquake preparedness, not hit or miss."

10 Emergency Supplies You Need

Yes, now is a good time to put together emergency supplies. So what do you need? Here is a list of the must-have bare essentials:

- Fire extinguisher

- Adequate supplies of medications that you or family members are taking

- Crescent and pipe wrenches to turn off gas and water supplies

- First-aid kit and handbook

- Flashlights with extra bulbs and batteries

- Portable radio with extra batteries

- Water for each family member for at least three days (allow at least one gallon per person per day) and purification tablets or chlorine bleach to purify drinking water from other sources

- Canned and packaged foods, enough for several days, and mechanical can opener; extra food for pets if necessary

- Camp stove or barbecue grill to cook on outdoors (store fuel out of the reach of children)

- Waterproof, heavy-duty plastic bags for waste disposal

For more information, contact *www.earthshakes.com*. Earth Shakes offers a full line of earthquake survival kits and emergency supplies for disaster preparedness.

Get Prepared for Your Pets

No matter how smart and intuitive your pets are, they can only protect themselves so far, according to experts for disaster services of The Humane Society of the United States (HSUS). So plan ahead. Here are some pet-friendly tips:

- If you evacuate, don't leave your pet behind.

- Pets should wear a collar and up-to-date I.D. tag at all times.

- Have a backup plan in case you aren't home when disaster hits. Contact friends and family members now to ask if they would be willing to get your pet and meet you at a prearranged place.

- Find out where you can go with your pet or board your pet for temporary housing. Most emergency shelters won't allow pets.

- Pack a disaster kit for your pet that includes food and water, bowls, leashes, carriers, a list of phone numbers, vaccination records, required medications, cat litter, and a cat box.

5 Steps to Planning Ahead for a Quake

- Make sure each member of your family knows what to do no matter where they are when earthquakes strike:

  - Establish a meeting place where you can all reunite afterward. Have a distant contact person to phone as a clearinghouse. It's easier to call out of a disaster area than into it.

  - Find out about earthquake plans developed by children's school or day care.

  - Remember, transportation may be disrupted; keep some emergency supplies—food, liquids, and comfortable shoes, for example—at work.

- Know where your gas, electric, and water main shutoffs are and how to turn them off if there is a leak or electrical short. Make sure older members of the family can shut off utilities.

- Locate your nearest fire and police stations and emergency medical facility.

- Talk to your neighbors—how could they help you, or you them after an earthquake.

- Take a Red Cross first-aid and CPR (cardiopulmonary resuscitation) training course.

Must-Do's Before an Earthquake Strikes

So what can you do to help minimize damage before an earthquake occurs? Take a look at these safety tips, gleaned from the Washington State Office of the Insurance Commissioner, and the American Red Cross:

Before

- Be sure that water heaters, gas appliances, and other such fixtures are fastened securely.

- Ensure that bookcases, wall hangings, and hanging plants are secured and fastened.

- Make sure that you have a family emergency plan and that all family members know what they should do in case of an emergency. Designate a meeting place outside the home where family members can gather once the danger has passed.

- Designate a distant relative or friend who can serve as a point of contact where you and family members can coordinate and communicate if you're separated.

- Plan ahead. Keep flashlights, batteries, and candles on hand. Make sure you have a portable radio.

- When shopping for earthquake insurance, ask the company to help you identify possible repairs and other improvements that will make your home safer and minimize damage.

- All members should know how to turn off utilities (electricity, water, and gas) at the home.

During

- If an earthquake occurs, be alert for breakable items that might be shaken and knocked down, especially glass items. Broken glass on the floor accounts for many of the injuries suffered in the aftermath of an earthquake, and glass-filled carpet is hazardous long after the danger posed by the quake has passed.

- If you're inside when an earthquake hits, stay inside and get under a heavy table or desk. Stay away from windows. Don't evacuate the building unless directed to do so by emergency personnel.

- Get out of the kitchen, which is a dangerous place (things can fall on you).

- Don't run downstairs or rush outside while the building is shaking or while there is a danger of falling and hurting yourself or being hit by falling glass or debris.

- If you're outside, get away from buildings and power lines, and remember that stone and masonry facings can break loose and fall away from upper stories of buildings.

- If you're in a car, stop safely away from structures, large trees, power lines, and other hazards. Stay inside the vehicle.

- Don't stop on or under a bridge or overpass, light posts, or large signs.

- When you begin driving, watch for breaks in pavement, fallen rocks, and bumps in the road at bridge approaches.

- If you're in the mountains, watch out for falling rock, landslides, trees, and other debris that could be loosened by quakes.

- Don't use candles until gas lines are checked. Also, check all areas of your home before using, including sewage connections, and especially utilities.

- Don't tie up phone lines except to report emergencies.

- Be prepared. Remember that you'll need food and water, even for the short term. Keep your family together and stay alert for after-shocks.

After

- Check yourself for injuries.

- Protect yourself from further danger by putting on long pants, a long-sleeved shirt, sturdy shoes, and work gloves.

- After you have taken care of yourself, help injured or trapped persons.

- If a person is bleeding, put direct pressure on the wound; use clean gauze or cloth if available.

- ◆ If a person isn't breathing, administer CPR.

- ◆ Don't attempt to move seriously injured persons unless they're in further danger of injury.

- ◆ Cover injured persons with blankets to keep them warm. Seek medical help for serious injuries.

- Check for life-threatening hazards.

  - ◆ Fire hazards—put out fires in your home or neighborhood immediately; call for help.

  - ◆ Gas leaks—shut off main gas valve only if you suspect a leak because of broken pipes or odor.

  - ◆ Damaged electrical wiring—shut off power at the control box if there is any danger to house wiring.

  - ◆ Downed or damaged utility lines—don't touch downed power lines or any objects in contact with them.

  - ◆ Spills—clean up any spilled medicines, drugs, or other harmful materials such as bleach, lye, or gas.

  - ◆ Don't use a damaged chimney (it could start a fire or let poisonous gases into your house).

  - ◆ Fallen items—beware of items tumbling off shelves when you open the doors of closets and cupboards.

- Check food and water supplies.

  - ◆ Don't eat or drink anything from open containers near shattered glass.

  - ◆ If power is off, plan meals to use up foods that will spoil quickly or frozen foods (food in the freezer should be good for at least a couple of days).

  - ◆ Don't light your kitchen stove if you suspect a gas leak.

  - ◆ Use BBQ or camp stoves, outdoors only, for emergency cooking.

- If your water is off, you can drink from water heaters, melted ice cubes, or canned vegetables.

- Avoid drinking water from swimming pools or especially spas—it may have too many chemicals to be safe.

The Upside and Downside of Earthquake Insurance

A few days before the August 6, 1979, earthquake, Berkland purchased earthquake insurance, getting ready for his August 7–15 seismic window. He also encouraged others to do the same during many of his talks to schools, service clubs and churches, the Red Cross, and emergency personnel.

"The August 6 Coyote Lake quake shook much of Central California, but our home was undamaged by the 5.9 event. I let the insurance drop when the rates were increased about 300 percent in 1983, and I have never been tempted to seek new coverage," says Berkland.

The fact remains, insurance rates were reasonable before the Coalinga quake of 1983 and the Loma Prieta quake of 1989. "By the time of the 1994 Northridge quake, many insurance companies had deserted the state of California. Those that remained raised the deductibles from 5 to 15 percent, and decreased the coverage. From 1910 to 1984, insurance companies were counting on earthquake insurance to add billions to their income. Suddenly, they were paying out more than they were receiving, and that wasn't acceptable," explains Berkland, who knows the pros and cons of buying earthquake insurance.

As a geologist, he knows that the type of bedrock, the depth of soil, the magnitude and distance of the earthquake, and the quality of construction all affect the intensity of damage from earthquakes, and should be considered before investing in earthquake insurance. Berkland suggests that it might be a good idea for people to self-insure by investing regularly into a fund reserved for natural disasters.

Should You Buy Earthquake Insurance?

Earthquake insurance isn't just a California deal. "When the Puget Sound area experienced a significant earthquake in early 2001, many homeowners and tenants learned a painful lesson—standard home-owner and tenant insurance policies do not cover losses that result from earth movement," explains Washington Insurance Commissioner Mike Kreidler.

Still not sure if you're a good candidate for earthquake insurance? "There isn't one answer for everyone, but for most people their home is their major asset. Protecting it just makes good sense," says Kreidler. Here are five facts, straight from Kreidler, to help you make your decision.

- It covers landslides, not floods. Beware. An earthquake endorse-ment generally excludes damages or losses from floods and tidal waves—even when they are compounded by an earthquake. However, loss caused by a landslide, settlement, mud flow, and the rising, sinking, and contracting of earth may be covered if the dam-age resulted from the quake.

- It covers major losses. It's sold with deductibles equaling 10 to 25 percent of the structure's policy limit. The limit works like the deductibles on your auto insurance. The result: The insurance pays only for damages that exceed the deductible. But note that, unlike car insurance, some earthquake policies treat contents and struc-ture separately.

- Relax, your car is covered by auto insurance. If your vehicle is dam-aged in an earthquake and you have comprehensive coverage, the loss would be covered under your auto insurance policy.

- You've gotta qualify. Some insurers may require an inspection of your property before they'll issue a policy. For instance, many com-panies require that your home be bolted to its foundation. This wasn't required by building codes until the early 1960s.

- It's not available after a shaker. Surprise. When a significant earth-quake hits an area, insurers in the earthquake market will declare a moratorium on new sales. This suspension of sales may last until the threat of aftershocks has passed.

Coping with It All

As you've read in the previous chapters, quake survivors often must cope with symptoms such as sleeplessness, depression, loss, anxiety, and flashbacks. As a self-professed earthquake sensitive and an excitable person, I can tell you that I had these symptoms after experiencing the Loma Prieta earthquake. Not only did I not sleep well for days (I slept in the living room with the lights on, completely dressed, shoes on the floor next to the dog leash), but I also had grueling flashbacks of the mainshock. And this is a scenario of post-traumatic stress disorder (PTSD); it's what war veterans and rape survivors deal with after the real-life nightmare happens.

"The severity of the PTSD and number of symptoms one experiences vary depending on your background, your personality, and the nature of the trauma. While some will experience more and some fewer symptoms, it makes no difference how strong or capable you think you are: If you are traumatized, you will experience at least some symptoms," notes *Anxiety, Phobias & Panic* author and therapist Reneau Z. Peurifoy. "Keep in mind that you do not have to experience the trauma directly to experience PTSD symptoms. Witnessing a trauma, or working or living with someone who has been traumatized, also triggers symptoms."

For instance, remember Rick Von Feldt, the tourist who experienced the tsunami at Phuket Beach, Thailand? As a keen observer of the natural disaster and a survivor, he wrote these words: "These days, I ask myself, 'Rick, why are you even writing about this? You didn't really suffer. You saw the whole thing. You felt the emotion. You listened. And sure, you were scared—but for you, life goes on.' For me, writing is a way of telling what is flashing in my mind. It is like the debris that is washed up on the beach. As I try to go about my days here in Singapore, a new thought will 'wash up' in my mind. It will lie on my beach until I pick it up and do something with it. And so the writing helps me to record it—wrap it up—and lay it away with the rest. And each morning, when I awake, there are so many little things that I am reminded of. Things that were small items in the moment, but like the bodies that wash up on the beach, they lie there, waiting to be taken away."

If you or someone you know experiences PTSD after an earthquake or related event (i.e., fire or tsunami), Peurifoy recommends using these statements to help you cope:

- I am a normal person who has been in an abnormal situation.

- Sometimes my mind takes snapshots of the disaster to try to make sense out of something that is actually senseless.

- The disaster is over. It's in the past.

- I'm safe now.

Now that you've got disaster preparedness strategies down, it's time to bring in earthquake projections for the future in Chapter 20, "Future Shocks, Wow!"

EARTHSHAKING FACTS
TO DOG-EAR

~ You can reduce earthquake risk by learning what to do when an earthquake hits and how to make your home more earthquake safe. Increased earthquake safety also can be achieved by strengthening existing buildings, and by building new buildings according to building codes.

~ Get earthquake-ready by putting together emergency supplies, getting prepared for your pets, and developing a solid family emergency game plan in case an earthquake strikes.

~ To help minimize damage to you and your home, learn what to do before, during, and after an earthquake occurs.

~ Consider earthquake insurance or self-insure by investing regularly into a fund reserved for natural disasters.

~ If you or someone you know is experiencing post-traumatic stress disorder, you can cope with it all. But note, PTSD can affect both people who experience the earthquake directly and those who have been traumatized by the effects of a quake even though they weren't "in" it.

~ Remember that earthquakes will occur whether or not they're predicted. If you're fatalistic about earthquake preparedness, it may prove fatal.

20 –ᴧᴧᴧ– Future Shocks, Wow!

The hardest thing to predict is the future, but I'm working on it.

—Jim Berkland

MOST LIKELY, NEITHER YOU NOR I WANT TO WAIT 20 YEARS TO FIND OUT WHAT'S IN store for our earth's changes, so I went to our nation's earthquake experts (and visionaries) and asked the question: What changes do you see for our earth in the next 20 years? Here's what they said.

USGS's Long-Term Forecasts

- USGS scientists conclude that there is a 70 percent probability of at least one magnitude 6.7 or greater quake, capable of causing wide-spread damage, striking the San Francisco Bay region before 2030.

- USGS scientists determined that there's a 30 percent chance of one or more magnitude 6.7 or greater quakes occurring somewhere on the Calaveras, Concord–Green Valley, Mount Diablo thrust, and Greenville faults before 2030.

- New data have allowed USGS scientists to calculate the first earthquake probabilities for the San Gregorio fault and to better estimate probabilities for the San Andreas fault. Combined, these two faults have a 25 percent chance of producing one or more magnitude 6.7 or greater quakes in these coastal areas before 2030.

- USGS scientists found that, of all the faults in the Bay region, the San Andreas, the Hayward–Rodgers Creek, and the Calaveras faults pose the greatest threat because they have high quake odds and run through the region's urban core. In fact, they believe the real threat to the San Francisco Bay region over the next 30 years comes not from a 1906-type earthquake, but from smaller (magnitude

about 7) earthquakes happening on the Hayward fault, the peninsula segment of the San Andreas fault, or the Rodgers Creek fault.

The Berkland Brief: "If you divide all known active faults into seg-
ments of potential activity, most earthquakes that occur over the next
30 years can be claimed to be expected, and some people will praise
the results as some great scientific achievement. Keep in mind that a
30 percent confidence that something will happen, means that the
dominant emphasis (70 percent) is that nothing will happen. The USGS
scientists did just that regarding the Loma Prieta segment of the San
Andreas fault. When the World Series quake occurred on October 17,
1989, the 70 percent forecast that it would NOT occur by 2030 was
wrong."

Prophet Nostradamus's Forecast

Welcome to the world of a renowned prophet of yesteryear, Michel
de Nostradamus, who still intrigues people today with what some see
as his astounding ability to foresee the future. Born in 1503 at St. Remy
in Provence, France, this man created mysterious forecasts in the form
of four-line poems, or quatrains. According to Victor Baines—director
of The Nostradamus Society of America, and author of *Remember the
Future: The Prophecies of Nostradamus*—the prophet made several references to earth changes. You only need to go to the specific quatrains
to see for yourself exactly what could take place around the globe
today or tomorrow.

Baines explains, for example, that in quatrain 2-65[3], "The sloping
park" could suggest shifting ground. The words "great calamity" might
refer to earthquakes through l'Hesperie (the "Lands of the West"—the
New World) and Lombardy, a region of northern Italy. Baines also notes
that "Mercury in Sagittarius, Saturn fading" is an astrological position
that will occur on November 25, 2015, then on November 23, 2016,

---

3. The sloping park great calamity
To be done through Hesperia and Insubria:
The fire in the ship, plague and captivity,
Mercury in Sagittarius Saturn will fade.

and again on December 7, 2044. "Could 2015 or 2016 be years that major earthquakes strike the New World and Italy? If the United States was one of the regions intended in this quatrain, it should be noted that according to the forecast of many geologists, a major earthquake could strike the San Francisco Bay Area at any time. An even greater danger exists in the New Madrid fault line located in the central region of the United States," says Baines.

In another quatrain, 9-83[4], words suggest an earthquake may occur between April 21 and May 21, but the year is not pinpointed. Baines cites Nostradamus's words and decodes them:

"The Sun in 20 degrees of Taurus" suggests May 10, the 20th day of the sun sign of Taurus. "A mighty trembling of the earth" could be a mighty earthquake, polar shift, or natural disaster. "The great theater filled up will be ruined" is perhaps a reference to mass gatherings of people who will witness and be involved in this event, or remotely it may be a reference to Hollywood, California—the location of film studios for "the great theaters"—which is located on a major fault line. Or, "the great theater" may be an allusion to the old Roman theaters in Rome, or perhaps a reference to a military theater. This event, possibly the eruption of volcanoes combined with earthquakes, "darkens and troubles the air and sky and land." Could nuclear blasts be a remote possibility here? But, the fact remains, Nostradamus doesn't provide specific clues as to the exact geographical area such a disaster will occur.

The Berkland Brief: Give me a break. Or perhaps I should say, give me an earthquake from a Nostradamus quatrain *before* the quake. Somehow, the "New City" destined for destruction was supposed to be

---

4. Sun twentieth of Taurus the earth will tremble very mightily,
It will ruin the great theater filled:
To darken and trouble air, sky and land,
Then the infidel will call upon God and saints.

Los Angeles, despite the fact that Naples, which existed at the time of Nostradamus, means "New City." Many bright people have made careers out of interpreting and re-interpreting Nosty. I think it is time to let him rest in peace.

Clarisa Bernhardt's Visions for Tomorrow

Ever wonder how visions come to the gifted (or "cursed")? Bernhardt's visions strike her at many different times—she could be awakening from slumber or walking down a street. "I never know when a 'cosmic bulletin' on a forthcoming event is going to arrive. I compare it to a sort of high frequency instant message from a divine source," she says. Take a look at some of her messages for your future.

United States

* West Coast—California is a little bit safer now than it was, because of the fact of all the little quakes (even though they're rattling everybody around). It's healthy, from my point of view. It's relieving some of the pressure. Yes, there could be changes. I've always said changes would not be something dramatic, but it would be because of the result of these minor ones.

  Now for Lake Tahoe, there's something about some volcano activity that could start. The southeast part of the lake, they might feel something—something about landfill. They might get some more settling than they want. It could happen by 2008 to 2010.

* The North—I was shown potential quake activity on a now quiet fault line that extends north and south through South Dakota. There could be a disruption. There's going to be a lot of earthquakes in places that haven't ordinarily had them before. I don't have a specific time line. If it is going to happen it could be by 2015.

* Midwest—I have felt a difference in the energies in the New Madrid region. I thought it was settled down a bit. But it seems like they have a tendency to have quakes toward Tennessee and then up above to the east and west of Louisville and a little to the north. So those are

the areas that still basically seem to be the sensitive areas.

- East Coast—In the Carolinas, there are some earthquake faults. I understand there are a lot of little quakes there all of the time. So, maybe because of those quakes it might relieve the pressure. I don't see a tsunami but it's not clear because I continue to see the hurricanes, water coming in. It's possible, but I keep seeing more hurricanes, so for that reason they overwhelm any tsunami.

Other Countries:

- South America—While I don't see the Pacific Northwest getting hit with a tsunami, I think it's going to be more toward South America. A great quake in Chile in 1960—yes, that could happen again anywhere from 2006 to 2020.

- Mexico—Had a glimpse of an earthquake fault in Mexico that is somewhat south of the pyramids. I have seen that a 6.5-to-7.0 quake will occur possibly before but more likely around 2012 or 2014. It seems to show a fault line area that will open up to show a long-lost city that will be of important archeological interest with some extremely interesting wall panels on a buried temple. There also will be a discovered entry to an area with a lost mine that will have minerals that will prove quite helpful for the Mexico economy.

- China and Japan—China will experience more and stronger quake activity with more 6.5 and 7.0 magnitudes. Japan unfortunately will also experience stronger seismic activity but basically the epicenters will be underwater. However, I do also see a bit of flooding on the northern coast of Japan, but I do not see the source of this.

The Berkland Brief: "I am convinced that she has psychic ability, as that has been demonstrated to me personally on several occasions. However, she deliberately avoids the scientific viewpoint, which might interfere with her innate impressions. Sometimes, her visions are of an impossible situation, such as a motorist being able to drive to Hawaii. Even millions of years won't help that commute, as the islands are moving away from the West Coast. Thus, care is necessary with interpretation of Clarisa's predictions, just as with USGS forecasts."

Jim Berkland's Seismic Circle

Unlike the USGS, Berkland doesn't do long-term forecasts. As a geologist, he prefers to make short-term predictions based on Mother Earth, not visions. "Prediction is to say something will happen before it does. Forecasting is like casting the dice and hoping to avoid snake eyes," he explains. "To me, a prediction is more timely, more honest, and more useful. Also, we don't need to wait 22 years or 30 years before we are motivated to make preparations."

Berkland is quick to point out that he isn't a prophet or a seer. But while his seismic windows do apply worldwide (remember, the Alaska earthquake of 1964, the Sumatra earthquake of December 2004, and the northern Sumatra, Indonesia, quake on March 28, 2005), he does provide monthly earthquake predictions in his seismic circle. To summarize, take a look at Berkland's earthquake targets.

Santa Clara County, where my hometown is located, is where Berkland began predicting earthquakes on January 8, 1974, since he was most interested in quakes in his county. So, for the first five years, he predicted quakes that would be felt in Santa Clara County. He explains, "It was suggested that my area of concern (my seismic circle) would be 70 miles from the approximate center of Santa Clara County (37.15 N; 121.75 W). The circle would just circumscribe the county, and any epicenter within that circle would meet the criterion, whether or not it was felt."

Here are the four areas he targets each and every month and publicizes in his newsletter and website:

- Mount Diablo: From 1970 to 1997, Santa Clara County was his local scoring area. Then, when Berkland relocated to Glen Ellen, California, about 100 miles north of Santa Clara County, "in order to share in my own predictions, and still include the old area," he extended his radius to 140 miles from Mount Diablo (peak at 37.9 N; 121.9 W).

- Southern California: He began predicting for Southern California around 1980. His predicted area was usually within 70 miles of Los Angeles (the county line). By 1990, he revised the L.A. region to within 140 miles of Los Angeles City Hall (34 N; 118 W), making it easier to evaluate the results of his predictions for the area.

- Washington-Oregon: Berkland didn't start predictions for the Pacific Northwest until January 22, 1995, when he made an earthquake prediction for the Seattle area. On January 28, 1995, Seattle was hit by the strongest quake since 1965, says Berkland. Within a week, he had received more than 2,000 requests for his newsletter. That's when he began to add the Northwest as one of his four regular areas involved in monthly predictions.

- Pacific Ring of Fire: Berkland also predicts quakes globally of 7.0-plus. He suggests that these earthquakes will most likely occur around the Pacific Ring of Fire, where 80 percent of the world's strongest quakes hit.

Berkland rarely makes predictions for other than the San Francisco Bay Area, Southern California, Washington/Oregon, and the Ring of Fire. But if there's good evidence, he'll do it. He did just that for the 7.8 quake that struck western Turkey just after the total solar eclipse passed over those countries on August 11, 1999.

So, while Berkland sticks to his monthly predictions for four regions, he does provide a look at the immediate and beyond the year 2020:

- China and Japan—The country comes right down into the mountain building areas that are close to Tibet. In the coastal part of China, there are some active faults that gave us Haicheng in 1975. And Taiwan gets a 7.0 magnitude quake almost every year. Japan is the number one country for large earthquakes, and New Zealand isn't far behind. Three plates are right underneath the Japanese islands, even the North American plate. So they're vulnerable always. They've been predicting a great Tokyo quake for the last 20 years. And it hasn't happened yet. They could have another great quake anytime because they have a section of a fault out there that hasn't moved since September 1, 1923, when more than 150,000 people died in a horrendous earthquake and resulting firestorm. (The quake occurred on day six of the August 26 to September 1 seismic window.)

- Europe—Italy, Greece, and Turkey are the most logical countries to have future earthquakes because that's where they've happened before—and they're closest to the plate boundary. Because history repeats itself, we need only review disastrous quakes in Naples, Avezzano, Messina, Salonika, Bucharest, Izmit, etc. Some strong seismic activity should be expected in the Mediterranean area within the next decade.

Yes, You Can Predict a Quake

Last, but certainly not least, it's a good idea for people from the California coast, New Madrid, Missouri, to Phuket Beach to learn how to use Jim Berkland's user-friendly do-it-yourself earthquake theories and put them to work. As Berkland says, "The lunar phases give maximum tides, which give maximum periods of vulnerability to quakes. Abnormal animal behavior, geyser and spring activity, magnetic aberrations, seismic patterns, etc., provide confirmatory data for 'where' and 'how big?'"

Like Berkland, you can predict an oncoming quake yourself. And today, there are countless amateur earthquake predictors who do get hits. In "Berklandese," that means monitor the lunar phases (get a calendar) and tidal flow (purchase an annual tide table), tune into your pets, and tally the lost cats and dogs in your local newspaper.

So what will you do next time Felix starts acting strangely or you notice significant earth changes? Will you roll your eyes, or get prepared? Is it really so far-fetched to monitor lost cats and dogs and pay attention to the tides? Berkland doesn't think so. Berkland hopes that "someday earthquake warnings will be announced along with the weather" and could save countless people's lives around the world. Jim Berkland, maverick geologist and the man who predicts earthquakes, believes Mother Earth's past and present quake warnings are sending us a message. Are you listening?

EARTHSHAKING FACTS TO DOG-EAR

- If you're looking for long-term San Francisco Bay Area forecasts, the USGS gives you the lowdown for the next 30 years.

- Do consider but remain skeptical about the prophet Nostradamus's vague worldwide projections.

- Pay attention to visionary Clarisa Bernhardt's earthquake predictions.

- Jot down on your calendar each month geologist Jim Berkland's seismic windows for the San Francisco Bay Area, Los Angeles, the Pacific Northwest, and the Pacific Ring of Fire.

- Remember, quake warnings can and do save possessions and lives. There isn't any reason to panic, any more than when you are reacting to a hurricane or tornado warning.

Aftershocks

ARE YOU SURPRISED BY THE FAR-OUT QUAKE WARNINGS THAT JIM BERKLAND AND other people in this book use for themselves? While mainstream scientists don't like the "P" word, people are predicting earthquakes every day. And often their predictions come true.

More and more people are turning to Mother Nature's clues and have monitored earth changes in their everyday world. These inspirational men and women who face the potential of earthquakes, like you and me, dare to be different. They follow their hearts and sixth sense, and use nature as their friendly guide, not their enemy.

Back in 1986, I wrote about earthquakes and sensitive pets in California. After writing this book, I realize that earthquake prediction is much bigger than I had ever imagined. It's in the works around the world. And most important, Berkland's seismic windows, strange animal behavior, tidal flows, and lunar phases are being talked about.

I focused more on four catastrophes: The 1906 great San Francisco earthquake, the 1964 great Alaska earthquake, the 1989 Loma Prieta earthquake, and the 2004 Indian Ocean earthquake-tsunami. It's not that I believe these disasters were more important than other earthquakes in the world. To me, these are the events that have made a big impact on my mind and spirit—and I will never forget them. But writing this book has helped me to get a handle on the exciting world of earthquake prediction, and how I, and you, can be prepared for the next big one.

As time goes on, I predict that Berkland will work hard to demystify earthquakes for the public. It's his calling. "The experts of high science state that earthquake prediction is currently a scientific impossibility. I maintain that the topic is too important to leave to the experts, and I continue to do the impossible with a better than 75 percent batting average, which is more than 300 percent greater than chance," concludes Berkland, who is making a difference in the world.

Berkland's Glossary

Active fault. A fault that will probably have another earthquake some-time in the future. Certainly the San Andreas and Hayward faults are active as they have had movement along them in the past 10,000 years. About half of the damaging quakes in California have been on faults not previously known to be active.

Aftershock. A quake that follows a mainshock closely in time and space. If it's stronger than the initial quake, then it becomes the main-shock, which is then reduced to the status of a foreshock. Commonly, the strongest aftershock measures within 1.0 of the mainshock, and occurs on the same fault system within about 30 miles of the main-shock. Just when an aftershock series ends is controversial, but larger quakes are usually followed by longer intervals of aftershocks. Quakes that start more than 20 miles deep tend to have fewer and smaller aftershocks.

Amplitude. The difference between the high and low wave drawn on a seismogram, which records the ground shaking. It's the critical factor for determining Richter magnitude, where it's the maximum length in millimeters between the highest peak and the lowest valley.

Apogee. The farthest point in the Moon's monthly orbit. It usually occurs in the secondary seismic window, with lower tides than in a primary window.

Blue Moon. A so-called blue moon is nothing more than the second full moon of a month. Only February can never have one, even in leap year, because it takes 29.5 days for a full lunar cycle, and February comes up short. All the other months can have a rare blue moon, but naturally a 31-day month has an advantage.

Body wave. This isn't how much the human body vibrates during a quake, but refers to definitions of P-wave or S-waves. These seismic waves can pass through the deep earth; however, the P-wave is slowed by the liquid core and the S-wave can't travel through liquids at all.

Continental drift. A term coined by German meteorologist Alfred Wegener between 1912 and 1915 for a process that he visualized to be a slow movement of a continental crust over mantle rocks to explain the jigsaw appearance of South America and Africa and other land-masses, as well as explaining the separation of matching rock forma-tions, mineral deposits, and fossils. The concept was ridiculed by most earth scientists as lacking a mechanism. However, by the 1960s, the theory was modified in many ways and is now known as the theory of plate tectonics, which has gained almost universal acceptance.

Depth. When applied to an earthquake, it refers to the original break (hypocenter) of a fault on a line between the epicenter on the surface of the earth and the center of the earth. If the depth of a shallow earth-quake isn't clearly determined, it's often assigned a default depth of 33 kilometers.

Earth tide. Like ocean tides, the solid earth tide also has two highs and two lows during a day but is detectable only through sophisticated instruments. The true earth tide shows amplitudes of up to three feet and can be measured only far inland from seacoasts because of distor-tions from ocean tides. But note, underground fluid pressure changes along fault lines from any kind of tidal loading have the potential to decrease frictional forces and stimulate fault movement and earthquakes.

Earthquake. Simply a shaking of the earth. (There are also moonquakes and marsquakes.) Earthquakes may occur tectonically (on faults), volcanically (from magma movement or eruptions), from extraterrestrial impacts by meteors or asteroids, from large explosions (such as nuclear tests), or even heavy-footed herds of cows. Modern seismographs can detect magnitudes of −3.

Earthquake sensitives. A term that refers to humans who have demonstrated an ability to detect precursors that signal an upcoming earthquake. This ability may take the form of dreams or visions, psychic impressions, or physiological symptoms (i.e., agitation, ear tones, headaches, etc.). Most sensitives are reluctant to discuss these symptoms publicly because of the common negative reaction by others, who ridicule the concept.

Echo quake. Sometimes strong quakes seem to rebound from one fault to another after the passage of several years. In the San Francisco Bay Area, historic examples are found between West Bay and East Bay faults, such as the pairs of echo quakes that occurred in the following years: 1836 to 1838, 1865 to 1868, 1890 to 1892, 1898 to 1906, 1906 to 1911, 1955 to 1957, 1979 to 1980, 1980 to 1984, and 1984 to 1989.

El Niño. An effect in the eastern Pacific in which oceanic currents change periodically and affect the weather of the Pacific Basin. The term was coined by Peruvian fishermen who noted the upwelling of deep cold waters and better fishing around Christmastime (like a present from the Christ child, or "el niño").

Epicenter. The point on the earth's surface intersected by an imaginary line from the center of the earth through a focal point, where an earthquake originates at depth. With a vertical fault, the epicenter is directly over the focus.

Extremely low frequency. The radio spectrum is divided into many categories depending upon the frequency of the waves. At the low end is extremely low frequency (ELF) of 3 to 30 hertz (Hz, vibrations per second). Next comes super low frequency (SLF) of 30 to 300 Hz. Then comes ultralow frequency (ULF) of 300 to 3,000 Hz. These electromagnetic waves are emitted from stress on the earth, and are detectable by special equipment, and apparently by animals.

Fault line. Faults are sudden breaks in rock and soil along which differential motion has occurred. With up and down faulting (normal, reverse, thrust, and transverse), there's usually a visible fault scarp or ridge. With sideways movement (strike-slip), there's usually a fault trough, marked by sag ponds, or offset roads or buildings. Some active faults don't reach the ground surface and have no surface expression such as a fault line. These buried faults are identified by patterns of epicenters, boreholes, geological mapping, or geophysical methods.

Full moon syzygy. The term *syzygy* is from the Greek *zygos*, meaning yoked together like a team of oxen. Twice a month, with every new and full moon, the Sun, Earth, and Moon are aligned, creating maximum spring tides. With every full moon, the Sun and Moon are on opposite sides of Earth, with the Moon rising as the Sun sets. If the alignment is perfect, there is a lunar eclipse. Two weeks later, the Moon rises and sets with the Sun, and we have a new moon. If the alignment is perfect, there is a solar eclipse. Only two to seven times per year does syzygy produce an eclipse.

Geology. *Geo* equals earth; *logos* equals "science of."

Geyser gaps. A fumarole erupts continuously with steam and water and thus has no gaps between eruptions. A geyser is a jet of hot water and steam that erupts periodically. Some geysers, like the Old Faithful of Yellowstone or Calistoga, California, have a fairly predictable pattern of eruption, with the time intervals informally called gaps or intervals.

Gone gatos. *Gatos* in Spanish means "cats," some of whom flee their homes prior to perceived danger. A small percentage of missing cats appear in newspaper classified sections. When the number of ads increases dramatically, it often signals an upcoming earthquake. Gone gatos is an essential part of the "Three Double-G" method of predicting earthquakes, as reported humorously in *Rolling Stone*. It refers to gravity gradients (from maximum tides), geyser gaps, and gone gatos (from anomalous numbers of missing pets).When all of these measurements increase dramatically, a quake is indicated.

Lat, latitude. The latitude is the number of degrees north (N) or south (S) of the equator and varies from zero at the equator to 90 at the poles.

Liquefaction. A term that means when saturated sandy or silty soil is shaken, it behaves like quicksand. Heavy objects (like buildings) sink; buried light objects (like gasoline tanks) will rise. The ground is typically fissured, and miniature "volcanoes" of sand can dot the landscape and continue to form for hours after a strong earthquake. And note, soils more than 40 feet deep are usually too compressed to liquefy, so buildings on deep piers can resist damage from liquefaction.

Lon, longitude. The epicenter is given by the latitude and longitude. The longitude is the number of degrees east (E) or west (W) of the prime meridian, which runs through Greenwich, England. The longitude varies from zero at Greenwich to 180, and the E or W shows the direction from Greenwich.

Magnitude. A term adopted in reverse from astronomy where a star magnitude of 1.0 is 10 times brighter than a star magnitude 2.0. Most humans can't see stars below magnitude 5.0 without artificial magnification. For earthquakes, people seldom feel a magnitude 2.0, but often recognize a magnitude 3.0 as a quake. The 3.0 makes a 10 times greater signature on a seismogram than does a 2M (see Richter scale). However, the energy released is about 32 times greater, so that a 2.2 has double the energy of a 2.0, etc. Many media people confuse magnitude with the felt intensity, which is usually based on the 12-level modified Mercalli scale (Roman numeral I to Roman numeral XII—total destruction). A great earthquake has a magnitude over 8.0; a major earthquake, a magnitude of 7.0–7.9; a strong earthquake, a magnitude of 6.0–6.9; a moderate earthquake, 5.0–5.9; a mild earthquake, 4.0–4.9; a minor earthquake, 3.0–3.9;. a very minor earthquake, 2.0–2.9; and a micro-earthquake, 1.9 down to –3.0 (possible to measure with newer instruments).

Mainshock. The largest earthquake in a sequence. It can be preceded by one or more foreshocks, and usually aftershocks will follow.

Modified Mercalli intensity scale. A scale based on what earthquakes do to people and things, and isn't directly dependent on the energy of the quake or proximity to an epicenter.

Moment Magnitude Scale (Mw). Now the most widely used measurement of earthquake energy. Unlike the Richter scale it considers the length and depth of fault movement, along with how rigid the rocks are. It is more accurate for large earthquakes.

Ocean tide. Ocean tides vary from a couple feet in mid-ocean to more than 50 feet in places like the Bay of Fundy. Each foot of seawater over each square mile amounts to a force of about one million tons per square mile, and the loading-unloading can affect the stability of faults. And note, any seaside observer can detect the six-hour change between low and high tide. The tides result from the 24-hour rotation of Earth beneath the bulges of water created by the gravitational pull of the Moon and the Sun, with the Moon's effect being 2.2 times that of the Sun.

Pacific Ring of Fire. An arc of earthquake and volcanic activity stretching from New Zealand, along the eastern edge of Asia, north across the Aleutian Islands of Alaska, and south along the coast of North and South America. The historic record shows that about 80 percent of the 6-plus quakes occur within the Ring of Fire. It's also been called the "Circle of Fire" to describe the pattern of volcanoes that encircle the Pacific Ocean. The volcanoes are now known to result from friction developed by movement of down-going slabs of oceanic crust and upper mantle as they slide beneath continental lithosphere, creating oceanic trenches and 80 percent of the world's largest earthquakes.

Perigee. A term that means the closest point of a satellite to Earth (*peri* equals near; *ge* equals Earth; compare with apogee, the far point). The perigee of the Moon can approach 221,428 miles from center to center. The tide-raising force varies with the cube of distance, which explains why moonquakes concentrate once a month at the time of the Earth-Moon perigee. It also explains why the Moon has 2.2 times the effect that the Sun has on terrestrial tides.

Perihelion. (*peri* equals near; *helios* equals sun) The closest point of a celestial body to the Sun. The Earth-Sun distance is at a minimum of about 91.5 million miles every year in early January. (Compare with aphelion, in early July, when Earth is 94.5 million miles from the Sun.)

Plate tectonics. A space age version of continental drift, the much ridiculed theory of geographer Alfred Wegener, who died in 1930 on the Greenland Ice Cap trying to prove that continents moved laterally, not just up and down. The plate tectonics theory matured in 1969, when scientists met to establish the phenomena of subduction, spreading ridges, thermal plumes, supercontinents, etc. This became known as the "revolution in earth sciences."

Postdiction. A term that means to report something after it happens.

Predict. (*pre* equals before; *dictio* equals word) This term means to report something before it happens. A meaningful earthquake prediction should contain four factors: A limited time window; a limited specified area (for rare major or great quakes in a much larger area may be acceptable); a significant or meaningful magnitude or range in magnitudes; and a high level of confidence.

P-wave. The primary seismic wave. It's the fastest one, and it travels like a sound impulse (compression; rarefaction, or push-pull).With a Slinky, push one end and watch the wave move to the other end. A P-wave can pass through liquids although much slower than it can through rock, where it averages about 3.5 miles per second. (See S-wave, the secondary seismic wave.)

Primary seismic window. The 8-day earthquake-prone period associated with the monthly highest tidal forces based on the alignment of the Sun-Moon-Earth (syzygy) and the monthly closest approach of the Moon (perigee). From two to five times per year, syzygy and perigee are on the same day, forming extreme perigean spring tides and especially clear seismic windows.

Q. The quality of the location. Two characters are used. Either a letter from A through D or a number from zero through four is used to show that the location quality goes from good to bad respectively. If the location was determined automatically, without review by a person, then this character is followed by an asterisk (*).

Richter scale. The measurement of seismic energy devised by Dr. Charles Richter of Caltech in 1935 for local quakes (ML). Essentially, it's the seismic size originally based on a standard Wood-Anderson seismograph at 100 kilometers from an epicenter. By measuring the maximum trace amplitude of wiggly lines on a seismograph, the wave action from earthquakes can be compared on a logarithmic scale, where a 5.0 quake produces an amplitude 10 times that of a 4.0 and 100 times that of a 3.0. This shouldn't be confused with the total energy of an earthquake, which is 1,000 times greater for a 5.0 than for a 3.0 event. Dr. Richter was often annoyed by people demanding to see his "scale," thinking that it was a mechanical device like a postal scale. There is no theoretical upper limit to the Richter scale, but the maximum recorded earthquake was 8.9ML. It's believed that the asteroid that ended the age of dinosaurs impacted the earth with a force equivalent to 15ML.

Secondary seismic window. The alternate eight-day period associated with the alignment of the Sun-Moon-Earth (syzygy) and the monthly farthest point in the Moon's orbit (apogee). The effect of this gravity transition point is similar to that found on the Moon, where moonquakes concentrate at the time of perigee, with a secondary flurry at the time of apogee.

S-wave. The slower seismic body wave, which moves like a sidewinder rattlesnake. It's a shear wave that is analogous to tying a rope to a post and shaking it sideways. Unlike a P-wave, it can't pass through a liquid, and thus can't pass through the liquid core of the earth. It travels through rock at about two miles per second. If an epicenter is 25 miles away, the S-wave arrives about five seconds after the P-wave. At a 50-mile distance, the time difference is about 10 seconds. It's similar to lightning and thunder. Note the arrival of the P-wave (like a truck hitting a house) and time the arrival of the S-wave (like on a boat in a choppy sea). If the epicenter is close, there's little difference in the arrival times.

Seiche. A wave set up in an enclosed body of water from a large earthquake. It's higher when the lake is deep, with a long axis parallel to the incoming seismic waves. The run-up from such a wave may be hundreds of yards. The body of water can be hundreds of miles from a large earthquake and still create a seiche (pronounced "saysh") of several feet.

Seismic window. A term I coined in 1974 to represent an eight-day period of extreme tidal changes, when earthquakes are most likely to occur, based upon my analysis of the timing of previous California quakes. It also applies to most other regions of the earth. The tidal forces determine the timing of the window, but the clarity may be affected by other factors. For example, the place, magnitude, and probability of the expected quake may be better fixed by unusual animal behavior, earthquake patterns, groundwater or geyser changes, and magnetic field changes.

Solar flares. Huge magnetic storms on the Sun that may create large eruptions of solar material (coronal mass ejections). If oriented toward Earth, they may create auroral effects far below polar latitudes, and create electric power failures and radio interference; they perhaps are responsible for some earthquakes through a process of magnetohydrodynamics.

Synchroneity. Hours between syzygy and perigee. When this number is less than 25 hours, it occurs only two to five times per year.

Syzygy. A word from the Greek *zygos* (yoked together like a team of oxen). It's an astronomical term that describes a conjunction of three bodies, such as the Sun, Moon, and Earth at the new moon stage, or the Sun, Earth, and Moon at the full moon stage. This cosmic tug-of-war is the major factor in raising ocean tides as well as solid earth tides, and is often considered as a triggering force for earthquakes. An eclipse is a near-perfect syzygy.

Tsunami. In Japanese, it literally means a "harbor wave." Sometimes called a "tidal wave," it's unrelated to tides. It requires a sudden movement on the sea floor, from an earthquake with a vertical component of fault movement, from a large sub-sea landslide, from an explosion of a volcanic island, or from an extraterrestrial impact. Significant tsunamis generally require the energy released along a fault to be a magnitude 7.5 or greater. A tsunami can travel 500 miles per hour in the deep sea, where it's only a few feet high. As it approaches coastlines, it can reach more than 100 feet high with a run-up of miles inland. Even a tsunami of 10 feet high can be highly destructive to life and property.

White noise. A steady background noise that provides a sound barrier, so that individual conversations can be conducted in relative privacy. It's like the background noise of a baseball game, or in a busy restaurant, where you can hardly hear someone talking next to you. For animals, the magnetic field may be analogous to a constant white noise. When it begins to fluctuate in some way, it may cause animals to become anxious, or even panicked. The magnetic field is known to vary prior to earthquakes.

Bibliography

ABC News Online, "Damaging Wave Hits Indonesian Island," March 29, 2005.

American Red Cross, "What to Do After an Earthquake: Talking About Disaster: Guide for Standard Messages." Produced by the National Disaster Education Coalition, Washington, D.C., 1999, *www.red-crosss.org/services/disaster.*

Baines, Victor, *Remember the Future: The Prophecies of Nostradamus*, Fort Worth, Texas: Holographic Books, 2005.

Bernhardt, Clarisa, "My Earthquake Predictions," *www.clarisabernhardt.com/quakes/predict.html.*

Brown, Jay, and David and Rebecca McClen Novick. *Mavericks of the Mind: Conversations for the New Millennium*, Freedom, California: The Crossing Press, 1993.

Brown, Jay, and David Brown, *Conversations on the Edge of the Apocalypse: Contemplating the Future with Noam Chomsky, George Carlin, Deepak Chopra, Rupert Sheldrake and Others*, New York: Palgrave Macmillan, 2005.

Bryson, Bill, A Short History of Nearly Everything, New York: Broadway, 2003.

Calico. "Earthquake Predictions by Calico: What I Have Learned," www.calicothepsychic.com/welcometocalico5.htm.

Chang, Kenneth, "Post-Tsunami Earthquakes Rumbled Around the Globe," The New York Times, May 24, 2005.

Gentry, Curt, Last Days of the Late, Great State of California, New York: Putnam and Sons, 1968.

Goodman, Jeffrey, We Are the Earthquake Generation, Ventura, California: Seaview, 1978.

Guerrero, L. Diana, Animal Disaster Preparedness for Pet Owners & Pet Professionals, Big Bear Lake, California: Diana Guerrero, 1996.

Hansen, Gladys, Emmet Condon, and David Fowler, Denial of Disaster: The Untold Story and Photographs of the San Francisco Earthquake and Fire of 1906, San Francisco, California: Cameron & Company, 1989.

Hsueh, Hungfu, "Lee to Stop Predicting Earthquakes," Taiwan News, November 17, 2004.

Ikeya, Motoji, Earthquakes and Animals: From Folk Legends to Science, Singapore: World Scientific Publishing Company, 2004.

Leake, Jonathan, "Geologist Gave Repeated Alerts," Times Online, January 2, 2005, www.timesonline.co.uk.

Lieber, Arnold L., The Lunar Effect: Biological Tides and Human Emotions, New York: Random House, 1976.

Live Science, "Deadliest Earthquakes in History," March 28, 2005, www.livescience.com/forcesofnature.

Joachim, Leland, "San Jose Geologist Is Suspicious: Was There a Cover-up of the 1906 Toll?" San Jose Mercury News, December 9, 1979.

Mason, Harry, "Sumatra Continuing Seismic Noise—Danger Continues," Rense.com, January 1, 2005, www.rense.com.

Mott, Maryann, National Geographic News, "Did Animals Sense Tsunami Was Coming?" January 4, 2005.

Nelson, Christina, "Future Looks Shaky: Large Temblors, Tsunami Could Occur in Region," Tahoe Daily Tribune, April 29–May 1, 2005, p. 1, 12.

Orey, Cal. PetFolio, "What Kitty Knows," October/November, 2004.

Orey, Cal. PetFolio, "Do Animals Have a Sixth Sense?" February/March, 2005.

Orey, Cal. PetFolio, "Want a Quake Warning? Ask Your Pet!" August/September 2005.

Orey, Cal, Doctors' Orders: What 101 Doctors Do to Stay Healthy, New York: Kensington, 2002.

Orey, Cal, 202 Pets' Peeves: Cats and Dogs Speak Out on Pesky Human Behavior, New York: Citadel, 2003.

Peurifoy, Z. Reneau, Anxiety, Phobias & Panic: A Step-by-Step Program for Regaining Control of Your Life, New York: Warner Books, 2005.

Plageman, John R., and Stephen H. Gribben, The Jupiter Effect: The Planets

As *Triggers of Devastating Earthquakes*, New York: Random House, 1976.

Shapley, Dan, "Earthquake Rattles, but Only a Little," *Poughkeepsie Journal*, October 16, 2004.

Sheldrake, Rupert, *Dogs That Know When Their Owners Are Coming Home*, New York: Crown, 2000.

Sheldrake, Rupert, "Listen to the Animals: Why Did So Many Animals Escape December's Tsunami?" *The Ecologist*, March 2005, pp. 1–2, *www.sheldrake.org/papers/Animals/tsunami_abs.html*.

Shou, Zhonghao, "Earthquake Clouds a Reliable Precursor," *Science and Utopya* 64, October 3, 1999 (in Turkish), pp. 53–57.

Spignesi, Stephen, *Catastrophe! The 100 Greatest Disasters of All Time*, New York, New York: Citadel, 2004.

Smith, Timothy, "Tidal Wave Memories 1964: Ouzinkie and the Great Tsunami," *tanignak.com*.

Swanson, Doug, "On Shaky Ground: Prediction of Earthquakes Far from an Exact Science," *The Dallas Morning News*, October 3, 1999.

Tributsch, Helmut, *When the Snakes Awake*, Cambridge, Massachusetts: The MIT Press, 1982.

U.S. Geological Survey, "Past & Historical Quakes," *www.earthquake.usgs.gov/activity/past.html*.

Von Feldt, Rick, "Tsunami Survivor Stories," *phukettsunami.blogspot.com*.

Walton, Marsha, "Temblor Big Enough to Vibrate the Whole Planet,"

CNN Special Report, May 20, 2005.

Washington State Office of the Insurance Commissioner, "Facts About Earthquake Insurance," *www.insurance.wa.gov/factsheets*.

Index

About the Author

CAL OREY is an accomplished author and intuitive specializing in topics such as health, science, and pets. She holds a B.A. and an M.A. in English (Creative Writing) from SFSU. Ms. Orey is the author of several books, including the popular HEALING POWERS series (translated in 20 languages). She works as a phone psychic for an international network, pens a monthly column for *Oracle 20/20 Magazine*, "Earth Changes: I Can Feel the Earth Move," and has been featured for her intuitive powers to sense oncoming earthquakes on msnbc.com, *Coast to Coast* AM, *The Mancow Show* and other national radio shows. She resides at Lake Tahoe, CA. Her websites are www.calorey.com and www.earthquakeepicenterforum.com.

Sentient Publications, LLC publishes books on cultural creativity, experimental education, transformative spirituality, holistic health, new science, ecology, and other topics, approached from an integral viewpoint. Our authors are intensely interested in exploring the nature of life from fresh perspectives, addressing life's great questions, and fostering the full expression of the human potential. Sentient Publications' books arise from the spirit of inquiry and the richness of the inherent dialogue between writer and reader.

We are very interested in hearing from our readers. To direct suggestions or comments to us, or to be added to our mailing list, please contact:

SENTIENT PUBLICATIONS, LLC

1113 Spruce Street
Boulder, CO 80302
303-443-2188
contact@sentientpublications.com
www.sentientpublications.com